THE AMERICAN WEST

AMERICAN WEST

NEW PERSPECTIVES, NEW DIMENSIONS

Edited and with an Introduction by
JEROME O. STEFFEN

240476

University of Oklahoma Press: Norman

by Jerome O. Steffen

William Clark: Jeffersonian Man on the Frontier (Norman, 1977)
The Frontier: Comparative Studies (co-editor) (Norman, 1977)
The American West: New Perspectives, New Dimensions (editor)
(Norman, 1979)

Library of Congress Cataloging in Publication Data

Main entry under title:

The American West, new perspectives, new
dimensions.

Includes bibliographical references and index.
1. The West—Civilization—Addresses, essays,
lectures. I. Steffen, Jerome O., 1942–
F591.A415   978   78–58097

FOR CHRISTOPHER AND JOSHUA

PREFACE

In assembling the essays in this volume, it was my intention to make the end-product reflect both humanistic and behavioral interests within the historical profession as well as to make it interdisciplinary. In keeping with the interdisciplinary spirit of the volume, the style of annotation of each author's discipline has been preserved. I wish to thank the contributors for the time and effort put into their essays. I am especially indebted to William W. Savage, Jr., whose considerate counsel was of the greatest benefit. In addition, I would like to express my appreciation to the University of Oklahoma, which supplied me with several grants to undertake this and other projects. My deepest gratitude must extended to Ms. Evelyn Weekes, an especially meticulous typist whose editorial alertness prevented me from making many unnecessary errors. She deserves more than the passing reference usually accorded typists of book manuscripts. Finally, there is my wife, Gloria, who was, as always, a constant source of encouragement.

JEROME O. STEFFEN

Norman, Oklahoma

CONTENTS

ix

THE AMERICAN WEST

INTRODUCTION

In 1964, W. N. Davis, Jr., reporting the results of a survey on the future of the West as a field in American history, announced that the field would perish unless scholars made "fresh efforts in the form of imaginative, modern analysis of the large issues and of imaginative, modern synthesis of the separate ends. On the evidence of the survey," Davis wrote,

one can trust that the efforts may be forthcoming. Certainly the challenge and the opportunities of the field lie open. But more than challenge and opportunity is involved. At the forefront now, in the very midst of the unsettling new forces, stand the field's responsibilities and obligations.[1]

Three years later Rodman Paul addressed himself to many of these same concerns. Paul indicated that efforts to resurrect western history need not lead to grandiose, sweeping conceptual frameworks to cover all western themes. Instead, he suggested, scholars should "take up, one by one, some of the major topics in western history and subject them to a reflective examination":

Out of the insights gained from scrutinizing a series of these individual major topics, presently it may become possible to discern new interrelationships between them, new and deeper explanations, and ultimately a new synthesis of western history as a whole.[2]

In a 1969 review of Robert Dykstra's *Cattle Towns* and Gene M. Gressley's *Bankers and Cattlemen,* Paul felt that he had found examples of the badly needed new western history. Both books, he concluded, illustrate that ''all our beleaguered field needs is a combination of well directed hard work and a determination to handle western themes with the same sophistication that is now so visible in the treatment of American history generally.''[3]

Paul's assessment of Dykstra's and Gressley's work is shared by most western historians. Indeed, in the past decade the field has witnessed occasional spurts of sophistication. In addition western history has experienced a back-door revival of sorts, owing to the recent widespread interest in Native American and Chicano studies.

Despite these positive trends, however, even the most die-hard loyalist must admit that the renaissance of western history is not as far along as reasonably could be expected. Several factors might account for this. First, the West is still ignored by too many serious scholars. In addition, there are a number of scholars who linger on the field's periphery, either terribly defensive of their western interests or, like the biblical Peter, denying any association with the victim of crucifixion. Another factor may be that historians, as part of the milieu that they attempt to understand, have had a tendency to assume about western scholarship what is popularly assumed about the West regionally—that it is a colorfully quaint retreat from the rigors of mainstream American life, but in the end unsophisticated. It is conceivable that these latent assumptions may, for example, cause historians unwittingly to view dreary narratives of American national political elections as acceptable scholarship, while at the same time they consider narratives of western military campaigns to be antiquarian. this tendency is exacerbated by the predilection of american elites to defer to Europeans in matters cultural and intellectual. As this phenomenon relates to scholarship, one can understand the American tendency to assume that an agricultural history of a French province is sophisticated but that a similar study of a county in rural Kansas might be considered parochial.

These assumptions, however, should not be confused with the realities of western scholarship. Indeed, western historical works are too often provincial and devoid of conceptual frames of reference. But a distinction must be drawn between the field of interest and the work completed therein. To ignore the field simply because it has not reached its fullest potential is rather like throwing the baby out with the proverbial bathwater. It is time once again to retrieve the baby and to decide whether it has life and, if so, what its future nourishment should be.

The chapters in this book derive from different but equally valid categories of inquiry into American western development. First, the environmental crisis, a matter of concern for all of civilization, has its roots in the evolution of man's view of his relation to nature. John Opie discusses the American frontier manifestation of this body of thought and how it has caused civilization to court disaster by ignoring the forces of the natural world. Opie reviews pertinent literature on the subject and calls for an "ecological thesis" of American history in which it is recognized that man's so-called victories over the environment are but short-lived interludes in the inevitable course of natural history.

Next, the American West must continue to be viewed in its frontier context. With its post–Civil War trans-Mississippi West temporal and spatial parameters, the frontier presents the scholar with an changing national laboratory in which to study man as a universal problem solver interacting with complex environmental constructs. John Hudson reflects this perspective in his chapter on population movements. Frontier populations, to Hudson, have "no ultimate origin in time or space," and therefore they must be studied in their broader demographic and geographic context. Hudson's chapter gives perspective to the American manifestation of frontier migration and provides scholars with methodological tools for future study.

Roger G. Barker discusses the nature of frontier environments and their possible effect on human behavior. He dissects the many components that ultimately comprise human environment and applies them to the new, unfinished, and undermanned frontier settings.

In my chapter I attempt to compare different American frontier settings with an eye toward change and continuity and those combinations of variables that served as causatives for each condition. I argue that only certain combinations of variables are exclusive to frontiers that experienced substantive change while other combinations are associated only with frontiers that experienced modal change.

The frontier as a natural setting for the study of culture contact is the focus of Reginald Horsman's chapter on Native American history. In addition to providing a review of the current literature in the field, Horsman discusses the changing relationships between Native Americans and the community of scholars long associated with their study. Horsman offers suggestions for new topics to be explored and new methods to be utilized.

Western fiction and symbolism is another category that looms large in the future of western scholarship. Richard W. Etulain reviews the major contributions and various approaches employed in the study of western fiction. He notes an increased interest in western literature in the past decade and juxtaposes this interest with a seemingly contrary rise in the popularity of social science methods in historical inquiry.

Ronald L. F. Davis explores the growth of urbanization in the West, reviewing pertinent works in the field, as well as suggesting new perspectives for the study of urban growth. Davis defines western urban growth in terms of the factors affecting national urban growth.

Gene M. Gressley discusses the impact on the West of such current problems as land use, resource, allocation, and conservation, bringing us back again to the crucial issues of environment. Gressley contrasts the realities of the need for intraregional cooperation and planning with the West's historical legacy of extreme independence and suspicion of eastern capital and the federal government.

The content, style, tone, and perspectives of these chapters are diverse. It is my hope that western scholars will read them with the inquisitiveness that has always been the benchmark of true scholarship. The perspectives and methodologies presented here are but a few that illustrate the field's rich potential.

Notes

1. "Will the West Survive as a Field in American History? A Survey Report," *Mississippi Valley Historical Review* 50 (March, 1964), 685.

2. "The Mormons as a Theme in Western Historical Writing," *Journal of American History* 54 (December, 1967), 511.

3. "The New Western History: A Review of Two Recent Examples," *Agricultural History* 43 (April, 1969), 300.

1. FRONTIER HISTORY
IN ENVIRONMENTAL PERSPECTIVE

John Opie

Frederick Jackson Turner built his frontier thesis of American history around an 1890 census director's report that indicated that the far reaches of the empty western lands had been conquered. Hence, Turner argued, the era of continuous open expansion that had molded the American character had come to an end.[1] On October 12, 1971, another census director of the United States, George H. Brown, in a speech in Pittsburgh, interpreted the statistics of the 1970 census in a way that pictured changes in American development that were as significant as the termination of the frontier in 1890. He forecast an emerging ''affluent majority'' in this country by 1985, with real purchasing power rising more than 50 percent.[2] It was an optimistic statement, but Brown took care to include a new and historically unexpected warning: The costs of preserving living conditions according to 1970 standards would be rapidly spiraling upward. He asked: ''Will we use our increase in affluence to pay for pollution-free cars and planes; for cleaned-up rivers and lakes; for better schools; for updating of penal systems and institutions—a gamut of public services and needs?'' By mid-decade much of Brown's prediction about these costs had come true.

Turner believed that the frontier provided the stimulus for American individualism, fortitude, democracy, and nationalism, and he was honestly shocked by the 1890 census director's judgment that American frontier history was over. The conclusions drawn from the 1970 census statistics are equally awesome.

9

Brown asked, Will our "national inheritance" be "greater pollution of our air and water . . . more consumption of each natural resource . . . more goods and services . . . gadgetry gone mad . . .?" Costs of maintaining a recognizable, useful, comfortable, and pleasant environment may continue to rise rapidly and surpass any potential development. The $1.00 spent washing clothes may in the future require an additional $1.20 to remove the suds and chemicals from the nearby river. Will there be a $0.70 pollution surcharge on our $0.60 gallon of gas?

Brown's report is only one indicator of an extraordinary, confusing, and troublesome conflict over priorities in American society in the 1970s and points to permanent changes in the expectations of Americans. Brown titled his speech "1985," pointedly the year after George Orwell's 1984. On balance the environmental costs of living in America are rising far more rapidly than environmental rewards. Turner's frontier thesis in the 1890s looked backward; we may now require an "ecological thesis" of American history that will project forward from the 1970's. Another era of American history may well have come to an end in the 1960s—the era of measuring American destiny in terms of an expanding gross national product. We may begin measuring our condition henceforth in terms of GNC—gross national consumption—and rewrite our past history in these altered terms.[3] Such an "ecological thesis" suggests a radical reinterpretation of American life and fortunes.

Briefly, what would be some characteristics of such an ecological thesis of American history? Negatively, it would indict any exclusively man-centered or man-isolated treatment of historical values, priorities, and objectives as a narrow and inadequate portrayal because of its discrimination against the permanent and intrinsic significance of the so-called nonhuman, or natural, environment. Positively, it would incorporate cross-disciplinary methods and resources, beginning with tools used by ecologists and members of the biological sciences, who point to a far more extensive "natural history of man."[4] Such an ecological approach would also draw to a much greater extent upon complementary resources available from geography, anthropology, sociology, economics, and other related fields. The resulting interpretation would place American civilization inside and dependent upon a comprehensive world view that pictures man as a cultural and biological entity interacting with an environment continuously compounded and recompounded of physical and organic elements, natural and man-modified.[5] Thomas Kuhn's model, or paradigm, of man-and-environment most adequately depicts the distinctive characteristics of American frontier history.[6] The outstanding environmental contributions thus far remain Wilbur R. Jacobs' 1970 essay in the *Newsletter* of the American Historical Association, and Roderick Nash's 1967 intellectual history of the conservation movement.[7]

Historians have evaluated environmental influences for some time, but without the breadth and biological insight now required. Geographical features, such as natural resources, food supply, and climatic conditions, are forces recognized as demonstrably affecting human life and cultural development.[8] The emergence of primitive man and the rise of early civilizations are pitted by historians precisely against the material world. Frontier historians, because of the very nature of their materials, devote unusual attention to geographical factors.[9] Twentieth-century man, presumably insulated against raw nature in his technological cocoon, is being described by an increasing number of scholars as primarily a long-term product of the agricultural or neolithic revolution.[10] But the trend unfortunately persists that defines the civilizing process and desirable human progress as the ability to win man's separation from and independence of the natural world.

The difficulty of the task is evident when the historian's historian, the philosopher of history, tends to suggest that the methods and content of the craft have become internalized. There is a persistent prejudice that favors an interpretative internal logic imposed upon external events. This stance invariably places more value upon strictly human objectives at the price of meaning and value appropriated from external resources. Carl Becker's denial of historical positivism, while methodologically informative, encourages the notion that historical priorities cannot be derived from the external world.[11] This trend is also represented in Gerald Heard's "superconsciousness," Arnold Toynbee's "etherealization," Pitirim Sorokin's "ideational culture," Robin Collingwood's existential history, and Henri Bergson's *élan vital*.[12] Not all these men are historians, but they have created a widely accepted framework of expectations within the discipline. In contrast, an ecological perspective, with its high priority in the nonhuman environment, would seriously question this "phenomenology of consciousness." Further, historical internalization is in turn supported by arguments that a useful consideration of the natural environment is impossible.[13] Oswald Spengler argued that any real experience of nature by man was unlikely, since nature had been supersaturated with human content and had no separate identity.[14] And even if mankind was forever in touch with the natural world, it was always blanketed with a mesh of law, custom, tradition, usage, and habit. Wild nature, without the presence of man, cannot be experienced without the distractions of cultural and psychological clutter.

An outstanding example of this civilizational masking of the natural world remains the mythology that greeted the discovery of the New World. A well-defined European image of paradise seemed realized with the warm climate, abundance of food, and gold artifacts discovered in America. The nude body in Renaissance paintings often symbolized innocence and a purified soul. This image was reinforced when Europeans first encountered the unashamedly naked Indians.[15] Only later was the Indian perceived as an inexplicable evil in utopia, akin to the rattlesnake, alligator, and poison ivy. An alternative vision likened the New World to a hell filled with strange monstrosities that contradicted known laws of nature that tidily governed the Old World. Was the New World the refuse heap of discarded phenomena, and was the discovery of America a ghastly mistake?[16] Nevertheless, heaven or hell, it was still a European mental construct. J. H. Plumb has called North America "the most conscious and deliberate creation of any human society."[17] Such mythologizing was corrupted by the crude manipulative "selling of the West" by nineteenth-century land speculators, railway companies, and immigration brokers.[18]

When faced with an environmental interpretation of his craft, the historian must wonder whether he suffers from the fallacy of misplaced concreteness. Usually compelled to comprehend a fleeting series of subjective impressions, can the historian consider physical concreteness with fervor equal to his persistent chase for the inner motivation of a man or movement? Within the faith, historians are aware of the disastrous results when a historical construct, like the Age of Reason or the National Period, is taken for a discernible reality.[19] From this point of view our proper interest should not be the role of nature in the larger history of man, but to position the activity of man properly within the larger framework of the monumental history of nature.[20] What is required is a newly devised "natural history of man." Historians have evaded the issues by treating the environment as an external idea or phenomenon in our intentional horizon. Hence the debate over misplaced concreteness. Any human awareness, and any respectable and useful description of the human condition, must more decisively depend upon interaction with the environment.[21] The modern mind seems to have a very limited awareness of nonhuman existence, particularly its abundance, complexity, intrinsic values, and constant interpenetration with humanity. Yet biological reality remains man's primordial reality. Two ecologists, Paul Shepard and Daniel McKinley, have said, "To those who have not looked carefully at anything but human faces and printed words, the world's magnitude, diversity, and richness are difficult to communicate."[22] Anything less is a kind of methodological and epistemological poverty. The wonder of man is unchecked by the wonder of anything else. People watching alone leaves historians with no norm.[23]

What does this ecological thesis say about specific aspects of the American frontier? My task here must be a severely restricted one, to provide only a sampling of the possibilities for reinterpretation. First, it is possible to explore two interlocking aspects of American history: the nature of the highly productive grasslands frontier of the middle American continent and the character of the invasion of this region by dynamic, imaginative, aggressive white Europeans, exemplars of the so-called Faustian man. The movement of Caucasian peoples into the American grasslands is not so narrow a topic that it is not representative, nor so broad that it becomes a meaningless abstraction. In this juxtaposition both European behavior and an existing environment can be brought into sharper relief. We do know that in North America the white man found a rich and varied land with a complex ecology. We also know that in a relatively short time these European adventurers reduced this variety and complexity to a far simpler and uniform environment. Ecologists always term this reductionism entropy as a weakening process. Extraordinary exploitation of an environment can drive it into its own form of "future shock."

Second, and equally important, is the need to awaken historians to the significance of a compelling environmental stance for them and their craft. Robert Oppenheimer once said that with the atomic bomb physicists had come to know original sin.[24] Is there a conscience-stricken element among historians today? Our sin of omission is to ignore totally the powerful and arrarently destructive role of man in a environmental system upon which he depends for survival. Inadequate attention given in the past to complex biological interactions has led to overgrazing and overfarming of the land and to the liquidation of forest resources. It has caused man to exploit resources when prices are high and, when appropriate, to sell out and to get out rather than build the land and its resources.[25] In his responsibility for this state of affairs the historian must be placed alongside unaware or indifferent scientists, economists, politicians, farmers, and industrialists. The effect in the academic world has been to place nature outside the immediate sphere of concern among humanists and social scientists, who look upon man as so far removed from his biological moorings that he stands as an "egocentric man in a homocentric world."[26]

The Faustian man to be considered is not the figure so strongly portrayed in modern literature, although the wandering charlatan with unsatisfied yearnings and foul preternatural gifts may be close to the mark. After all, Faust bartered away his soul for a specified period of pleasure and power. It seems even more appropriate to begin with Western man's Faustian powers described by futurists as they look toward the year 2000.[27] The year 2000 is only fifteen years after the census director's 1985, which in turn is only fifteen years after the 1970 census. More often than not the futurists identify Faustian man as "technological man," particularly as technology has allowed the species to have a permanent impact upon the world. The origins of this stereotype date back to Judeo-Christian traditions, Greco-Roman culture and imperialism, Renaissance humanism, and Enlightenment rationalism, as well as to the scientific and industrial revolutions, the Puritan ethic, and the economic adventures of capitalism. this white western European had acquired substantially different cultural traits from those of, for example, the inhabitants of sub-Sahara Africa or China's Middle Kingdom or the Indian of America. Europeans believed man had to remake the earth to have it really usable. Wild nature was chaotic and formless, the nest of danger and anarchy until given some plan and orderliness by man. It was fruitful only when cultivated. The more man controlled nature the more liberated he would be to serve his own strictly human purposes.[28] And there were reasons to believe that Europeans had acquired these Faustian powers by the nineteenth century. Mechanical inventions did mean a remarkable multiplication of human productivity. Prodigious resources of energy were uncovered that promised limitless abundance of goods and services. Europeans acquired a very high capacity to reorganize human and natural societies. Most comforting was the apparent ability to bring about cumulative changes and self-sustaining development of wealth and power.[29] Finally, Western man acquired, through science, an incredible increase in the acuity of his human senses. Developments from the telescope, microscope, and maps to the rifle, from the invention of perspective in Renaissance paintings to the perspective of earth gained from air and space travel, gave man a unique sense of the environment.[30] This awareness expanded his own wealth and power. Such is the paradigm most often employed by the writers of history textbooks: a consistent yet constantly expanding human power that can make the species independent of time, place, and circumstance. It is presumably most adequately expressed in Western civilization and embodied in American society.

Alongside these Faustian powers we must place the familiar narrative of the westward march of the American Frontier.[31] These two stereotypes, and the adequacy of their juxtaposition, concern us here. Successful expansion meant precisely a truimph for Western man's Faustian powers over alien cultures and environments. The question before us now is whether this triumph became a Pyrrhic victory. When we join natural history (geology, biology, agronomy, and so on) with human history, the following picture emerges.

When the newly arrived pioneer farmer took a handful of soil, allowed it to run between his fingers, and said, "This will be a good piece of land to farm," he also indicated a good place for the historian to begin. It is said, "If man is to civilize, he must deform the environment that he enters." To acquire his own food out of nature, he takes it away from other organic process or physical entity. He interferes with a natural process and sets up his own preferred version of food production. So far in the United States, with a few exceptions, man-controlled production continues to be highly rewarding. But the ecological thesis raises the question whether we know what we are up to. Man has never been passive in his relation to nature, but his Faustian powers in commercial agriculture and the technological revolution may have far surpassed his understanding.

A fertile soil, upon which man is almost entirely dependent, is one of his least stable resources.[32] Any region of good soil is in only a momentary equilibrium, for soil can be described as "a temporary interlude for rocks and minerals on their way to solution and to the sea." Man's domestic plants are specialized in their ability to regroup these soluble minerals and chemicals from a physical to an organic state and to hold them until consumed. We are dealing with a successful or unsuccessful storage and retrieval system.

Paradoxically, the difficulty arises when man speeds this geologic interlude on its way. The farmer must work the soil to unlock its chemical dynamics. The nutrients of the soil cannot enter the roots of plants upon which men and animals feed unless the minerals in the rocks are put into solution and chemical exchanges take place.[33] But the process called entropy takes place when a demand for high productivity accelerates a natural process beyond its capacity. The farmer soon concludes, "This once was a good place to farm but is no longer." The other side of the paradox is that conservation of the soil presumably means the delay or even an attempt to halt this process. It is said that the soil should not be allowed to weather or erode, go into solution, and go into the sea. But there is no getting around the fact that only by this continuous process can life survive on earth. The rocks must go into solution, and the plants must capture the nutrients, or there is no food. What is not clear in frontier history are the steps by which man became more involved in soil destruction than in soil construction. Surely both are geologic processes. Can we determine a turning point, if there is one, when man began to break up the habitat in which he had his niche?

Initially the homesteaders avoided the midcontinent grasslands.[34] They believed that the region was a desert, unable to support anything but the prairie grass, since it could not support trees. they called the prairie "the Great Obstacle."[35] The expansion of civilization earlier in Europe and later in the eastern United States had almost always been in heavily forested country. The initial civilizing task had been to clear out the excess trees in order to plant domestic crops. Hence the settler who arrived on the western plains was truly a stranger in a strange land.[36] To him the grasslands were desolate because of the lack of trees and water, excessive heat and cold, interminable winds, and thick matted grass that grew in a heavy, unmanageable soil. But eventually these novel challenges to survival were either conquered or accepted for the sake of the rewards involved.[37] The highly polished light shear plow sliced readily through the matted and heavy sod that clogged or broke older, heavier plows. The settlers, of course, did not desire to maintain these grasslands but wanted to transform them into agricultural preserves. That change is what we need now to explore.

A well-known thesis proposes that the grasslands area was not after all a natural wilderness—a so-called "climax" region.[38] Supposedly, wherever forest and grassland meet, trees and shrubs spread into the grassland and take over. But the forest did not move into the American grasslands. The reason may have been fire. The American upland plains had enough dry weather and combustible material to feed and spread the fires, which in turn kept out woody plants. It is argued, however, that the burning had to be regular and systematic in order to hold back the trees. Spontaneous combustion and lightning therefore provide only partial and unsatisfactory explanations. Since about A.D. 1000, the argument goes, the existence of the American grasslands may well be ascribable to a man-nature symbiosis. The American Indian, for example, can be described as a major agent in a biotic system that he maintained to his satisfaction by repeated human intervention.

This historic balance preserved the grasslands, but the plains region to the west moved toward another plateau of equilibrium. The invasion of Europeans provided a workable ecological substitute for the earlier Indian inhabitation. Plows, draft animals, and the mowers and harvesters had brought about some stability by 1850. The plains region became a mixed agricultural economy, defined and controlled for the whiteman's purposes.[39] The fertility of the land was maintained, and it did exist as a self-sustaining ecological system with the European and his domestic plants and animals inserted into it. Prairie settlement seemed capable of continuous and improved productivity, without the exhaustion of the land that occasionally happened in the eastern United States. But presently the land, no longer primarily grassland, has its equilibrium and potential entirely in man's hands. This frontier represented man's biological universality and was part of the worldwide expansion of European techniques, which completely domesticated the earth for economic practicality.[40] It has been suggested that the Industrial Revolution was made possible by cheap human food and animal feed provided through plowing up the great grasslands of the world.[41]

The change, however, came with commercial agriculture. Earlier farming and animal grazing had created a total human lifestyle that functioned within the limits of an agricultural equilibrium, in a system that generally replenished the land. But by the opening of the twentieth century the balance had been broken because the tempo of land use had changed. This change in tempo pushed the land into its own form of future shock.[42] Commercial agriculture accelerated land use through exclusive concentration upon row or cash crops. It brought in "outside help"—capital, machines, manpower, markets—and effectively concentrated vast human resources in a relatively small geographic region. Commerical agriculture requires the infusion of large amounts of outside capital, intensive and comprehensive mechanization, and the immense load capacity of railroad transportation. In the semiarid western Great Plains, mechanized farming may have been the only means for productivity, but it was exploitative.[43] Technology was substituted for organic processes.[44]

If there is any validity to an ecological interpretation of American history, then pure anthropocentrism—human history apart from nature history—is clearly a forced abstraction. Man cannot be described except as an element—albeit enormously powerful—within a larger phenomenon, the environment. But to speak of any entirely nonhuman or wilderness environment alone is also an abstract—nature history apart from human history.[45] The frontier historian cannot properly speak of pure wilderness, without man, any more than he can consider man in isolation from nature.

We need to borrow from the physical sciences the principle of indeterminacy. This principle illustrates, for example, that one cannot know the temperature of a container of water because the thermometer will change the temperature of the water it is supposed to measure, just as the observer of the wilderness modifies what he reports on. Attempts to preserve environmental systems do in fact alter them. This indeterminacy makes historical precision conditional and establishes the interaction between man and nature, which then controls the historical evaluation. Only relatively speaking, then, with man as a highly ambiguous point of reference, can one refer to any so-called natural landscape before the introduction of human activity.[46] What we can say is that hunting and fishing, clearing the land, bringing plants under cultivation, general domestication, and mechanized food production each meant a different symbiosis between man and his environment.

The presence of the Indian, of course, precluded any valid notion of a land devoid of human occupancy. But until recently frontier historians wrote as if the native inhabitants did not significantly modify the landscape.[47] The argument was that, if the Indian was unable to stand up against white intervention, surely he was culturally weak and technologically helpless before the environment as well. Indian cultures were sophisticated, however, and had their own priorities over intensive land use. Frontier history is more adequately described in part as a contest between remarkably different cultures for the use of a landscape.[48] Even aside from native inhabitants an indeterminacy principle of human penetration into nonhuman surroundings would prevent a serious misunderstanding of the so-called empty wilderness in American history. This is the first fallacy of frontier history. Wilderness determinism is nonsense. The land was not devoid of human influence. The land cannot be interpreted without human interference. Descriptions of wilderness are both impossible and irrelevant.

The second fallacy of frontier history is that the land was a perpetual cornucopia, unchanged and unchanging throughout American history. The geographical base of American expansion has been improperly interpreted as a fixed, permanent, and constantly rewarding foundation for human development. The habitat is resilient, but it is a moving base, involved in a continuous process of decay and development. For example, the prairie soil at best is a moving point on a moving line.[49]

Hence again the behavior of an ecosystem may be somewhat analogous to physical indeterminacy. The geography of American history is by definition unstable. The historian must pay attention to this ever-changing base to comprehend the cultural experience built upon it. What if the cane lands of Kentucky had not become bluegrass when the region was settled, but instead a succession of worthless brush and weeds? The southwestern United States had no bluegrass to replace its original green fertility and consequently went through a progressive and mutual deterioration of plants, land, animals, and people. Aldo Leopold suggested the importance of the bluegrass when he asked:

Would Boone and Kenton have held out? Would there have been any overflow into Ohio? Any Louisiana Purchase? Any transcontinental union of new states? Any Civil War? Any machine age? Any depression? The subsequent drama of American history, here and elsewhere, hung in large degree on the reaction of particular soils to the impact of particular forces exerted by a particular kind and degree of human occupation.[50]

A forest-or-prairie site is not simply a place. It is a qualitative expression of ecological dynamics, far less in some form of equilibrium or homeostasis than in relative instability. The environment is never being but always becoming.

Thus controlled by complex interactions and a lack of fixity, this relationship between man and his surroundings can be clarified by the framework suggested in contemporary ecological thought. Unlike the independence claimed for Faustian man, man in ecological terms is properly identified when he is positioned in a niche in the environment. But in occupying his niche, he also has a role in continuing the dynamic stability of his surroundings. This is an incredibly complex notion because the niches themselves are not stable but constantly changing.[51] This ecological perspective is particularly important to the frontier historian, who is so prone to distinquish between wilderness and settled land. No matter whether a landscape is wild or cultivated, one of the laws of ecology is that no niche remains empty long. When a frontier settler would move on and leave his forest clearing untended, the forest returned. When man departed after exploiting and destroying the grasslands, his place was taken by scrub and weeds.[52] Land is always under full use, though it may be so bereft of contents desirable to man as to appear barren. Desert exists only from a perspective of human desirability. This stance also clarifies the relative ease with which Europeans conquered the North American continent and its inhabitants. There is evidence that the white man's expansion into the West may have been coincidentally assisted by niches that were weak or emptying, either because of ecological change of because of the decline of the Indians.[53]

What has been almost entirely ignored by historians is that one of the primary functions of human existence is the role man plays in his ecosystem. To survive, man in his niche must at least not play a destructive role. The habitat furnishes the niche, and if any species breaks up the habitat, the niche goes with it. The landscape is made up of processes that are very easily disrupted. It is this fact made possible for so long the white man's productive occupation of the grasslands frontier. The question remains, How much human pressure can be placed upon such an unstable environment, made doubly so by its natural indeterminacy and man's intensive interference?

To what extent do environmental conditions control human potential? Is an ecological thesis of the American frontier a formidable form of environmental determinism?[54] Human history has an inescapable physical setting, with intensive interaction between man and the external world. The processes of human thought and action take place not in a spatial vacuum but in some definite geographical setting that defines in varying ways and degrees the character and power of human effort.[55] In most historical periods and geographical regions the physical setting has, in human terms, a permanent order. The land has witnessed and survived the advent of man and the ephemeral episodes of his civilizing impulse. The natural landscape shows remarkable stability.[56] In this vein, when one considers the vast and rapid transformations of the American grasslands, the American middle western frontier experience is a remarkable experience of external change involving temporary equilibrium, artificial use, intensive balance, and potential future disintegration.

Nevertheless, even amid dynamic and extraordinary changes in a landscape, climate, soil and relief condition the *modes de vie,* "the ways in which a livelihood is got."[57] The basic task is to discover the physical properties of a milieu and out of this to consider the potentialities of a region (economic, personal, aesthetic) and then to determine what human use was made of the physical potential.[58] Environmental determinism—the doctrine that a mode of life is forced upon people by their habitats—remains an oversimplification. Nor can life be led without regard to the potentials of a place. The road usually taken leads to the "possibilist" position, which allows that any given area offers possibilities within limits and that human settlers act according to their needs, powers, and whims.[59] The results can be as diverse as tobacco exploitation in Tidewater Virginia, the bluegrass displacement in Kentucky, the plains Dust Bowl of the 1930s, or the irrigation of the southwestern desert.

This metabolic connection with the environment involves a crucial shift of real and interpretative priorities. Historical responsibility must be grounded in the breadth of all life, not merely in the singularity or address of man. The pioneering naturalist Paul Shepard writes of "the current agony of human isolation," the result of depersonalization through scientific "reduction" of man to material and statistical traits, and through the romantic-existentialist reaction to science, this latter subjectivism leading to "the excruciating sickness of self-consciousness."[60] According to this stance the locus of interpretation is not in man but in the ecosystem that is revealed as the relation between man and nature becomes clarified. Reinterpretation of American frontier agricultural history along environmental lines produces new results and new conclusions. Shepard continues:

... in the rich soils of the Midwest where the farms are prosperous it is necessary to drive many miles to find a farm in biological equilibrium with its environment, for these "model" farms are operated by drawing on the accumulated capital of a deep till soil, force-feeding with nutrient elements, the broad-scale use of chemical herbicides and pesticides, and increasingly efficient extractive machinery.[61]

The biologist Paul Sears has written:

I am assuming that it is not enough for man to live by bread alone. But that intangible, as well as tangible values are necessary to justify his persistence. If this be true, the question is, not how many people can exist on earth, but what kind of life will be possible for those who do.[62]

Aldo Leopold was on the track of some positive man-nature values when he said that an ecological ethic concerns the relative kinds of restraints and freedom written into environmental systems. An ecosystem guarantees a variety of rights and privileges of survival and existence to all its members.[63] Leopold argued that man's separation from nature and freedom of action from ecological limits threatens other forms of life. Sears and Leopold have both argued in their own ways that the game of life had its ethical rules. An environmental interpretation of human affairs invariably includes ethical considerations.

In conclusion, since neolithic times, plant and animal domestication meant discord between human needs and natural processes. This conflict is particularly evident with the rise of advanced civilizations, which are more demanding of their environments. The depth of the conflict reached in the United States has not received its deserved attention from historians. The way of the future seems to lie in our ability to look upon human life, civilization, and technology as not self-contained and distinct from the dynamics of land and the successful continuation of non-human life. Faustian man, and his reincarnation in technological man, is merely one of many distinctive expressions of biological existence, and it may not be the most workable.

Man gains his independence and builds up his civilization by breaking into the ongoing dynamic processes of the land. This is all dependent on the surplus growth of vegetation apparently not required for the survival and annual renewal of plants. The surplus production, determined by the biological capabilities of the land, is a sufficiently reliable base for the development of civilization. The grasslands of America have been immensely supportive of the hyperactive industrial development of the United States, not only by their natural wealth, but also by their ability to sustain, for a time, an equally hyperactive commercial agriculture.[64]

The American Indians received a certain level of available food from the fertile soil they possessed. Europeans made of the same soil an unprecedented source of productivity. Yet the early farmers had no conception of the productivity that would be developed by entrepreneurs after the Civil War. One must agree with David M. Potter that the environment does not wholly explain American civilization.[65] The value of natural resources depends upon the aptitude of a people to use them. The physical capacity of a land is not the entire story. Productivity depends not only upon physical resources but also upon economic organization and technological advancement. But, unlike Potter, we must ascribe American success to environmental luck and immensity—the existence of highly supportive grasslands that could endure radical change.

As with Melville's Ahab, all our methods are sane, but our

objective is insane. American history is now aware of a shift from ecological plenitude to entropy, a condition of environmental weakness and decline. A healthy system in the environment depends upon organic complexity, diversity, and interdependence and a large variety of species. Ill-health in an ecosystem is a turn toward simplicity, uniformity, separateness, and a small number of species, a case of high entropy or environmental retrogression.[66] What is required for the continuation of American history is the development of an "antientropic system." What should be sought out is a large set of constant variables in an ecosystem, like a set of self-sustaining dynamics of soil, plants, animals, climate, and man. As one writer notes: "Constancy of environmental variables generally represents, if not a good position, at least a non-deteriorating one. Any failure of constancy in the absence of strong evidence to the contrary must be considered as a danger sign."[67] When the soils of the grasslands were excessively plowed or grazed, they reverted through a successive series of more and more worthless grasses, shrubs, and weeds to a condition of unstable deterioration, with less and less usefulness to man, until even the woods gave way to sterile earth.

Let us recognize frontier history—whether pro-Turner or anti-Turner—for what it is. Americans, like their European forebears, made the new land into a "dream landscape," the invention of concepts, history, and patterns that color the seeing eye. "In such model building the individual feels that he is discovering rather than making the world."[68] The issue at hand is not whether or not to make interpretative models but which model is the most adequate screen by which to view the artifacts that one is analyzing. The frontier remains a primary myth in American history.[69] An environmental approach can more adequately act as an effective model to evaluate this remarkable experience.

The task of this chapter has been to evaluate ecology as an alternate interpretative context for frontier history. Man's total organic being is the referential complex—his basic interconnectedness with all other living things and his dependence upon the physical world as his "living tether." It may be that the Darwinian revolution has finally caught up with historians. How much longer could we have retained our traditional distinction between man, who is presumably rational and unique, and nature, which is unified and organic?[70]

A basic premise of conventional historical inquiry—indeed of the humanities at large—is that "man has no biology any longer, just history."[71] Unlike traditional humanists, ecologists do not praise this slogan but rather fear it, first for the future of any species that thinks and functions this way and second for the limits such an idea sets upon historical knowledge. Today's ecologists argue that there is no next step in human history unless it is the creation of an ecologically responsible humanity. The changes man induced into the environment are at best rational and orderly. If man and his environment do form a single interacting system, and if the reciprocal fate of man and environment is a focus of concern, then orderly modifications of human behavior are fully as reasonable.[72] This requires serious criticism of man-centeredness. We are in the position of the transcendentalist Margaret Fuller when she said, "I accept the universe." The historian Thomas Carlyle retorted, "Gad! She'd better!"

Note: The documentation for this chapter must be considered preliminary notation only. As with most interdisciplinary approaches there exists a vast literature that can be properly covered only in an extensive bibliographical review. The notations here are neither comprehensive nor definitive. References are often made only to materials that are readily available. I hope to develop an extended bibliographical comment in the near future.

Notes

1. Turner's 1893 essay, "The Significance of the Frontier in American History," is available in many editions. He incorporated his better-known essays in *The Frontier in American History* (New York, 1920, 1947).

2. George H. Brown, "1985" (speech delivered October 12, 1971, to the National Conference for Editorial Writers, Pittsburgh, Pa., available in *United States Department of Commerce News,* Washington, D.C., 1971).

3. This stands in direct contrast to the position taken, for example, by David M. Potter in his *People of Plenty: Economic Abundance and the American character* (Chicago, 1954); see particularly chaps. 3 and 7.

4. Literature in ecology is enormous and growing rapidly. A representative list would include George Perkins Marsh, *Man and Nature* (New York, 1864); Aldo Leopold, *A Sand County Almanac* (New York, 1947); Rachel Carson, *Silent Spring* (Boston, 1962), Marston Bates, *The Forest and the Sea* (New York, 1960); René Dubose, *So Human an Animal* (New York, 1968); Loren Eisley, *The Immense Journey* (New York, 1946–57), Ian McHarg, *Design with Nature* (Garden City, N.Y., 1969); the excellent collected papers and essays in Paul Shepard and Daniel McKinley (eds.), *The Subversive Science* (New York, 1969); William L. Thomas, Jr., *Man's Role in Changing the Face of the Earth,* 2 vols. (Chicago, 1965); William R. Ewald, Jr., *Environment and Change, Environment and Policy, Environment for Man,* 3 vols. (Bloomington, Ind., 1967–68); F. Fraser Darling and John P. Milton, *Future Environments of North America* (New York, 1966), and my collection, *Americans and Environment* (Boston, 1971). There is also important related work in the fields of geography and anthropology; for example: Philip Wagner, *The Human Use of the Earth* (New York, 1960); and Paul Bohannan and Fred Plog, *Beyond the Frontier* (Garden City, 1967); and two historical studies on the relation of man and nature: Clarence Glacken, *Traces on the Rhodian Shore* (Berkeley, 1967); and

Roderick Nash, *Wilderness and the American Mind* (New Haven, 1967).

5. Important parallels can also be developed out of studies in energy systems, systems analysis, and futuristics. A recent classic and controversial example of such interdisciplinary integration is contained in Donella H. Meadows et al., *The Limits to Growth,* Club of Rome (New York, 1972).

6. Thomas S. Kuhn, *The Structure of Scientific Revolutions* (Chicago, 1972), pp. 77–79, 95, 107–29, 149; see also the discussion in Glacken, *Traces on the Rhodian shore,* pp. 471ff.; and Isaiah Bowman, *Geography in Relation to the Social Sciences* (New York, 1934), pp. 3–4, 164.

7. Wilbur R. Jacobs, "Frontiersmen, Fur Traders, and Other Varmints: An Ecological Appraisal of the Frontier in American History," *American Historical Association Newsletter* 8 (November, 1970): 5–11; studies in the history of conservation, such as Roderick Nash, *Wilderness and the American Mind* (New Haven, 1967); or studies of natural resources, such as Joseph M. Petulla, *American Environmental History* San Francisco, 1976), are extremely useful and relevant, but no specific history has yet been written from a clearly articulated environmental stance.

8. The spectrum of interpretations of environmental influences is very broad and extensive, making up by itself an entire academic discipline. a bibliographical essay for historians has been prepared by the geographer Gary S. Dunbar in *Environmental History Newsletter* 3 (April, 1976,); see also *Historical Geography Newsletter* (Northridge, Calif.).

9. Typical of a traditional approach are Ray Allen Billington, *Westward Expansion* (New York, 1974); and Robert E. Riegel and Robert G. Athearn, *America Moves West,* 5th ed. (New York, 1971); for a more recent specialized attempt to integrate environmental perception and geographical studies with historical inquiry, see an interesting work by Ruth E. Sutter, *The Next Place You Come to: A Historical Introduction to Communities in North America* (Englewood Cliffs, N.J., 1973).

10. See particularly Henri Frankfort, *The Birth of Civilization in the Near East* (Garden City, N.Y., 1956), pp. 29sff.; Lewis Mumford, *The Transformations of Man* (New York, 1956); Edgar Anderson, "The Evolution of Domestication," in Sol Tax, ed., *Evolution After Darwin* (Chicago, 1960; Kenneth Boulding's article in John d. Roslansky, ed., *The Control of Environment* (Amsterdam, Holland, 1967), pp. 62–69; Glyn Daniel, *The Idea of Pre-History* (Harmondsworth, Middlesex,

1962–64), and J. D. G. Clark, *Prehistoric Europe: the Economic Basis* (London, 1952).

11. See Carl L. Becker, *Everyman His Own Historian* (New York, 1935); P. L. Snyder, ed., *Detachment and the Writing of History* (Ithaca, N.Y., 1958); R. O. Rockwood, *Carl Becker's Heavenly City Revisited* (Ithaca, N. Y., 1958); C. W. Smith, *Carl Becker: On History and the Climate of Opinion* (Ithaca, N.Y., 1956); and Cushing Strout, *The Pragmatic Revolution in America* (New Haven, 1958). Alongside Becker, Charles Beard said that he could not work his craft without a guiding "frame of reference." See Charles A. Beard, *The Discussion of Human Affairs* (New York, 1936); Howard K. Beale, *Charles A. Beard: an Appraisal* (Lexington, Ky., 1954); Lee Benson, *Turner and Beard* (Glencoe, Ill., 1960); and Robert A. Skotheim, *American Intellectual Histories and Historians* (Princeton, N.J., 1966), pp. 89–106.

12. For a representative sampling see Pitirim A. Sorokin, *Sociocultural Causality, Space, Time* (Durham, N.C., 1943), *The Pattern of the Past* (Boston, 1949); Pitirim A. Sorokin, *Social and Cultural Dynamics* (New York, 1937–41); Henri L. Bergson, *Mind-Energy: Lectures and Essays,* trans. H. Wilson Carr (New York, 1920); thomas Hanna, *The Bergsonian Heritage* (New York, 1962); Gerald Heard, *The Ascent of Humanity* (New York, 1929); Gerald Heard, *The Emergence of Man* (New York, 1932); Arnold Toynbee, *An Historian's Approach to Religion* (New York, 1956); Robin G. Collingwood, *The Idea of History* (New York, 1946); Patrick Gardiner, ed., *Theories of History* (Glencoe, Ill., 1959); Arthur C. Danto, *the analytic Philosophy of history* (Cambridge, England, 1965); Morton White, *The Foundations of Historical Knowledge* (New York, 1966); and Frank E. Manuel, *Shapes of Philosophical History* (Stanford, Calif., 1965), pp. 136ff.

13. There are striking parallels between this and the classic methodological argument that broke out around the turn of the century with the publication of Albert Schweitzer's *The Quest for the Historical Jesus* (New York, 1950), and reached its climax in the 1950s with the publication of Rudolph Bultmann's *Jesus Christ and Mythology* (New York, 1958), which set limits on the relevance and possibility of historical evidence and inquiry. For a summary statement see Robert M. Grant, *An Historical Introduction to the New Testament* (New York, 1963).

14. See the discussion in Watsuji Tetsuro, *A Climate: A Philosophical Study* (Tokyo, 1961), p. 57; see also H. S. Hughes, *Oswald Spengler* (New York, 1952).

15. See the useful study by Howard Mumford Jones, *O Strange New World* (New York, 1964), particularly chaps. 1 and 2.

16. See G. Chinard, ''Eighteenth Century Theories of America as a Human Habitat,'' *Proceedings of the American Philosophical Society* 91 (1947): 27–57; Glacken, *Traces on the Rhodian Shore,* pp. 681–98; Durand Echeverria, *Mirage in the West* (Princeton, 1957), particularly chap. 1; and the useful collection in Henry Steele Commager and Elmo Giordanetti, eds., *Was America a Mistake?* (New York, 1967).

17. In Plumb's introduction to John R. Alden, *Pioneer America* (New York, 1966), p. xxiii.

18. One of the most useful recent compendiums of the promotion of the West is available in the popular book by Kieth Wheeler et al., *The Chroniclers,* The Old West, Time-Life Books Series (New York, 1976).

19. See the discussion in Trygve R. Tholfsen, *Historica; Thinking* (New York, 1967), p. 167.

20. The debate is hardly contemporary. To paraphrase Francis Bacon, when scientific knowledge is sought, men should realize that they are dealing with physical reality, not a construct of the human mind; see Glacken, *Traces on the Rhodian Shore,* pp. 471–74. David Hume argued that man's vision is hardly transcendent or definitive: ''What peculiar privilege has this agitation of the brain which we call thought, that we must thus make it the model of the whole universe!'' David Hume, *Dialogues Concerning Natural Religion* (New York, 1962), pt. 2, p. 23. A striking popular attempt to position human history within the context of natural history is James Michener's *Centennial* (New York, 1975), particularly the opening chapters.

21. See Hans Jonas, *The Phenomenon of Life* (New York, 1966), p. 20; and H. S. Hughes, *History as Art and as Science* (New York, 1964), pp. 31sff. Also note the pioneering essay by Paul B. Sears, ''Ecology—A Subversive Science,'' *Bioscience* 14 (July 1964): 11–13.

22. Shepard and McKinley, *The Subversive Science,* p. 210.

23. Daniel McKinley, ''The New Mythology of 'Man in Nature,' '' *Perspectives in Biology and Medicine* 7 (Autumn 1964): 93–105.

24. See Paul Goodman, ''Can Technology Be Humane?'' *New York Review of Books,* November 22, 1969, reprinted in Robert Disch, ed., *The Ecological Conscience* (Englewood Cliffs, N.J., 1970), pp. 103–17; and Derek J. de Solla Price, ''The Science of Science,'' in John R. Platt, ed., *New Views of the Nature of Man* (Chicago, 1965).

25. See the discussion in Raymond R. Dasmann, ''Man in North America,'' in Darling and Milton, *Future Environments of North America,* p. 328.

26. Quoted by Alexander Spoehr, ''Cultural Differences in the In-

terpretation of Natural Resources,'' in Thomas, *Man's Role in Changing the Face of the Earth,* 2: 100.

27. Futuristic literature grows almost beyond human comprehension. Aside from the Meadows volume (*The Limits to Growth*) mentioned above, representative writing include Herman Kahn and Anthony J. Weiner, ''The Next Thirty-three Years,'' *Daedalus* 96 (1967): 705–32, and the important work by Bertrand de Jouvenel, *The Art of Conjecture* (New York, 1967).

28. Glacken devotes most of his book (*Traces on the Rhodian Shore*) to developing these themes. See particularly pp. 70, 72, 117, 134.

29. See Darcy Ribeiro, *The Civilizational Process* (New York, 1968), pp. 98ff., 128.

30. See Leo Marx, *The Machine in the Garden* (New York, 1964), p. 96.

31. A ''moving line'' of frontier development is questioned on the grounds, first, that the agricultural frontier jumped across the plains and worked backward and that farmers were attracted to existing mining towns, military posts, transportation centers, and lumbering towns. See Walter P. Webb, *The Great Plains* (New York, 1931), p. 205; John A. Hawgood, *America's Western Frontiers* (New York, 1967), pp. 312–13; Ray Allen Billington, *Westward Expansion,* 3d ed. (New York, 1967), pp. 479–80; and Gilbert C. Fite, *The Farmer's Frontier, 1865–1900* (New York, 1966), pp. 11–12. Second, civilized man retains too many of the sophisticated attributes and activities of his particular civilization when he transfers himself to a frontier community. See Ray Allen Billington, *America's Frontier Heritage* (New York, 1966); Billington's collection of essays, *The Frontier Thesis* (New York, 1966); and G. R. Taylor, *The Turner Thesis,* rev. ed. (Boston, 1956), for the debates involved. For another illuminating stance see Carol O. Sauer, ''Historical Geography and the Western Frontier,'' in John Leighly, ed., *Land and Life* (Berkeley, 1967), pp. 48–49; Paul Sears, *The Living Landscape* (New York, 1966); and Paul Shepard, *Man in the Landscape* (New York, 1967).

32. See William A. Albrecht, ''Physical, Chemical, and Biochemical Changes in the Soil Community,'' in Thomas, *Man's Role in Changing the Face of the Earth,* 2: 648ff.; and Firman E. Bear, ''Highly Productive Lands of North America,'' in Darling and Milton, *Future Environments of North America,* pp. 136ff.

33. See Albrecht, ''Physical, Chemical, and Biochemical Changes in the Soil Community,'' in Thomas, *Man's Role in Changing the Face of the Earth,* 2: 649.

34. See the description and definition of the grasslands, prairie, and plains in Webb, *The Great Plains,* pp. 3–7.

35. Ibid., p. 149; Billington, *Westward Expansion,* pp. 413–14.

36. Carl O. Sauer, "Conditions of Pioneer Life in the Upper Illinois Valley" (1916), in Leighly, *Land and Life,* pp. 11–13, 23–24.

37. See the essay by René Dubose in John D. Roslansky, ed., *The Control of Environment* (Amsterdam, 1967), pp. 62–69.

38. See especially James C. Malin, "The Grassland of North America" (Lawrence, Kans., 1967), and the appended bibliography in Thomas, *Man's Role in Changing the Face of the Earth,* 1: 350–60; and Sauer's revision of his earlier view, "The Agency of Man on the Earth," in ibid., pp. 55–56, 62.

39. Carl O. Sauer, "Homestead and Community on the Middle Border" (1962), in Leighly, *Land and Life,* especially p. 35.

40. Spoehr, "Cultural Differences in the Interpretation of Natural Resources," in Thomas, *Man's Role in Changing the Face of the Earth,* 1: 95.

41. Ibid., p. 65.

42. Ibid., p. 66.

43. Billington, *Westward Expansion,* pp. 691–92.

44. Three brief examples must suffice. First, in the long run, localized capital in the land is destroyed. Plowed land with row crops has a very low water-infiltration rate, whereas so-called wild or uncultivated soil does not become so "soupy." Second, much of our food has come out of grasslands not only by human consumption of plants but extensively by the far less efficient feeding of grains to livestock and consuming their meat and milk (some 80 percent of the energy and protein values of grains is lost in the process). Third, the very success of commercial agriculture encouraged Americans to use it even when the land is only marginally efficient or can easily wash or blow away. The dramatic and artificial rise of food prices during World Wars I and II encouraged exploitation of a great deal of land that probably never should have been utilized for agricultural production. See Bear, "Highly Productive Lands of North America," in Darling and Milton, *Future Environments of North America,* p. 139; the commentary by Paul Sears in Thomas, *Man's Role in Changing the Face of the Earth,* 2: 477–79; and George Wald, "Determinacy, Individuality, and the Problem of Free Will," in John R. Platt, ed., *New Views on the Nature of Man* (Chicago, 1965), p. 47.

45. See Carl O. Sauer's classic essay, "The Morphology of Landscape" (1925), in Leighly, *Land and Life,* pp. 315–30; and John A.

Jakle, "Time, Space and the Geographic Past: A Prospectus, *American Historical Review* 76 (October, 1971): 1084ff.

46. Sauer, "Morphology," in Leighly, *Land and Life,* p. 333.

47. Billington, in *Westward Expansion,* p. 409ff., treats Indians as part of the natural setting. Jack D. Forbes argues for an "Indian Frontier" in "Frontiers in American History," *Journal of the West* 1 (July, 1962).

48. Carl O. Sauer, "Forward to Historical Geography" (1941), in Leighly *Land and Life,* see especially pp. 377–78.

49. Wald, "Determinacy, Individuality, and the Problem of Free Will," in Platt, *New Views on the Nature of Man,* pp. 18, 40; and Sauer's comments on the work of P. Vidal de la Blance, "The Morphology of Landscape," in Leighly, *Land and Life,* p. 325.

50. Aldo Leopold, "The Conservation Ethic" (1933), in Disch, *The Ecological Conscience,* especially p. 46.

51. Sauer, "The Agency of Man on the Earth," in Thomas, *Man's Role in Changing the Face of the Earth,* 1:57; and the comments by Omer C. Stewart in ibid., p. 428.

53. See the discussion by Glacken in ibid., pp. 404–405.

54. For an important discussion on environmental freedom, possibilism, and determinism, with an extremely useful typology, see Harold and Margaret Sprout, *The Ecological Perspective on Human Affairs* (Princeton, 1965).

55. A representative approach from historical geography is available in W. Gordon East, *The Geography Behind History,* rev. ed. (New York, 1965), p. 204.

56. Ibid., pp. 8–10.

57. Ibid., p. 43.

58. Ibid., p. 10; see also note 8.

59. Ibid., pp. 116, 121 ff.

60. Shepard, *Man in the Landscape,* pp. xi–xii.

61. Ibid., p. xiv.

62. Paul B. Sears, "The Inexorable Problem of Space," *Science* 127 (January 1958): 9–16, especially p. 11.

63. Leopold, *A Sand County Almanac,* pp. 202–207; see also Paul B. Sears, "The Steady State: Physical Law and Moral Choice, *Key Reporter* 24 (January, 1959): 2–3, 8.

64. See Artur Glickson's comments in Thomas, *Man's Role in Changing the Face of the Earth,* 1: 432–33.

65. Potter, *People of Plenty,* p. 85.

66. See Ian L. McHarg, "An Ecological Method for Landscape

Architecture,'' in Shepard and McKinley, *The Subversive Science,* p. 332.

67. Lawrence B. Slobodkin, ''Aspects of the Future of Ecology,'' in Disch *The Ecological Conscience,* especially p. 80.

68. Shepard, *Man in the Landscape,* pp. 35–40.

69. John Opie, ''Turner, Traditional America, and the Abolition of American History'' (essay, forthcoming), based particularly upon the writings of Mircea Eliade, notably *Cosmos and History: The Myth of the Eternal Return,* trans. W. R. Trask, (New York, 1959), which explores frontier history in terms of myth and traditional societies.

70. See the discussion in Stephen Toulmin and June Goodfield, *The Discovery of time* (New York, 1965), pp. 240–42.

71. Or, in the words of Collingwood, ''Nature has no history; only human beings have history,'' quoted in ibid., p. 10.

72. See George Mackinko, ''Land Use and Urban Development,'' in Shepard and McKinley, *The Subversive Science,* pp. 369–83.

2. THE STUDY OF WESTERN FRONTIER POPULATIONS*

John C. Hudson

Everyone is familiar with the balance-sheet approach to population study: A population grows because of additions by births and immigration; it declines through the subtractions caused by deaths and out-migration. Values and norms condition the biological model of natural increase, but the system is closed because population can change in these four ways only. The simplicity of the basic model and the long-term and widespread habit of collecting population data have provided the basis for a well-developed field of demography that today has much to offer the scholar interested in reconstructing the past. Population numbers are interesting for their own sake, but they are even more useful for making inferences about human institutions. Mate selection, family size, household composition, and migration patterns are some of the variables that emerge from a detailed study of rather more mundane counts of people.

A population has a history and a geography that are carried with it over time and space. The number of females born this year defines the number available to give birth in a generation; a high death rate for young men in one year is carried through the population for generations to come in the form of a constricted

*I would like to thank Kay Weisman, Dawn Wrobel, and Jeannie Frank for their participation in the research. The financial support of the National Science Foundation is gratefully acknowledged.

age structure. Migration rearranges the population, blurring geographical differences in the tempo of growth and extending the territory occupied by a group. The removal of people from some places and their agglomeration in others rearrange the future potential for population growth, especially because migration is selective of young adults.

Frontier populations in the American West have no ultimate origin, either in time or in space. The frontier was part of a process of growth and change that is still with us and has always been with us. During most of the nineteenth century this process had a peculiar configuration in North America that never was and never could be repeated: a steady, outward, and usually westward advance of a line of settlement density of roughly two persons per square mile. The frontier thus defined was peculiar neither to this continent nor to that century. Its great significance lies in the initial impress of people and institutions on the landscape and in the legacy for future generations given by the circumstances of initial settlement. If the frontier was indeed a phenomenon cyclically re-created each time people pressed toward unoccupied territory, it was made possible by an intrinsic process of rebirth and redistribution of population.

Frontier Population Dynamics

Populations undergo many changes in size and composition that have little or nothing to do with migration. There are famines, epidemics, wars, economic cycles, and changes in living arrangements that would continue to produce ups and downs if migration ceased. Each fluctuation would also be present in a dampened form in successive generations. If such fluctuations take place in a series of migrations that are selective by age and by sex, and if the selection operates over and over again as longer-settled areas are depleted to colonize others, then at some future time each colonized area will have a different age distribution reflecting past demographic changes and age-selective migration.

In each community "behind" the frontier a similar sequence of demographic events occurred, but with a different starting date.

One hundred years after the frontier moved across Iowa, the great-grandchildren of the pioneers held community centenniel celebrations that began in the eastern part of the state and took exactly as many years to reach the western border as it took the frontier to travel that distance. Not all the great-grandchildren were still living in the Iowa pioneers' communities of residence; many of them were not even born there, nor were their parents. Some had moved west; others went to the city, and they became part of subsequent redistributions. When some pioneers moved on, others stayed and became community leaders; some of their children stayed eventually to fill their parents' places.

Although this kind of history really cannot be seen, a good visible landscape surrogate is the mix of buildings in a community. Original frontier structures were replaced with more substantial homes and business blocks, which then became obsolete, were converted to other uses, or were continued in disuse down to the present. This "look" of a place varies as one travels from east to west; styles changed with time, but the construction, aging, and conversion of buildings begun at the time of first settlement are carried over time just as is the underlying demographic structure.

The past does not determine the present, but neither can the present be understood without a knowledge of when the relevant processes began. There are demographic similarities from one frontier to the next because similar processes were in operation; the timing of subsequent demographic changes varied from one frontier to the next because each was settled at a different date. These restraints thus define the conditions under which frontier population processes are studied.

Types of Migrants to the Frontier

Descriptions of the frontier refer to time and place, the same coordinates necessary to locate an individual by age and residence. Isolines on a map of population frontiers are labeled by dates, just as a place possesses the attribute "frontier" for a limited amount of time. A simple graphic model can be used to classify individuals into several ideal types in terms of their mi-

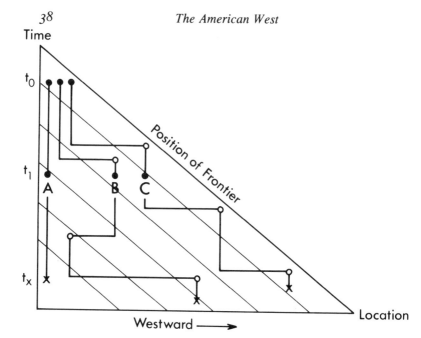

Fig. 1. Lifetime migration behavior for three frontier-born individuals.

gration behavior (Fig. 1). All individuals move downward with time, and they may also move horizontally, representing migration. Westward migration (shifting to the right) advanced the frontier of settlement over time. Three types of individuals with identical life spans illustrate some of the migration syndromes associated with the frontier.

Individual *A* made no moves in a lifetime. This person, the son or daughter of a pioneer family, was born on the frontier but grew to maturity in what became an established community. He or she perhaps achieved upward occupational mobility and a position of community leadership and may have reared children who moved either to a later frontier or to other established communities.

The opposite extreme is illustrated by individual *C*. He made his first moves with parents, brothers, and sisters but later moved westward independently of the household into which he was born; probably he married and took his own children through a similar series of advances to the margins of settled territory. This is the "Daniel Boone syndrome," which is sometimes portrayed as typical of all frontier migrations but was in reality an extreme case. Individual *C* was not able to exploit successive frontier opportunities to the extent of growing attached to any single location. He lived in the same kind of society (or lack thereof) for his entire life, keeping pace with a mode of existence as it kept disappearing to the west.

Individual *B*, born at the same time as *A* and *C*, probably was the most typical frontiersman. He joined in the westward movement at an early age, but after spending some time in the West decided that it was not for him. Men and women who first advanced toward the frontier and then turned away from it often returned to their previous communities of residence. Some were drawn to the urban centers of the Northeast. When new tracts were opened for settlement, many of these individuals succumbed to the lure of new opportunities and again joined in the westward movement. Individual *B* moved forward and backward, from city to frontier and back again, perhaps searching for the right opportunity but often pursuing the same line of work through successive moves.

In very general terms a steady westward migration was more characteristic of the agricultural population than of merchants, clerks, and professional people. A tenant farmer or farm laborer lured west by the promise of free land sometimes returned to the community he left, but he was less likely to move back east than was an individual who saw land ownership more as an investment than as a means of livelihood. Each of these syndromes (and others, of course) set in motion a demographic cycle of growth and redistribution that simultaneously became part of the urbanization process and of the westward push of the frontier.

Migration Data

My argument to this point has been in the form of a plea not to isolate the study of frontier populations from the demographic contexts that produced them and that frontiers, in turn, brought about. It is frustrating to conceive of a historical topic with no beginning or end and no absolute geographical boundaries. Whether we are interested in broad demographic changes or in local history, it is necessary to break down the problem to a manageable scale and to find appropriate sources of data. Empirical research need not abandon a broader view, however, simply for the sake of convenience in delimiting a problem.

What we know depends on the questions we ask (and answer), but what we ask is often guided by the data available. The study of migration "flows" or "streams" is one example. Our hydrologic terminology results from collecting data by area units. Sometimes many individuals from one place move to the same destination, but we speak of flows in general, as though there exist certain channels, when in fact we know that migrants move from one specific place to another. Our models of migration need data; data are collected in areal units, and hence we model migration flows. Studies of population turnover are suggested by data availability also. It is possible to examine manuscript censuses for two time periods to determine the number of new individuals, the number who left, and the amount of persistence. If we lacked such data, or if the usual means of recording residence was by life histories, then we probably would not have so many studies of population turnover. To be sure, many ingenious ways have been devised to escape the limitations of data, but it is also true that much of what we know arises from these very efforts. This suggests the importance of ingenuity in data collection, as well as the desirability of analytical reasoning to deduce the expected results of processes that no one has bothered to record.

The frontier migration process can be thought of as a projection of one set of culture areas onto another; migrants from many environments were put into contact with one another in an environment new to all of them. The frontier did not develop a cultural mirror image of its antecedents partly because of intrinsic differences in the frontier environment and partly because of cultural contacts on the frontier that resulted in new patterns independent of the physical landscape. Detailed information on migrants' origins and their intermediate places of residence help us understand the totality of experiences new settlers brought with them to the West. If we could obtain a complete map of the previous residences of a new frontier population, chances are it would be a baffling pattern of clusters, blank spaces, and intervening areas of low density from which only few were drawn. It is unlikely that two adjacent counties, say in central Nebraska, would have very similar patterns of population origin, although at the state level the origins would be similar.

The process that produced migration patterns is not well understood, and few migration maps exist partly because of data limitations.[1] Manuscript census data provide little in the way of details; intermediate residence sometimes can be inferred from the birthplaces of children, but the locational precision is usually no more than the state or national level. County histories are one source of migration data that could be used to a greater advantage. Many histories give detailed though brief descriptions of the early settlers, their origins, and how they came to move west. If one traces these origins, a picture of the preemergent frontier can be assembled. It goes against common demographic usage to call such a widely scattered group of unacquainted individuals a population, yet the traits learned in the formative years were brought along in the minds of men and women who made up the frontier population. The population existed ten years before the frontier was occupied, though of course no one identified it as a population.

Longitudinal data, in the form of biographical or autobiographical accounts, provide a clearer picture of the people who settled the frontier. Life histories tell us about the frontiersman before and after he qualified for the label. During the late 1930s the Works Progress Administration and the State Historical Society of North Dakota undertook the ambitious Historical Data Project, collecting autobiographies and questionnaires from several thousand pioneer residents of the state. These data on the northern plains frontier are unique in scope and detail. Migration maps, showing birthplaces, the sequence of moves, and the occupations of Dakota frontier settlers classified by national origins, have been constructed from these data (Fig. 2).[2] Any notion of a frontier slowly inching westward is destroyed when one

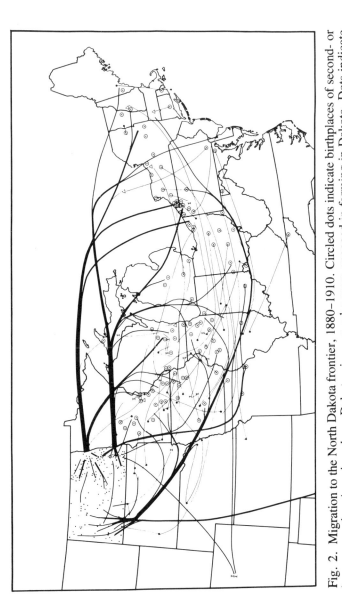

Fig. 2. Migration to the North Dakota frontier, 1880–1910. Circled dots indicate birthplaces of second- or later-generation American-born Dakota pioneers who were engaged in farming in Dakota. Dots indicate previous employment in farming; I indicates previous employment as a farm or nonfarm laborer; triangle indicates previous employment as a craftsman, clerk, or professional. Source: J. C. Hudson, "Migration to an american Frontier," *Annals of the Association of American Georgraphers* 66 (1976): 242–65.

observes the vast territory and the range of urban and rural environments that sent their sons and daughters west to Dakota. The map illustrates only a small part of the total migration, but it is enough to suggest what could be accomplished by detailed studies of population shifts in the general westward movement of the late nineteenth century.

The Frontier Life Cycle

Migration literature today refers to certain peaks in an individual's lifetime propensity to move in terms of stages in a lifecycle. The first independent move is usually associated with college or a first job; marriage produces another move; rearing a family often leads to a search for a larger home; and possibly there are other moves associated with job transfers. When grown children leave home, parents may move to a smaller residence; retirement often brings another migration. These stages identify the crucial associations between migration propensity and age. Migratory behavior is not a recent phenomenon characteristic of a rootless society; with slight modification the stages are equally applicable to historical frontier populations. The creation of new households and the formation of families were most characteristic of the age group represented in greatest abundance on the western frontier.

Eblen studied the age and sex composition of eighty-eight counties between the Great Lakes and the Pacific Coast listed in the Census of Population of 1840, 1850, and 1860.[3] The age composition of a composite frontier county showed an excess of persons in the 20–29 age group. Frontier counties showed deficits in the over-40 ages and in the adolescent years, compared with the national-average age distribution. On the frontier young couples just starting out were far more common than middle-aged couples with children. The degree of difference was most pronounced in areas just being settled, and the tendency was most apparent in areas where initial settlement was rapid. With minor adjustments the same generalization about the age composition of recent arrivals could be made about the booming suburbs around major American cities in the 1950s. New households are most likely to occupy new territory, no matter whether the frontier is Minnesota, 1850, or Park Forest, 1950.

The frontier age distribution for women was far closer to the national average than was the age pattern for frontier men. The surplus of men in the 20–29 age group meant that there were few single women of this age and that frontier women tended to marry at a younger age. Those "extra" young men often had more success finding a bride when they went back home to have another look. This was more than the stuff from which melodrama is fashioned: it was a demographic fact. When the surplus of young men disappeared, it was a sure sign that the young adventurers saw greater opportunities elsewhere and that the frontier was passing.

The Dakota Territorial Census of 1885 illustrates these general sex and age characteristics in all the counties for which records were published.[4] Wells County, in central North Dakota, was on the cutting edge of the frontier at this date (Fig. 3). The 25–29 age-group bulge for men in 1885 did not appear in the 30–34 age group in 1890, but in 1890 there was again a large surplus in the 25–29 age span, most of whom had not been in Wells County in 1885. This group of young men was the most mobile segment of the frontier population.

Marriage

Anyone who has seen a western movie knows that, although the action is left to the young gunslingers on horseback in the foreground, the planks laid in the mud in the background carry an endless parade of bonneted women in calico dresses, arm in arm with men dressed to look like husbands. The folk in the background are there in order to duck and run when the shooting starts, but at least Hollywood did not forget the frontier family. It is easy enough to identify stereotypes, but it often proves more difficult to provide accurate generalizations from facts. The frontier family varied in size and composition from place to place and from time to time, but in all areas where agricultural settlement occurred, the nuclear family as we know it today—husband, wife, and children—was a basic part of the social fabric beginning with the first effective occupation of the land.

Since new household formation is characteristic of the peak

Male　　　　　Female

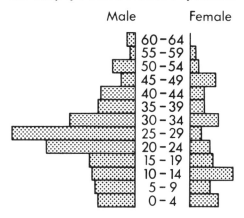

Fig. 3. Age-sex pyramid for Wells County, Dakota Territory, 1885.
Source: Dakota Territorial Census of 1885.

migratory age span among young adults, it follows that frontier
household formation and the westward movement were contemporaneous. A sample of 790 first marriages within the Dakota
pioneer group showed that women married younger than men (the
median age at marriage was 21.7 for women and 26.4 for men).[5]
Of these marriages 43 percent occurred before migration; the rest
took place in Dakota. Early marriage was more common for
women than for men, but there is little evidence that early marriage itself was a frontier characteristic. Endogamy prevailed
among the foreign-born and was only slightly less prevalent
among the first-generation offspring of foreign-born Dakota
pioneers. The customs surrounding marriage were largely preserved in the westward movement, at least for the later frontiers.

Fertility

About 10 percent of the Dakota sample families remained child-
less. Among married couples with one or more children the median length of time between marriage and birth of the first child
was slightly more than twelve months.[6] Migration, marriage, and
family start were collapsed into a short span of time, although

The American West

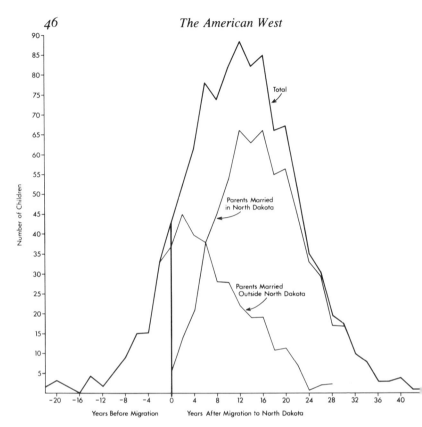

Fig. 4. Childbearing before and after migration to Dakota frontier.
Source: Historical Data Project (sample).

that was not peculiar to the nineteenth-century West either. Awareness of the importance of this timing is crucial to understanding subsequent demographic events because it meant that an especially large frontier-born cohort came into the childbearing years about thirty-five years after initial settlement. Migration to and from the postfrontier society evened out the peaks and valleys in the age distribution, but successive frontiers produced a surplus population attracted to the "next West" with cyclical regularity.

In the early years, then, frontiers grew almost entirely by inmigration; later growth was due to natural increase. In North Dakota the peak in childbearing occurred about twelve years after the pioneer settlers arrived (Fig. 4). The childbearing patterns can be subdivided into those households formed before migration to the West and those begun by young couples who married after they settled on the frontier.

Pioneer Dakota mothers who married back East or in Europe had completed a little less than 30 percent of their lifetime fertility by the time they reached the frontier; according to the graph about 15 percent of them were pregnant when they arrived in Dakota. Those marrying after settlement completed half their childbearing within fourteen years after migration. The twelve-year lag between migration and the peak in childbearing resulting from the sum of these two distributions may or may not be characteristic of other frontiers, but it is likely to be a close approximation for areas that were settled rapidly and whose women had a similar age at marriage.

There is some evidence that fertility was higher in the frontier stage of settlement than it was after the frontier had passed.[7] That is difficult to assess because of the long-term decline in national birthrates that persisted during the entire period of initial settlement in the West. New, lower fertility norms were passed to the frontier by successive generations, although it seems likely that a given husband and wife on the frontier raised a larger family than they would have had they remained in an older, established community.

There were variations in family size among frontier families as great as or greater than those between frontiers and longer-settled areas. The median completed-family size for Russian-German women in North Dakota was 7.5 children; for Norwegian-born mothers the figure was 6.6; and for American women whose parents also were born in this country, the median number of children was 3.9. The Russian-German settlements in the American West, along with heavily Mormon areas, continued to have among the highest child-woman ratios of any predominantly white areas of the country. Fertility norms held by various religious and national groups probably had more effect on the spatial variation of nineteenth-century fertility than did the existence and position of a settlement frontier.

Data on completed family size are difficult to obtain; fertility ratios (such as the number of children aged 0–9 years, divided by the number of women aged 15–44) can be computed from census data. On the Indiana frontier in 1820 this fertility ratio varied between 1.75 and 2.64 among the thirty-three organized counties.[8] Among the nine counties listed in the published Dakota Territorial Census of 1885 in which there were at least ten children recorded, the ratios varied from 0.74 to 2.14. All these Dakota counties were ahead of the "two-persons-per-square-mile" frontier at this date.

The sixty-five years that elapsed between frontier settlement in southern Indiana and the beginnings of white occupancy in western North Dakota saw a decline in national fertility levels that were reflected in the frontier community. Fertility began to fall markedly in some rural areas of the country in the latter half of the nineteenth century.[9] Rural fertility began to converge with urban levels at that time, although urban fertility was declining slowly also. The men and women who left the rural and urban Middle West to take up land in the Great Plains evidently carried these more up-to-date family plans with them. Again frontier demographic patterns emerge as reflections of values and norms held in the pioneers' previous communities of residence.

Household Types

It is common to label a single individual as a household if he or she constitutes an independent economic unit, regardless of the number of other persons living under the same roof. This practice poses a special problem in identifying households on the frontier, where single individuals sometimes made up a large share of the population. Most of them belonged to some sort of outfit, but it stretches the imagination to call such a bunch a "household."

Excluding the population enumerated at the Fort Buford military post, about 49 percent of the white households in the published Dakota Territorial Census of 1885 were single males, 2 to 3 percent were single females, and 3 percent were single heads with children present (Table 1). About 33 percent of the households were nuclear families, with or without children. The remaining 13 percent were multiple-person households including relatives or unrelated individuals. In terms of the total population, however, more than twice as many adults lived in multiple-person households as in the single category, and virtually all children were parts of larger households. These percentages reflect the youthful age structure of the population and the low proportion of single women over twenty-five years of age.

The first group of counties (McIntosh, Towner, and Wells) were on the agricultural frontier in 1885. While these three counties were experiencing a rush of homesteaders, the next group (Mercer, Oliver, Renville, Stanton, and Ward) were about to receive settlement, but they were about three years away from their peak, measured in terms of the dates of pioneer home building. The last group (Bowman, Dunn, McKenzie, Villard, and Wallace) was receiving some new settlement in 1885, but stock raising, rather than farming, was a more usual way of life. Most of these counties received agricultural settlement after 1900; boundary changes and renaming affected all counties in the third group.

If there was a marked change in household composition that accompanied the transition from range livestock to an agricultural economy, these data do not reflect it. Fertility ratios were highest in the third group of counties, and households with children were slightly more common; but single-person households were no more prevalent in the western North Dakota ranch country in 1885 than they were on the farming frontier two hundred miles east. The slightly larger family size in the westernmost group of counties reflects an older population that dated from the beginnings of the range-cattle era there in the late 1870s.

The "honyockers" may have brought with them a different way of life—one dreaded by the range-livestock men, who had hard years of readjustment ahead of them in 1885—but the nuclear family was an institution firmly established before the farming population arrived. If anything, the early years of transition

Table 1. Household Types, Dakota Territorial Census of 1885

Date of Frontier	Counties	Single Households		Married Household Head			Single Head		Fertility Ratio (Range for Group)
		Male	Female	No Children Present	Children Present	Unrelated Individuals Present	Children Present	Other Relatives Present	
1885	McIntosh, Towner, Wells	207	6	23	99	22	14	28	1.00=1.52
	Percentage	51.9	1.5	5.8	24.8	5.5	2.4	7.0	
1888	Mercer, Oliver, Renville, Ward, Stanton	178	12	27	119	34	6	22	0.74=1.83
	Percentage	44.7	3.0	6.8	29.9	8.5	1.5	5.5	
1900–1905	Bowman, Dunn, McKenzie, Villard, Wallace	89	2	6	56	3	4	13	1.34=2.14
	Percentage	5.4	1.2	3.5	32.4	1.7	2.3	7.5	
	All counties	474	20	56	274	59	24	62	
	Percentage	48.8	2.1	5.8	28.2	6.1	2.5	6.5	

from open range to fenced pasture and cultivated fields probably saw a decrease in the ratio of established families to the total population, but as the fertility data show, this was soon reversed by the new wave of settlers, who lost no time in marrying and starting families.

Migration of Frontier Families

What of the rest of the frontier life cycle? Did the families reared by the new arrivals stay put, or did they follow their parents' example and move on? As for the parents themselves, the story of their frontier hardships, battling blizzards, droughts, insect plagues, low prices, and other privations, is well known. Thousands of settlers left before bringing their lands to patent and sought a less precarious existence elsewhere. For those who stayed and there raised their children to maturity, it was often with relief that they saw their offspring leave to seek out opportunities on the next frontier or anywhere else.

Part of the story has already been told, because to some extent the population of a later frontier was drawn from earlier ones. The story is far from complete, however, because the frontier also helped supply the young urbanites of the nation. The westward shift in the mean areal center of the United States' population occurred as urbanization all over the nation drew in the farm families from frontier and postfrontier settings, and it is not surprising that attraction to "the West" and attraction to "the City" show up on a migration map of frontier sons and daughters (Fig. 5).

In 1939, when the Historical Data Project questionnaires were completed, most of the offspring of the Dakota pioneers were at least forty years old. They had already passed through the early adult years of peak mobility, and most of them were older than their parents had been when they settled on the frontier during the 1880s. Some of the frontier-born children continued the westward movement, especially to Montana and to the Prairie Provinces of Canada. They participated in virtually the last large-scale occupation of new agricultural regions in the West—the spring-wheat country of northeastern Montana, the "wheat triangle"

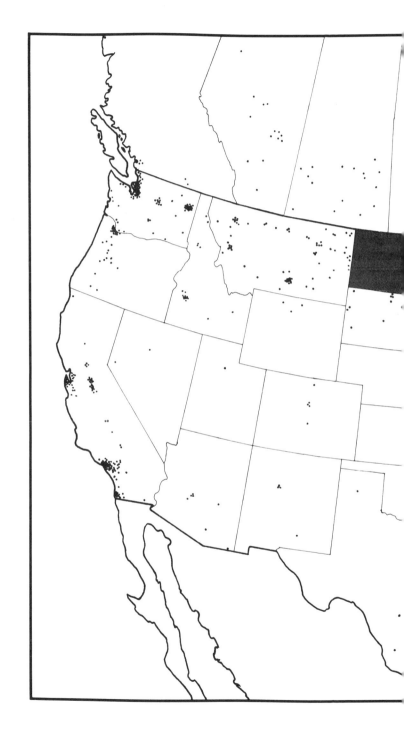

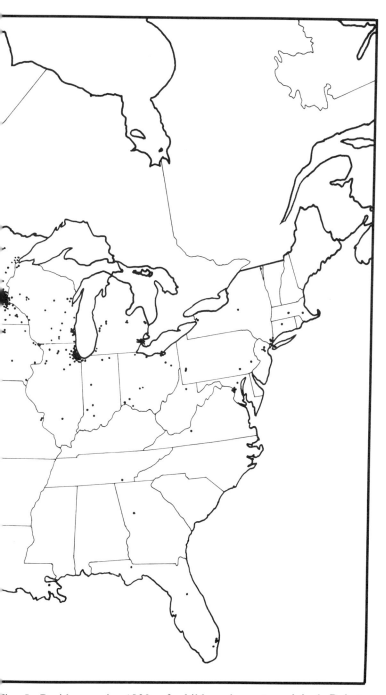

Fig. 5. Residences in 1939 of children born to original Dakota pioneers. Source: Historical Data Project (sample). Only interstate migrants are shown.

north of Great Falls, and the "last best West," in Saskatchewan and Alberta. Few in this sample went to dry-farming areas in central Montana or east-central Washington. Another group fell back from the Dakota frontier, and were found on scattered farms in Minnesota, especially in and around the forested eastern margins of the Red River valley. There was a scattering in other rural areas, but the principal story is to be found in the attraction to urban areas.

Minneapolis and St. Paul attracted large numbers, as did Seattle, Portland, Los Angeles, and Chicago. Billings, Boise, Spokane, Sacramento, San Diego, Milwaukee, Detroit, and New York also drew Dakotans. In 1939, just before military duty imposed a new pattern of circulation on the population, Dakota frontier children had grown to maturity, and, if they had left the state, most of them were raising their families in the rapidly growing cities of the West, where many had sought work during the "dirty thirties." A small proportion returned to the state of their birth.

The dominant direction of movement was to the west, either to urban or to rural locales; eastward migration retraced earlier steps back to established farming areas of the upper Middle West and to the industrial centers of which most of their parents had known but little. The least likely destination of out-of-state migrants was one of the plains states to the south. North–south stratification of migration streams began with the early expansions beyond the colonial eastern seaboard, and they were continued from one frontier to the next across America. The long-distance pattern of migration of pioneer sons and daughers continued the trend.

With the exception of the migration to Canada, which all but dried up after 1920, these patterns of out-migration differ only in degree from those prevailing today.[10] Puget Sound, California, the Twin Cities, and other urban areas continue to be the peak attractions for out-of-state migrants from North Dakota. Postfrontier out-migration patterns established by the first-generation offspring have continued and indeed have been reinforced by information feedbacks similar to those that induced migration to the frontier nearly a century ago. The Dakota frontier was a late one, and it is doubtful that the generalization could be made for the immediate trans-Appalachian West that was settled before large-scale urbanization in the central and western states, but the pattern might well be extended as far east as Illinois and Wisconsin.

It would be erroneous to say that conditions facing young people growing up on the western frontiers of the nineteenth century were similar to those perceived by young people today. The frontier condition contained different stimuli to move or to remain, and cities have a different range of attractions today from those they had then. Still the origins of long-distance population mobility patterns in this country might be traced to the patterns of in- and out-movement established in frontier days. There are traditions of migration, just as there are traditions surrounding other demographic events. Frontier migration established and postfrontier migration extended the national system of population mobility, which is too often treated only in a recent context.

Those pioneer offspring who were still living in North Dakota in 1939 show a similar trend toward urban life (Fig. 6). The pattern is simplified by excluding all but nine counties as origins; moves within those counties are not shown. A slight westward trend was produced by pioneer children reared in eastern counties of the state who moved to farms and ranches on the Missouri Slope, but the noticeable shift is toward the growing urban centers. A similar pattern of urbanization in a westward-drifting frontier context has been documented for late-nineteenth-century Iowa.[11] Turnover on the farm brought in the offspring of the pioneer settlers, but the steady increase in the average size of farms suggests that here, as on other frontiers, the large frontier-born group had to look elsewhere for opportunities. The young folks turned to the towns and cities both nearby and far away. Many of these 1939 residences were not first moves but represent a stage in the population-redistribution process; they by no means reflect all of the lifetime migration of the second-generation frontier population.

It has been asserted that intermarriage within frontier communities produced a kind of clannishness that offered opportunities for individuals who married into certain families.[12] This custom discouraged migration by those who had become well connected and stimulated the migration of those left "outside."

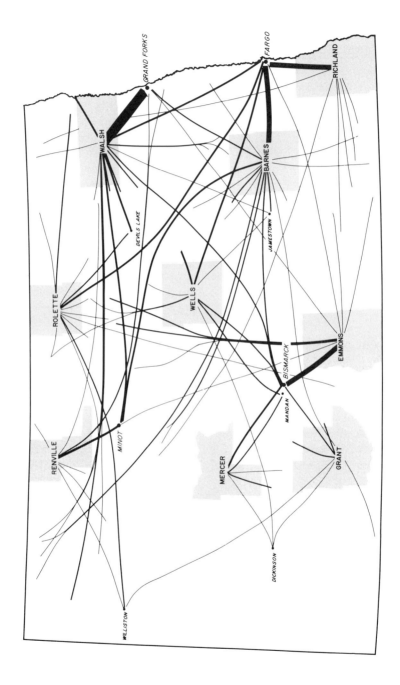

Fig. 6. Residences in 1939 of children born to original Dakota pioneers in nine Dakota counties. Only intrastate,

Social cohesiveness may have been born in many a frontier community, but it is also likely that certain of the settlers brought the tendency with them. The most endogamous groups were those with a tight internal structure often governed by religious principles and further reinforced by non-English-speaking origins. The stronger the common ties the less likely was migration out of the area, regardless of the cultural meaning of those ties.

In North Dakota there was a statistically significant relationship between national origin and the tendency to leave one's home community (Table 2). A sample of 1907 pioneer offspring whose parents were Russian-German, Norwegian, or second generation or later American-born pioneers reveals that the Russian-German children were less than half as likely to leave the state as were children born to the American-stock population; children of Norwegian-born pioneers occupied an intermediate position. Three of five children born to Russian-German families grew to maturity in the same counties where their parents had settled; fewer than one in five had left the state by 1939. Roughly similar proportions in all groups (about one in five) moved elsewhere in North Dakota.

Traditions brought to the frontier by various ethnic and religious groups persisted longest in those communities whose populations also persisted. If no large group of postfrontier migrants arrived to disrupt the initial trait complex, group cohesiveness was maintained as the population itself was retained; retention, in turn, reinforced traditional patterns. New frontiers disrupted community solidarity in older frontier communities by attracting their sons and daughters to the West. As such, the frontier may have been a cultural homogenizer of at least as great proportions as twentieth-century urbanization is said to be. This was so not because frontiersmen shed old customs when they moved west; there is much evidence that they did not. It was the act of outmigration from the postfrontier community that disrupted the passage of local customs to later generations.

Conclusion

What is to be gained by refocusing the study of frontier populations to include their broader geographic and demographic con-

Table 2. Out-Migration Patterns for Children of Dakota Pioneer Settlers

Parents' Nationality	Residence of Children in 1939		
	Same County as Parents	Other North Dakota Counties	Outside North Dakota
Russian-German	230	78	61
Percentage	62.3	21.1	16.5
Norwegian	408	163	238
Percentage	50.4	20.1	29.4
United States (second or later generation)	314	128	287
Percentage	43.1	17.6	39.4

Source: Historical Data Project files. Chi-square test for significance of association = 62.684, four degrees of freedom; significant at 0.01 level.

texts? It is to be hoped that the richness of community case studies would not be lost but rather would be enhanced by the availability of comparative data in which case studies can be interpreted more meaningfully. It is perhaps a geographer's bias not to be content with a series of case studies but to seek generic processes that accommodate the many similarities and differences from place to place. This bias is not at all inappropriate for the study of the evolving American West, because the frontier can scarcely be defined without reference to movement, change, and succession. We do not need a grand theory that can accommodate all possible frontier variations, but we could stand to have a better stock of concepts with which to examine the whole as well as the parts.

Finally, my comments should not be confused with those made by individuals who are urging massive computer-based models for processing historical data. I can state that not one shred of the data analyzed here has been punched on a card, fed onto a tape, or otherwise manipulated by any machine larger than a desk calculator. At the beginning of my analysis of the Historical Data Project questionnaires, I realized that there would be some benefits from computerized data processing. I decided not to pursue that course, not because of any inherent dislike of computers but because I realized that there was no way that my data, especially the unsystematic and wholly unscientific bits and pieces, could be computerized without making far too much work for the results that would be obtained. The alternative was to discard such information. Instead of neat piles of clean, crisp, computer printouts, I have a filing cabinet full of dog-eared pieces of paper that have provided more insights in their rereading than any amount of computer output would ever provide. Each time I look at the data I congratulate myself on that decision.

Notes

1. Two such maps, based on county histories, are found in J. Hudson, "Two Dakota Homestead Frontiers," *Annals of the Association of American Geographers* 63 (December, 1973): 442–62.

2. J. Hudson, "Migration to an American Frontier," *Annals of the Association of American Geographers* 66 (June, 1976): 242–65.

3. J. E. Eblen, "An Analysis of Nineteenth-Century Frontier Populations," *Demography* 2 (1965): 399–413.

4. "The Dakota Territorial Census of 1885," *Collections of the State Historical Society of North Dakota* 4 (1913): 338–448.

5. Hudson, "Migration to an American Frontier," 11. See also B. T. Williams, "The Frontier Family," in H. Hollingsworth, ed., *Essays on the American West* (Austin: University of Texas Press, pp. 40–65.

6. A similar lag was observed among couples in the frontier community of Benzonia, Michigan, between 1868 and 1889; see R. E. Bieder, "Kinship as a Factor in Migration," *Journal of Marriage and the Family* 35 (August, 1973): 429–39.

7. Y. Yasuba, *Birth Rates of the White Population in the United States, 1800–1860* (Baltimore: Johns Hopkins University, 1962).

8. J. Modell, "Family and Fertility on the Indiana Frontier, 1820," *American Quarterly* 23 (December, 1971): 615–34.

9. This was observed in a manuscript census study of southern Michigan; See S. E. Bloomer, M. F. Fox, R. M. Warner, and S. B. Warner, Jr., "A Census Probe into Nineteenth-Century Family History: Southern Michigan, 1850–1880," *Journal of Social History* 5 (Fall, 1971): 25–45.

10. The major difference between the 1939 and the 1965–70 outmigration patterns is the more recent preference for cities in the Great Plains and the Southwest, such as Denver, San Antonio, Phoenix, Dallas, and Tucson.

11. M. P. Conzen, "Local Migration Systems in Nineteenth-Century Iowa," *Geographical Review* 64 (July, 1974): 339–61.

12. Bieder, "Kinship as Factor in Migration," n. 6.

3. THE INFLUENCE OF FRONTIER ENVIRONMENTS ON BEHAVIOR

Roger G. Barker

In this article I will set forth some assumptions about the nature of frontier environments and make some predictions about their consequences for pioneer behavior in terms of particular theories of behavior-environment relations. It is for historians to discover if the assumptions and predictions are true, and for behavior scientists to evaluate the theories of behavior-environment relations. So the article raises theoretical issues and makes research proposals but settles nothing. In fact, no historical data are presented; records are used to illustrate the assumptions and predictions, but they have been selected for their clarity as illustrations, not for their adequacy as data. The general hypotheses related to issues of behavior-environment relations originate from a series of empirical and theoretical studies in the work of Kurt Lewin. Because of the general nature of the presentation, specific references are not usually given; relevant publications are cited in the Bibliography.

Attributes of the Frontier Environment and Their Consequences for Behavior: An Overview

Among the many attributes of the western American frontier, three seem to be crucial for understanding important features of the settlers' behavior:
  1. The frontier was *undermanned;* there were fewer than the

optimal number of people at hand to operate the farms, stores, schools, governing bodies, churches, and so forth.

2. The frontier was *new* to the pioneers; living conditions imposed by geography, weather, prevailing customs, social organizations, and so forth, were unknown or poorly known to them.

3. The frontier environment was *unfinished;* many of the physical-social structures required for the life the settlers desired had to be created.

These frontier characteristics are frequently reported in contemporaneous and retrospective accounts. Below are examples from the novelized reminiscences of Laura Ingalls Wilder.

Undermanned Environment

It was haying time on the Ingalls' homestead on the Dakota plain. Pa needed help to stack the hay. But "he could not borrow work, because there were only a few homesteaders in this new country and they were busy on their own claims." The homestead was undermanned:

"Pa," Laura said, "why can't *I* help you make hay? Please let me, Pa. Please."

Pa lifted his hat and ran his fingers through his sweat-damp hair, standing it all on end and letting the wind blow through it. "You're not very big nor strong, little Half-Pint."

"I'm going on fourteen," Laura said. "I can help, Pa. I know I can." . . .

"Well," Pa said, "maybe you can. We'll try it. If you can, by George! we'll get this haying done all by ourselves!"

Laura could see that the thought was a load off Pa's mind and she hurried to the shanty to tell Ma.

"Why, I guess you can," Ma said doubtfully. She did not like to see women working in the fields. Only foreigners did that. Ma and her girls were Americans, above doing men's work. But Laura's helping in the hay would solve the problem. She decided, "Yes, Laura, you may." . . .

. . . Pa walked beside the wagon and drove the horses between the rows of haycocks. At every haycock he stopped the horses and pitched the hay up into the hayrack. It came tumbling loosely over the high edge and Laura trampled it down. Up and down and back and forth she trampled the loose hay with all the might of her legs, while the forkfuls kept coming over and falling, and she went on trampling while the wagon jolted on to the next haycock. . . .

Laura rested in the prickly warm hay while Pa drove near to the stable. Then she slid down and sat in the shade of the wagon. Pa pitched down some hay, then climbed down and spread it evenly to make the big, round bottom of a stack. He climbed onto the load and pitched more hay, then climbed down and leveled it on the stack and trampled it down.

"I could spread it, Pa," Laura said, "so you wouldn't have to keep climbing up and down."

Pa pushed back his hat and leaned for a minute on the pitchfork. "Stacking's a job for two, that's a fact," he said. . . .

. . . when they came back with the next load he gave her a pitchfork and let her try. The long fork was taller than she was and she did not know how to use it, so she handled it clumsily. But while Pa tossed the hay from the wagon she spread it as well as she could, walking around and around on the stack to pack it tightly. In spite of the best she could do, Pa had to level the stack for the next load.

Now the sun and the wind were hotter and Laura's legs quivered while she made them trample the hay. She was glad to rest for the little times between the field and the stack. She was thirsty. . . .

Dinner was ready when they went to the shanty. Ma looked sharply at Laura and asked, "Is the work too hard for her, Charles?"

"Oh, no! She's as stout as a little French horse. She's been great help," said Pa. "It would have taken me all day to stack that hay alone, and now I have the whole afternoon for mowing."

Laura was proud. Her arms ached and her back ached and her legs ached, and that night in bed she ached all over so badly that tears swelled out of her eyes. . . . [Wilder, 1940, pp. 3–10]

New Environment

A cutter-bar section of Pa's mowing machine had broken, "There's no help for it. . . . Laura, I wish you'd go to town and get [one]. . . . I don't want to lose time. I can keep mowing after a fashion." Laura dreaded to go to the unfamiliar town and hardware store, and so her sister Carrie accompanied her. But it was when they were returning that the environment became entirely new and strange:

... Their errand was done and off their minds, and the sun was shining, the wind was blowing, the prairie spread far all around them. They felt free and independent and comfortable together.

"It's a long way around to where Pa is," Carrie said. "Why don't we go this way?" and she pointed toward the part of the slough where they could see Pa and the horses.

Laura answered, "That way's through the slough."

"It isn't wet now, is it?" Carrie asked.

"All right, let's," Laura answered. "Pa didn't say to go by the road, and he did say to hurry."

So they did not follow the road that turned to cross the slough. They went straight on into the tall slough grass.

At first it was fun. It was rather like going into the jungle-picture in Pa's big green book. Laura pushed ahead between the thick clumps of grass-stems that gave way rustling and closed again behind Carrie. The millions of coarse grass-stems and their slender long leaves were greeny-gold and golden-green in their own shade. The earth was crackled with dryness underfoot, but a faint smell of damp lay under the hot smell of the grass. Just above Laura's head the grass-tops swished in the wind, but down at their roots was a stillness, broken only where Laura and Carrie went wading through it.

"Where's Pa?" Carrie asked suddenly.

Laura looked around at her. Carrie's peaked little face was pale in the shade of the grass. Her eyes were almost frightened.

"Well, we can't see him from here," Laura said. They could see only the leaves of the thick grass waving, and the hot sky overhead. "He's right ahead of us. We'll come to him in a minute."

She said it confidently, but how could she know where Pa was? She could not even be sure where she was going, where she was taking Carrie. The smothering heat made sweat trickle down her throat and her backbone, but she felt cold inside. . . .

She listened for the whirr of the mowing machine, but the sound of the grasses filled her ears. There was nothing in the flickering shadows of their thin leaves blowing and tossing higher than her eyes, to tell her where the sun was. . . .

"Come along, Carrie," she said cheerfully. She must not frighten Carrie.

Carrie followed trustfully but Laura did not know where she was going. She could not even be sure that she was walking straight. . . .

The slough went on for a mile or more of bending, swaying grasses, too tall to see beyond, too yielding to climb. It was wide. Unless Laura walked straight ahead they might never get out of it.

"We've gone so far, Laura," Carrie panted. "Why don't we come to Pa?"

"He ought to be right here somewhere," Laura answered. She could not follow their own trail back to the safe road. Their shoes left almost no tracks on the heat-baked mud, and the grasses, the endless swaying grasses with their low leaves hanging dried and broken, were all alike. . . .

They went on. They must surely have passed the place where Pa was mowing. But Laura could not be sure of anything. Perhaps if they thought they turned back, they would really be going farther away. They could only go on. Now and then they stopped and wiped their sweating faces. They were terribly thirsty, but there was no water. They were very tired from pushing through the grasses. Not one push seemed hard, but going on was harder than trampling hay. Carrie's thin little face was gray-white, she was so tired.

Then Laura thought that the grasses ahead were thinner. The shade seemed lighter there and the tops of the grasses against the sky seemed fewer. And suddenly she saw sunshine, yellow beyond the dark grass stems. . . .

Close together, Laura and Carrie looked out from the edge of the standing grass. The hayfield was not Pa's hayfield. A stronge wagon stood there and on its rack was an enormous load of hay. On the high top of that load, up against the blinding sky, a boy was lying. . . .

[A] strange man lifted up a huge forkful of hay and pitched it. . . .

[Then the boy] stood up on the high load of hay against the sky and saw Laura. He said, "Hello there!" They both stood watching Laura and Carrie come out of the tall standing grass—like rabbits, Laura thought. She wanted to turn and run back into hiding.

"I thought Pa was here," she said, while Carrie stood small and still behind her.

The man said, "We haven't seen anybody around here. Who is your Pa?" The boy told him, "Mr. Ingalls. Isn't he?" he asked Laura. . . .

"Yes," she said. . . .

"I can see him from here. He's just over there," the boy said. Laura looked up and saw him pointing. . . .

"Thank you," Laura said primly and she and Carrie walked away, along the road . . . the wagon had broken through the slough grass. . . .

"Were you much scared, Laura?" Carrie asked.

"Well, some, but all's well that ends well," Laura said. [Wilder, 1940, pp. 18–26]

Unfinished Environment

Although two whole blocks on the west side of Main Street were solidly filled with new yellow-pine buildings, there was no church and no place for general entertainment:

Pa said that the town was growing fast. New settlers were crowding in, hurrying to put up buildings to shelter them. One evening Pa and Ma walked to town to help organize a church, and soon a foundation was laid for a church building. [Wilder, 1941, p. 27]

Suddenly the door [of their house] opened and Pa burst in, saying, "Put on your bonnets, Caroline and girls! There's a meeting at the schoolhouse!"

"Whatever in the world—" Ma said.

"Everybody's going!" said Pa. "We are starting a literary society."

Ma laid aside her knitting. "Laura and Carrie, get your wraps on while I bundle up Grace."

Quickly they were ready to follow Pa's lighted lantern. When Ma blew out the lamp, Pa picked it up. "Better take it along, we'll want lights in the schoolhouse," he explained. . . .

The seats were filled and men were standing thick behind them, when Mr. Clewett called the room to order. He said that the purpose of this meeting was to organize a literary society.

"The first thing in order," he said, "will be a roll call of members. I will then hear nominations for temporary chairman. The temporary chairman will take charge, and we will then proceed to nominate and ballot for permanent officers." . . .

. . . Then Pa stood up by his seat, and said, "Mr. Clewett and townfolks, what we've come here for is some fun to liven us up. . . .

. . . I take it we're pretty well agreed right now on what we want. . . . I suggest, let's just go straight ahead and do what we want to do, without any officers. We've got the schoolteacher, Mr. Clewett, to act as leader. Let him give out a program, every meeting, for the next meeting. Anybody that gets a good idea can speak up for it, and anybody that's called on will pitch in and do his share in the programs the best he can, to give everybody a good time.''

''That's the ticket, Ingalls!'' Mr. Clancy sang out, and as Pa sat down, a good many began to clap. Mr. Clewett said, ''All in favor, say 'Aye!' '' A loud chorus of ''Ayes'' voted it should be so. [Wilder, 1946, pp. 213–16]

It is the thesis of this article that these behaviors of Laura, Carrie, Pa, and Ma Ingalls were not idiosyncratic but rather resultants of undermanned, new, and unfinished environments that they inhabited. The less-than-optimal manpower of the region generated for Laura hard work, difficult actions, an enlarged range of activities and experience, the approbation of important people, enhanced self-esteem, fatigue. For Pa it produced tolerance of Laura's marginally adequate performance and appreciation of her contribution. For Laura, Pa, and Ma it instigated urgent and earnest interactions and obvious interdependence. For Laura and Carrie the new environment of the big slough produced uncertainty, alertness, carefulness, fright, bravado, false moves, surpirses, and fatigue. And the unfinished frontier environment, the lack of social-physical structures for the behavior Pa and Ma desired, instigated actions by them directed at creating a church and a literary society. The *degree* and the *manner* in which the members of the Ingalls family and other inhabitants of the frontier exhibited these behaviors were unique to them as singular individuals, but, to the extent that these conditions held across the frontier, behavior of these kinds was general.

This was also the view of Frederick Jackson Turner and his students. They described many attributes of the frontier environment and behavior, including the environment's ''demand'' for exertion (Turner, in Taylor, p. 29) and the necessity of ''hewing out a home, making a school and a church'' (Turner, in Taylor, p. 32); they saw the frontier as a ''place where men are scarce'' (Craven, in Taylor, p. 96), with an ''intense pressure for labor'' (Craven, in Taylor, p. 99). They did not, however, spell out how the frontier environment produced frontier behavior. This I shall attempt to do for the three environmental attributes I have identified.

The Environments of Behavior

It is necessary first to consider the general nature of the human environment. A person has many environments. The ones that are relevant to the issue at hand must be identified. Here we are concerned with the frontier environments that are involved in the molar behavior of its inhabitants, that is, in goal-directed behavior such as putting up hay, organizing a church, taking a shortcut. We are not concerned with such molecular actions as the manner in which Laura gripped the pitchford, the grammar Pa used at the meeting of the literary society, the length of the girls' paces in the slough. Molar behavior is linked with two environments: the objective, or *ecological, environment* and the subjective, or *psychological, environment*. The ecological environment consists of the regions surrounding the person as they *exist independently of his perception of them,* that is, as it is described by independent observers and instruments. The psychological environment is the regions and objects outside the person *as they are perceived by him.* Wilder provides a description of the Big Slough as both ecological and psychological environments. Ecologically it was a mile-wide depression in the prairie covered with dry soil on which coarse, 40-inch-high grass plants grew 1 to 3 inches apart. Psychologically, for Carrie and Laura the Big Slough was a rustling, hot, luminous, homogeneous, head-high medium of yielding grass stems that closed behind them after each step and obscured their vision in all directions; it was a fearsome, directionless place. Both the ecological and psychological environments have parts with differing properties.

The ecological environment is a nesting series of ever-more-inclusive regions surrounding a person. In the instance of Laura and Carrie in the Big Slough, the most proximal ecological region was the immediately circumjacent grass-covered depression that ended with upward-sloping sides surrounded by the level prairie, spotted with irregularly occurring farmsteads and a single town, with a few businesses, a school, and some residences within it. Beyond this other geosocial regions without limit finally encompassed the whole world for them. The psychological environment of Laura and Carrie consisted, likewise, of ever-more-distant regions. Beyond the directly experienced surrounding wall of grass, there was the area Pa was mowing, the house where Ma was waiting, the town and the store the girls had recently left. Far from these regions was the little house in the big woods where Laura had once lived.

It is essential to specify these aforementioned surroundings, as well as the exact part of each. On the western American frontier the ecological environment encompassed the settler's homestead with its buildings, soil, surface contours, flora, and so on, and also, hundreds of miles away, the eastern seaborad, with its industries, financial institutions, government agencies. Both influenced his behavior, but in different respects and degrees, and by way of different mechanisms. The psychological environments of the pioneers included the immediately surrounding situation as they saw it, that is, the "real" psychological environment closely corresponding to the ecological environment—what they may have called the "actual situation" (open spaces, isolated shacks, the general store, wandering tracks, the saloon, and so on)—and it included also an envisioned environment determined to an important degree by their own needs, or what they may have called "hopes and aspirations" (farms, roads, a school, a mill, a postoffice, and so on).

So we are faced with questions of the component parts and the structures of ecological and psychological environments. I shall consider the ecological environment first.

The Proximal Ecological Environment: Behavior Settings*

If a satellite with cameras for recording human behavior were positioned over any considerable portion of the world, whether a frontier or a settled region, it would show that human activities are by no means uniformly or randomly distributed over the earth but are clustered within relatively small, widely separated areas.

---

*This section is adapted from Barker and Associates, *Habitats, Environments, and Human Behavior* (San Francisco: Jossey-Bass Publishers, 1978), pp. 192–201.

These are towns (and settlements, villages, cities). Outside these areas, and the roads connecting them, there are minor concentrations of human activity around farmsteads and other isolated habitations. Behavior otherwise is very sparsely distributed.

If the cameras were focused on a particular town, they would show again that human activites are not uniformly or randomly distributed but are concentrated in bounded regions. These are *behavior settings,* an important class of ecological regions because they form the proximal environments of most molar actions. They are especially important for an understanding of the frontier, because behavior settings on the frontier differed from those in the settled regions in ways that produced differences in behavior.

Towns and their component behavior settings are easily seen and commonly reported. Travelers often describe the "life" of a country in terms of its towns, the behavior settings of the towns, and the behavior of the towns' inhabitants within their settings. An example may be found in Dr. Alexander Hamilton's 1744 travel diary of a trip along the eastern seaboard through England's American colonies that were still frontier areas (Bridenbough, 1948). The description leaps from town to town (Boston, Dedham, Wrentham, Providence, Bristol, Newport . . .), each a unit of colonial life with only occasional mention of roadside inns and farmsteads. As Hamilton approached Newport, Rhode Island, he described it as a unit with a few outstanding structures and regions:

The town of Newport is about a mile long, lying pritty near north and south. It stands upon a very levell spot of ground . . . with one long, narrow street and several branching lanes, one large market house, the town house, two Presbyterian meeting houses, one large Quaker meeting house, one Anabaptist meeting house, one Church of England, and the town's fort.

As a visitor to Newport, Hamilton described the town in terms of nine behavior settings (his own behavior within them is in parentheses): White Horse Tavern (dining, "putting up" for the night), streets (walking about, sightseeing), Baptist meeting (attending church), rooming house and apothecary shop (lodging), coffeehouse (drinking coffee, spending the evening with acquaintances), Hog's Hole, shaded park area (gallantly "romping with the ladies"), Philosophy Club meeting (conversing with members), prison (talking with prisoners), Little Rock, another park area (promenading with ladies). The behavior of Hamilton and his associates is always described within the context of one of these behavior settings.

Behavior settings are bounded, stable, objective entities whose properties are independent of the perceptions of the inhabitants; nonetheless, they coerce the inhabitants. This would be shown clearly if the satellite cameras were brought nearer with lens and film arrangements to penetrate the walls of particular behavior settings and to record movements within them. It would not be difficult to focus on particular settings, for each is surrounded by a conspicuous wall or boundary zone. It would be found that the pattern of activity within each setting is stable and characteristic even when the inhabitants vary greatly in psychomotor characteristics. The pattern within Weylin's Grocery Store, of Oskaloosa, Kansas, in the 1960's, for example, with the main current of the inhabitants and grocery carts flowing along the aisles between the shelves, past the check-out counter and out the exit, was radically different from that within County Engineer's Office, with a small stream of people moving into and out of one region (the secretaries' room) and a few of these branching off into a connected region (the engineer's private office). If the cameras were lowered still more and focused on particular individuals, they would reveal that the behavior of persons who move between behavior settings conforms to the pattern prevailing in the setting they currently inhabit. Weylin's Grocery Store and County Engineer's Office are not passive places where people assemble and behave solely in accordance with the intentions and abilities they bring to these settings. Rather these and other settings mold the behavior of their inhabitants. How do they do this? And how do behavior settings on the frontier generate behavior that differs from that of settings in settled regions?

Characteristics of Behavior Settings

Behavior settings have many characteristics. These have been expounded in technical detail in a number of publications (see especially Barker, 1968, and Barker and Schoggen, 1973). Here we shall consider in a general way only the most important characteristics.

ECO-BEHAVIORAL PHENOMENA AND PROGRAMS OF EVENTS

Dictionary definitions identify two important attributes of behavior settings: they are mixes of physical and human components (they are eco-behavior phenomena), and they are ongoing occurrences (they are programs of events). Here, for example, are definitions of two classes of behavior settings:

Hardware store: A business establishment where metal goods are bought and sold at retail

Homestead: A tract of land and its interjacent buildings and appurtenances on which the owner and his family live and raise crops and/or livestock

According to these definitions, hardward stores are more than rooms, shelves, boxes, cutter-bar sections, nails, stoves, and so on; they are also standing patterns of customers' buying behavior and storekeepers' selling behavior. And homesteads are more than fields, buildings, and equipment. They are also ongoing programs of housekeeping, milking, and putting up hay. All other behavior settings involve both human and nonhuman components in particular programs of events.

VARIED AND INTERDEPENDENT PARTS

Behavior settings have various parts that are interdependent. Within Weylin's Grocery Store, for example, some human components are young, some old; some are buyers, some sellers; some are male, some female; some are butchers, some checkers. The nonhuman components range from black pepper to refrigerators and fluorescent lights. In view of such variety, one can ask, What makes Weylin's Grocery Store a unitary phenomenon? Why do not its refrigerators and all other refrigerators in the town form an ecological unit? The answer is that each part of the store is dependent on every other part, because the store functions as a unit. If the refrigerators break down, meat cannot be sold; if the check-out counter is blocked, customers cannot buy soup. It is the interdependence of the parts rather than their similarity that makes a behavior setting a unitary entity.

HOMEOSTATIC CONTROLS

Related to the interdependence of its parts is the fact that a behavior setting is a self-governing entity with homeostatic-control mechanisms that enforce, within limits, conformity of its diverse components to its standing pattern and level of functioning in the presence of internal and external disturbances. The Ingalls' homestead, for example, bought very strong forces to bear on Pa, Ma, and Laura to use extraordinary means to carry out the essential operation of putting up the hay before winter closed in. Likewise, Weylin's Grocery Store enforces its characteristic pattern upon its customers and staff, in that the customers enter not a passive region but one that incorporates them into its ongoing program. A customer with the intention of quickly buying a can of soup for lunch, for example, finds that one door resists his entrance while the other flies open at his approach. Once he gains entrance, the one-way turnstiles require him to proceed to the right, away from the soups. The tide of other customers further opposes the most direct path, and so he takes a longer way along the meat counter; here the friendly butcher urgently recommends to him a great bargain in chuck roast that he cannot resist. He insists, however, that the somewhat reluctant butcher cut the roast into two pieces and wrap them for his home freezer. Finally, proceeding to the check-out stands the customer learns that only one stand is in operation, furthering the delay. This troubles him greatly, and in his agitation he hoists the can of soup and packages of meat into the view of the clerk, who signals him to exit by the neighboring unmanned check-out counter. However, just as the automatic exit door is closing behind him, he is called back by the clerk because, in his haste, he has failed to sign the charge slip. He must make a short loop back through the ever-eager entrance door to the check-out counter, to be released again by the exit door. Our customer is not a free spirit; the store exerted a claim over him.

NUMBER OF HUMAN COMPONENTS

Behavior settings have optimal numbers of human components. The number varies with the prevailing standing pattern and level of functioning of the setting. A Bridge Game as a behavior setting requires four human components, no more no less. Weylin's Grocery Store in the 1960's on the other hand, operated smoothly with five employees and 150 regular customers, though it could function with both fewer and greater numbers, within limits.

GEOGRAPHICAL AND TOPOLOGICAL POSITION

Three characterisitcs of behavior settings are related to their locations. Every behavior setting has a precise geographical and temporal locus. Weylin's Grocery Store exists in Oskaloosa, Kansas, at 503 Delaware Street from 7:30 A.M. to 8:30 P.M., Monday through Saturday, and from 8:00 A.M. to 12 noon on Sunday. Every behavior setting also has a boundary that completely surrounds it; this frequently is a wall with entrances and exits and properties that regulate the flow of human and physical components and influences across it. Weylin's Grocery Store, for example, excludes dogs at its entrance with the sign "No Dogs Allowed," and it insulates its interior space from rapid changes in the outside temperatures by ventilating devices and by the structure of its walls. Finally, every setting has a definite topological position; it occurs within a nesting set of units consisting, in the case of Weylin's Grocery Store, of the town (Oskaloosa), the setting (the grocery store), components of the setting, both physical and human (customers, cans of soup), and parts and attributes of the components, including movement and actions (a customer's desire for a can of chicken soup and the price stamped on the can). When it is remembered that almost all behavior in a town occurs within its behavior settings, it will be clear why those settings are so important. Although towns have many other parts (buildings, oxygen gas, institutions, social classes, business areas, families, organizations), the topological position of behavior settings means that only they form the most proximal, circumjacent environments of the inhabitants. They intervene between a town's inhabitants and the wider environment through their selective boundaries and their coercive programs. In other words, a town's inhabitants are almost always subject to influences residing in its behavior settings.

SMALL SIZE

On a scale encompassing the whole world, behavior settings are small entities. Their spatial extents and populations in Oskaloosa range from the setting Telephone Booth, $3' \times 3'$ in area, with a single inhabitant at each occurrence, to the setting School Football Game, in an area $400' \times 500'$ in extent with six hundred inhabitants on some occasions. Most churches, schools, manufacturing concerns, and government institutions and many businesses consist of a number of behavior settings housed in one or more buildings. For example, County Engineer's Office in Oskaloosa is a behavior setting located in the Courthouse along with a dozen other behavior settings. Behavior settings are man-sized units, and they are the ecological units most proximal to people.

These characteristics of behavior settings hold equally for those on the frontier and for those in settled regions. In the nineteenth century a hardware store on the western frontier and one on the eastern seaborad were in these respects the same; and this was true, too, for school classes, worship services, homesteads, and so forth. But there were differences, such as their spatial and thermal properties, the sex and age distribution of their inhabitants, and the nature and prominence of aesthetic, recreational, and governmental behavior in their programs. Here I shall consider one difference that I have already mentioned: The behavior settings of the American frontier more frequently than those of the settled regions had fewer than the optimal numbers of human components; they were more often undermanned. I consider this difference to be crucial for the behavior of the pioneers; it is an environmental difference whose *modus operandi* we are beginning to understand.

The Undermanned Frontier Environment

If the number of human components of a behavior setting is less than the optimal number, there are predictable resultants along its operating and maintenance circuits. Operation is continued unaltered, within limits, by controls that redistribute the available forces among the fewer inhabitants, so that, on the average, there are more and stronger forces per inhabitant in a wider range of directions. If the friendly butcher is absent, the store manager waits on some customers, the stockman moves part time from the storeroom to the meat counter, and the manager's secretary carries out essential tasks of the manager under his direction; all work harder than usual. A similar redistribution occurs if there is a shortage of nonhuman components. If trolleys for transporting goods from storage rooms to shelves are in short supply, pressures arise to use those available more continuously, to load them more heavily, and, in extremities, to use customers' carts as trolleys. The nature of the redistribution depends upon the precise arrangement and properties of the control circuits, Nevertheless, the general consequences of having less than the optimal number of parts are as stated: Fewer parts are, on the average, foci of more and stronger operating forces in a wider range of directions.

Undermanning has the same resultants along the maintenance circuits of behavior settings: Controls redistribute the forces among the fewer human components, but in this case the consequences are more severe and wide ranging. Settings with fewer than the optimal numbers of inhabitants or other components have smaller reserves for meeting the inevitable interferences with normal operation; thus they are vulnerable to more frequent and serious breakdowns. The program of Ingalls' homestead with its single mowing machine, single operator, and no spare parts was almost brought to a stop by the broken cutter-bar section; both maintenance (repairing the mower) and operation (keeping "mowing after a fashion") were most urgent. The greater vulnerability of undermanned settings has two consequences: (1) the strength of both operating and maintenance forces is enhanced when the more frequent breakdowns occur, and so the fewer inhabitants are subject to even greater pressures at these times; (2) the prevailing direction of the forces is altered. The latter consequence requires explication.

There are two ways of dealing with a behavior-setting component that interferes with normal operation: eliminate the deficient component or correct the defect. If a checker in Weylin's Grocery Store makes errors, he may be fired or he may be retained and more closely supervised. Behavior-setting controls compare the costs of these two procedures and select the least costly procedure. Two facts are relevant to the selection: (1) it often requires less effort to eliminate defective components than to correct them; (2) reducing the number of components by eliminating the defective ones may, by increasing vulnerability to breakdowns, increase the effort required to operate and maintain the setting at an adequate level. The likely smaller cost of eliminating a defective component must be balanced against the possibly greater cost of maintaining the setting with reduced components. *This balance usually differs for undermanned and optimally manned behavior settings. For undermanned settings the cost of correcting the behavior of a deficient inhabitant is often less than the combined cost of eliminating him and of maintaining the setting with the reduced manpower. The reverse more often holds for optimally manned settings with their reserves of manpower.* Efficiency decrees that undermanned behavior settings favor correcting the deficiencies of inhabitants, whereas optimally manned settings favor eliminating inhabitants with defects. That is one manifestation of a more general difference in the dynamics of the kinds of behavior settings. The forces within an undermanned setting are prevailingly centripetal; they unify and integrate the setting by molding and strengthening its parts. They do this by discriminating between deficient attributes of components (which are corrected) and the components themselves (which are conserved). On the other hand, the forces within an optimally manned setting are prevailingly centrifugal. They shunt defective components out of the setting without discriminating between their attributes and the components themselves. This is of greatest significance for the inhabitants of behavior settings, for it means being essential and valued in undermanned settings and expendable and less highly regarded in optimally manned settings. This difference holds too for the nonhuman components of behavior settings. A homesteader's meager, irreplaceable implements must be most carefully conserved, whereas a big operation cannot afford to retain unreliable equipment.

I cannot map out here the detailed arrangements involved in the control, operation, and maintenance of behavior settings—arrangements that determine the particular consequences of undermanning for the behavior and experiences of the inhabitants. However, the most important resultants of undermanning can be indicated from what has been presented, namely, that forces bearing on the inhabitants of undermanned behavior settings are, relative to those of optimally manned settings, (1) more numerous, (2) stronger, (3) more varied in direction, and (4) more prevailingly centripetal, involving in the case of inhabitants with inadequate performances forces that are more frequently directed (5) toward removing inadequacies of behavior and (6) toward retaining the inhabitants themselves. I shall, therefore, list the behavioral resultants of undermanning relative to optimal manning and identify (by number) which of the above behavior-setting conditions are primarily involved.

The theory of behavior settings and the assumptions I have made about frontier behavior settings imply that in comparison with inhabitants of settled regions, on the average:

Frontiersmen *carry out more actions* (1); they are busier.

They *work harder* (2); their actions are more vigorous.

They *engage in a wider variety of behavior* (3); they are more versatile.

They *act to sustain the settings they inhabit more frequently* (4) they are more behavior-setting–oriented.

They *more frequently act to remove behavior deficiencies of behavior setting inhabitants* (5); they are more implicated in correcting the behavior of their associates.

They *more frequently act to retain behavior setting inhabitants* (6); they appreciate their associates' contributions more highly.

These are the immediate, primary attributes that distinguish the behavior of frontiersmen from that of their fellows in the settled regions. But this is only the beginning, for these differences lead, singly and in combination, to other behavior differences one or more steps removed from the direct adjustments to undermanning; namely, on the average:

Frontiersmen *attempt to carry out difficult actions more frequently,* that is, actions that are near the top of their ability ranges, actions that tax their capabilities. They, therefore, suffer *greater wear and tear and fatigue.* For those who are unable to stand up to the greater difficulties, a further outcome is *reduced stamina and vigor, higher morbidity and mortality, more experience of failure, and lower self-regard and self-esteem.* These are the broken men of the frontier, and their greater number is one of its important features; but since these casualties contribute little to the active life of the frontier, and many of them leave, they will not be considered further. For those who are able to cope, the more difficult actions lead to *greater hardiness,* to *more experience of success and failure,* and to *enhanced self-esteem and self-confidence.*

Frontiersmen *engage in important actions more frequently.* Importance is defined as the amount of impairment a setting would suffer if the action did not occur. This difference is a manifestation of the more vigorous, more varied, and more setting-sustaining actions of the frontier. Because of their more important actions frontiersmen are, in fact, *more often persons of consequence,* and even indispensable people, so they are *more highly valued* by their associates for their contribution to the maintenance of essential behavior settings. This, in turn, contributes to a self-image of a *person of importance* (to whom others look up) and a *person with responsibilities* (on whom others depend).

Frontiersmen *accept lower levels of performance;* their standards of workmanship are lower. This arises because they must engage in a greater variety of activities, some of which are likely to involve mutually interfering skills and in some of which they are not proficient by endowment or training. Furthermore, being busier, they have less time for preparation, and their greater fatigue hinders highest achievement. Nevertheless, lacking replacements, they must accept their own behavior and that of their associates if it is minimally adequate for the continued operation of the setting.

Frontiersmen *are less evaluative of personality differences;* they are more tolerant of their associates. This is an aspect of the more centripetal direction of forces and setting-sustaining actions in undermanned settings. If personnel are in short supply, the operative basis for evaluating a person is the particular actions he can provide; the personality of the only person available to do an essential task is secondary. On the frontier the balance of questioning is less toward What kind of a person is he? and more toward What has to be done? and Can he do this job?

Frontiersmen *have more urgent interactions with their associates;* they are more interdependent. This is a consequence of the more frequent actions to remove behavior deficiencies and to retain essential human components, through stronger, more varied, and more important actions. Frontiersmen have *richer and tenser* interactions.

Frontiersmen *engage in actions with less certain outcomes.* Under pressure of engaging in more difficult behavior within behavior settings that are more vulnerable to breakdown, frontiersmen are in greater jeopardy of being unable to achieve their goals.

Frontiersmen *are more involved with the ecological environment* and less so with their own inner states; worldly concerns are more salient and personal concerns are less salient; frontiersmen are more reality-oriented. They are so busy with vigorous and varied activities required to implement and maintain the undermanned frontier settings that they have less time and energy for the life of the mind, for contemplation, for scholarship, for art, and so forth.

These behavior characteristics of frontiersmen relative to the inhabitants of settled regions hold for those who cope with the demands of the frontier, not for casualties of the frontier. They refer to generally prevailing differences. For various reasons there are exceptions: some frontiersmen are lazy, some contemplative, some irresponsible, and so forth. the exceptions occur because frontier behavior settings differ in degree of undermanning (and some are not undermanned). The exceptions occur because people differ in sensitivity to behavior-setting conditions, and because the differences may be masked or contravened by countervailing circumstances, such as the migration of a particular cultural group into a limited and highly populated frontier area, or by a period of drought where casualties are great and only a subsistence life is possible.

The differences refer to overt actions, not to the cognition, emotions, and motives that may accompany them in particular cases. A versatile frontiersman may not realize that he is widely competent and may not aspire to be so; he merely does what the behavior settings require. The pioneer who tolerated the rough carpentry of of his helpful neighbor may not have approved of the poor workmanship. The early settler who got along with a variety of people on the school board, in the work crews, at the general store may have disliked and disapproved of many of them; but these behavior settings would be jeopardized without his and their implementation, and within them he satisfied more urgent needs than the need for congenial associates. We have seen that, in comparison with optimally manned behavior settings, undermanned settings more often correct their inhabitants' deficiencies and retain the inhabitants, whereas the former more often eliminate inhabitants with deficiencies. this means that on the frontier *conformity of overt behavior occurs at the cost of cognitive, emotional, and motivational nonconformity,* whereas this is less true of settings in settled regions. The result is that within frontier behavior settings there is *greater unity through mutually supportive actions but also greater tension through cognitive, emotional, and motivational diversity.*

The New Frontier Environment

The behavior of the pioneers vis-à-vis the undermanned environment of the frontier was not, as we have seen, a response to their perception of it as undermanned; rather it was a syndrome of reactions to the characteristic pattern of discrete, objective inputs from the undermanned settings. In the examples given earlier, Laura's behavior was responsive to the pitchfork that was taller than she was and to Pa's request, "Laura, I wish you'd go to town and get it" (the cutter-bar section). In contrast, the behavior of the pioneers vis-à-vis the new environment of the frontier, to which we now turn, was directly in response to their perception of it as *new, unfamiliar, untried,* in the same way as they behaved in response to their perception of it as extensive, productive, hot, cold, windy, and so on.

An environment that is new to the inhabitants has three simultaneous attributes for them:

1. *Directions not known.* The actions that will result in a desired effect are unknown. This is the situation confronting a homesteader intent on locating a good claim, and it was Laura and Carrie's situation in the Big Slough.

2. *Valence* (attraction) simultaneously positive and negative. Each action is seen as having possible good consequences (bringing the person closer to his goal) or bad consequences (moving him further from his goal). This again is the situation of the homesteader: if he goes north, he may be advancing toward the best land, or he may be leaving it behind; similarly this is the case if he goes south, east, or west. This was the situation of Laura and Carrie, too: "Perhaps if they turned back they would really be turning away [from Pa]."

3. *Perceptual structure unstable.* The pattern of the stimulating field is indefinite and ambiguous; it changes in important ways with small changes in the viewpoint or motivation of the person. The sight of trees means, momentarily, good soil and water to the homesteader, but the almost immediate realization that many trees are broken and misshapen means trouble; perhaps there are buffeting winds.

These three attributes apply to social and intellectual situations as well as to those with spatial dimensions. A homesteader on meeting his neighbor with whom he wants to be on good terms but about whom he knows nothing is in a new social situation: social actions that will foster harmony between them are not known; each action may elicit a harmonious or a disharmonious response from the new neighbor. With each interchange the homesteader and his neighbor reveal first this and then that side of themselves.

Certain characteristics of behavior within a new environment can be derived from these attributes. To the degree that the frontier confronts its inhabitants with more new situations than the old established regions, we can predict some differences between the behavior of frontiersmen and that of old settlers.

1. *From directions not known:*

Frontiersmen *more frequently engage in nonparsimonious, exploratory behavior;* they less often take the most direct path to their goals. The first homestead claim is relinquished for a (it is hoped) better one.

Frontiersmen *more frequently make errors, false steps, and radical moves.* At the very moment the pioneer with the thirsty family and animals searches for water, he moves away from the only spring in the region.

Frontiersmen *more frequently experience frustration.* They are prevented by the unknown directions from reaching goals and achieving satisfactions. On digging the third dry well, the homesteader becomes desperate.

2. *From valence simultaneously positive and negative:*

Frontiersmen *are more frequently in a state of conflict.* The hungry, snowbound homesteader simultaneously wants to eat his wheat and save it for seed.

Frontiersmen *more frequently advance and retire alternately* as the balance of positive and negative components shifts. The snowbound homesteader starts for town only to return after thinking better of it.

Frontiersmen *are more cautious and alert.* Because of the opposing tendencies the pioneer neither advances nor retires freely; he feels his way, "plays it by ear." The pioneer storekeeper carefully balances stocking sufficient goods (which he cannot replenish) against overstocking merchandise (he cannot return).

3. *From perceptual structure unstable:*

Frontiersmen *are more vacillating and unstable;* their behavior shifts as their perceptions of the situation shift. The emigrant family suddenly pulls up stakes and returns to the old home when their perception of the situation (''on the ground'') contradicts their perception of it from a distance.

Frontiersmen *are more sensitive* to small cues. Emigrants by boat tie up to the riverbank and investigate on foot when they hear a sound like that of a waterfall (which turns out to be wind in a poplar grove).

These primary properties of behavior in new frontier situations have secondary properties, too, and in combination and under particular conditions they are sometimes altered and even take on the appearance of their opposites. In new social situations conflict and caution may take the form of a *bold front.* In a potentially very dangerous situation, such as a prairie fire, the conflict between the opposing tendencies to advance and fight the fire and to retire and flee from it can result in *immobility.* The inevitable errors and conflicts produce *particular fears* and *persisting anxiety.* Severe frustration is accompanied by *emotional outbursts* and *behavior disruption.* Exploratory behavior, conflict, and being easily influenced foster the support of *hopeless projects* (new townsites, railway lines) and panaceas (medical nostrums).

There are serendipitous consequences, also, in life on the new frontier. Errors and frustration are not the only consequences of unknown directions. Sometimes pioneers have *strokes of luck* and strike it rich. The possibility of good outcomes is always present, and even the perceptual instability of the frontier—the ever-changing landscapes and townscape—fosters the hope that something good will turn up. In fact, this possibility, and the knowledge and rumors of its occasional occurrence doubtless more than balance the negative attributes of the new frontier environment for many pioneers.

Psychological environments on the frontier relative to those in settled regions have something in common with the environments of adolescents relative to those of adults. Adolescents, too, are confronted with new situations as they grow into adulthood, and so it is not surprising that we have used terms commonly used in connection with adolescents in our consideration of pioneers in their new frontier environments: exploration, errors, false steps, radical moves, frustration. Indeed, adolescents and pioneers are both frontiersmen; they are both entering new territory.

The Unfinished Frontier Environment

The undermanned frontier, which we first considered, refers to a particular feature of the objective, ecological environment (meager manpower); the new frontier environment, which we considered next, refers to a feature of the subjective, psychological environment (strange surroundings). We come now to the unfinished environment. This refers to a discrepancy between the psychological environment the pioneers saw spread out before them—the real environment—and the psychological environment they brought with them, in other words, an envisioned environment determined to an important degree by their own needs. In the adjustment to the frontier there was a reduction in the discrepancy between these environments. That reduction came about in two ways. When a pioneer actually settled on the land, inputs from the ecological environment undoubtedly increased the salience of the real environment at the expense of the envisioned environment and altered the latter toward greater conformity with the former. For example, the dream home in the west took on some of the dimensions of a soddy. In an extreme case the envisioned environment collapsed, and the pioneer abandoned his earlier hopes and aspirations and became a permanent marginal homesteader (mountain man, backwoodsman, hillbilly) with goals appropriate to the real situation as he saw it. On the other hand, to the degree that inputs from the pioneer's own needs were dominant, his envisioned environment became a template for building the transformation of the ecological environment toward conformity with his envisioned environment. Put simply, the soddy became a mere prelude to the house of dreams, and in the extreme and ideal case the pioneer completed what, in terms of his hopes and aspirations, was an unfinished ecological environment. This chiefly involved creating new behavior settings in the likeness of those of the envisioned psychological environment. The urgent task was to create behavior settings rapidly: to prove up on a claim, to build a sawmill, to establish a trading post or store, to start a school and church, and so forth, all of which are, as we have seen, self-governing entities that take charge of their inhabitants. This required behavior that differed from joining an established church, buying a functioning farm or store, or sending the children to an ongoing school. It required, on the physical side, building a suitable structure and furnishing it with the essential equipment; it required, on the social side, assembling committed people; and it required, on the organization side, laying down and gaining acceptance of a program of operation. Every viable frontier settlement had to have among its members persons with requisite initiative, foresight, energy, social skills, and organizing ability to create an ecological environment of behavior settings congruent with that envisioned by the inhabitants.

These adjustments between the envisioned and the real environments are not peculiar to the frontier, of course; they occur in settled regions whenever a new dwelling is built or an old one redecorated or remodeled (altering the ecological environment) and whenever plans for these are abandoned and the status quo is accepted (modifying the envisioned environment). However, these adjustments involved very different problems on the frontier and in the settled regions for two important classes of inhabitants. Some pioneers were conservers, who aimed to replicate the familiar environment of the settled region. They sometimes brought to the frontier the name, plat, building designs, and furniture of the home town, as well as the constitution, bylaws, and programs of its behavior settings. Others were innovators, who brought with them plans for a different environment, one that would support a new way of life; they aimed to create a New Jerusalem. Both classes of pioneers had to cope with the real frontier environment: its geography, its weather, its soil, its flora and fauna, its "natives," its limited local materials, its meager manpower, its newness, and its unfinished state. In many cases

this required alteration in the guiding templates of both the conservers and the innovators, but there is no reason to think the
frontier was in this respect more favorable to one class than to the
other.

The settled regions posed different problems for conservers
and innovators who were on the move. Newcomers to a settled
region who were conservers had minimal difficulties in securing
an environment of behavior settings in accordance with their
aspirations; many were already present, and the establishment of
new ones was a matter of using materials readily at hand in
accordance with generally approved plans and programs of organization. It was easier for conservers to move from one settled
region to another where the same environmental conditions were
obtained than to move to the frontier. The converse was true for
the innovators. Whereas the frontier environment resisted their
efforts to build a New Jerusalem, as it did the conservers' efforts
to replicate the home town, it was not as recalcitrant as a settled
environment with its established behavior settings that were in-
compatible with their envisioned environment. It was easier for
innovators to move from an uncongenial settled region to the
frontier than to another uncongenial settled region.

The unfinished frontier environment was not neutral; it modified the hopes and aspirations of both conservers and innovators,
and it elicited from both greater *flexibility, initiative, foresight,
energy, social skills,* and *organizing ability* than the settled regions required. In addition, for the innovator the frontier was a
region of at least temporary freedom from the restraints of established, self-governing behavior-setting environments, thus encouraging *building the Promised Land.*

Escape from Redundancy

Did the frontier and the settled regions affect only the current
actions of their inhabitants, or were the enduring bases of their
behavior modified? Some attributes of frontier behavior continued in frontier communities long after the historic frontier
period passed them by. This could mean that the frontier selected
or developed a western American personality; or, on the other

hand, it could mean that the behavior-coercive frontier environment outlasted frontier days. There is evidence for the latter. Behavior attributes that have continued are the busyness, vigor, importance, difficulty, and so forth associated with undermanned behavior settings, a feature of the environment that has also persisted beyond the frontier era. The evidence of these behavioral and environmental continuities comes from a comparative study of a modern American town whose century-old roots are in the western American frontier and an English community with no frontier history (Baker and Schoggen, 1973).

The study shows that in the 1960s undermanning of behavior settings persisted in the American town three generations after the frontier had passed and that the English town was much more adequately manned, as it had been for generations. There were 884 public-behavior settings in the American town and 830 inhabitants to man them, whereas in the English town 758 settings were manned by 1,310 inhabitants. Moreover, the average setting of the American town required more human components to operate and maintain it, so that in terms of essential jobs to be filled it had half as much manpower as the English town. In other words, one inhabitant of the American town and two inhabitants of the English town were available over a year's time to carry out 12 essential community tasks. The data of the study are in accord with the theory of undermanning that we have presented. On the average, the inhabitants of the American town were busier than the inhabitants of the English town in public settings. They spent 25 percent more time within them; they carried out 2.5 times as many important tasks within them; and they were leaders in twice as many behavior settings. We can safely assume that the secondary consequences of these immediate adjustments also occurred and that the inhabitants of the American town experienced greater fatigue, more success and more failure, more widespread feelings of self-esteem and self-confidence (and also defeat), lower standards of acceptable performance, greater tolerance of deviancies in associates, and more urgent involvement in practical affairs and less in private, subjective concerns.

But our interest here is why the American town with 63 percent as many inhabitants as the English town creates and maintains

117 percent as many behavior settings and 132 percent as many essential jobs (208 percent as many per town inhabitant). A number of possible explanations come to mind. Perhaps the behavior settings of the towns are not comparable and have different programs with different manpower requirements. In fact, however, three-quarters of the settings are fundamentally identical in the two towns (for example, Dentists Offices, Cooking Classes, and Auction Sales), and only 12 percent are unique to one town (for example, Cricket Games in the English and Baseball Games in the American town); furthermore, the unique settings do not differ in manpower requirements. Perhaps the American town serves a tributary area with a greater population. In fact, the opposite is true. Within the English town and a four-mile radius about it, there are 238 percent as many inhabitants as in the American town and district; and within a ten-mile radius the English region has 283 percent as many inhabitants. Perhaps the differences in behavior settings and essential jobs are imposed by outside authorities, and the American town is required to have more settings and more essential positions than the english town. In fact, the American town has 251 percent as many locally controlled settings as the English town, and within them there are 311 percent as many essential positions to be filled. There appears to be a dynamism within the american town that creates and maintains a more demanding environment for its inhabitants than the English town. It does this, for example by scheduling seven lodge meetings instead of one, twenty cultural meetings instead of seven, seven parades instead of two, twenty-eight plays and programs instead of eleven, forty-two religious classes instead of eleven, forty-two religious classes instead of eleven, seven Scout meetings instead of one, and so forth. this does not mean that the American town is more nearly complete than the English town, only that it is more prodigal in replicating behavior settings.

Why does this occur? Why does the environmental attribute of undermanning continue as in frontier days after the conditions that produced it then have gone? Why, by multiplying behavior settings, does a former frontier town continue the relative manpower shortage characteristic of the frontier? The answers to these questions appear to reside partly in the ecological environment and partly in the psychological environments of the inhabitants.

Two bases for the persistence of undermanning are found in the ecological environment. The first is the homeostatic nature of behavior settings that we have discussed earlier; their self-governing controls operate to maintain their programs (including the number of human components) and within limits in the face of varying external conditions. Once it is established as an effectively functioning unit, a behavior setting resists both decrease and increase in its manpower. The second basis is the greater ease of replicating an existing behavior setting than of fashioning a distinctive one. The designs and components of established settings are at hand, and so the effort and obstacles involved in inventing, planning, and testing a new setting are completely bypassed. These two features of the ecological environment tend to maintain its behavior settings with their existing complements of human components even if these are less than optimal.

Another basis of the persistence of undermanning is found in the psychological environments of the pioneers. We have pointed out that those pioneers who did not give in to the frontier and go native, so to speak, or give up and return to the East developed a workable congruence between the envisioned and real psychological environments through modification of the envisioned environment toward the real environment and alteration of the real environment toward the envisioned environment. Goals were set in accordance with the compromise. Some important satisfactions of the compromise were threatened with destruction by the tide of later arrivals, namely, satisfactions derived from undermanning: being persons of some power and importance, being self-reliant and self-respecting, doing difficult and essential tasks, being versatile, being needed and valued by associates. The pioneers knew that a church with three hundred rather than thirty members would greatly reduce opportunities for these satisfactions; they knew that it would require much fewer than ten times as many important people (board members, preacher, choir members, ushers, organist) to implement its programs and that, in general, an inhabitant of a small behavior setting is less expendable than an inhabitant of a large setting. Abundant manpower threatened frontiersmen with redundancy, an endemic condition in many settled regions and the precise condition from which some pioneers had fled. In addition, new arrivals threatened the New Jerusalems they had established, which provided them with particular religious, political, economic, educational, and other satisfactions. The members of the little church found that its special creed and form of worship could not be maintained with a tenfold increase in its membership through the addition of heterogeneous strangers. And, finally, it threatened established and effective operating procedures. The large church would require new operating arrangements, but what arrangements? Discovering them would inevitably involve trouble, mistakes, conflict, tension.

The answer to these problems was at hand: build more behavior settings into the ecological environment. It was the aim of the pioneers to complete an incomplete environment according to their envisioned environments; environments that, when completed and tempered by frontier experience, did not have expendable people, uncongenial programs, or untried procedures. So, coping with the later arrivals was as simple as adding new rooms to the house as the family increased. When the little church (literary society, lodge) was invaded by many newcomers, the present members became redundant, the sacred program attenuated, and the tried and true service altered, a new church for the true believers was established where the chosen people were still important, its program inviolate, and its procedures familiar.

Many American regions had prolonged frontier periods, and so we would expect many small, disparate behavior settings to characterize American society and undermanning with its behavioral resultants to be attributes of its built environment and its national character.

Bibliography

Citations

Barker, R. G., and Schoggen, P. *Qualities of Community Life. Methods of Measuring Environment and Behavior in an American and an English Town.* San Francisco, 1973.
Bridenbaugh, c., Ed. Gentleman's Progress. *The Itinerarium of Dr. Alexander Hamilton, 1744.* Chapel Hill, 1948.
Taylor, G. R., ed. *The Turner Thesis.* Boston, 1949.
Wilder, L. I. *Little Town on the Prairie.* (New York, 1941.
———. *The Long Winter.* New York, 1940.

General References

UNDERMANNED ENVIRONMENT

Barker, R. G. *Ecological Psychology: Concepts and Methods for Studying the Environment of Human Behavior.* Stanford, Calif., 1968.
Barker, R. G., and Gump, P. V. *Big School, Small School: High School Size and Student Behavior.* Stanford, Calif., 1964.
Gump, P. V. "Persons, Settings, and Larger Contexts." In B. Indik and K. Barrien, eds. *People, Groups, and Organizations: An Effective Integration.* New York, 1968.
Wicker, A. W. *Introduction to Ecological Psychology.* Monterey, Calif., 1978.
———. "Undermanning Theory and Research: Implications for the Study of Psychological and Behavioral Effects of Excess Population." *Representative Research in Social Psychology* 4 (January, 1973): 185–206.
Willems, E. P. "Sense of Obligation of High School Activities as Relative to School Size and Marginality of Students." *Child Development* 38 (December, 1967): 1247–60.

NEW ENVIRONMENT

Barker, R. G. *Adjustment to Physical Handicap and Illness: A Survey of the Social Psychology of Physique and Disability* New York, 1953.
Lewin, K. "Behavior and Development as a Function of the Total Situation." In L. Carmichal, ed. *Manual of Child Psychology.* New York, 1946. Reprinted in K. Lewin, *Field Theory in Social Science.* New York, 1951.

————. "Field Theory and Experiment in Social Psychology: Concepts and Methods." *American Journal of Sociology* 44 (May, 1939): 868–96. Reprinted in K. Lewin, *Field Theory in Social Science*. New York, 1951.

UNFINISHED ENVIRONMENT

Lewin, K. *Principles of Topological Psychology*. New York, 1936.

4. INSULAR *v.* COSMOPOLITAN FRONTIERS:
A Proposal for the Comparative Study
of American Frontiers

Jerome O. Steffen

The western scholarly community has become for all practical purposes a closed society. With some notable exceptions, communication between western historians and the American historical profession in general has been minimal. The source of this problem seems to be the lack of dimension in most western history. This chapter represents one small attempt to generate a larger approach to western history. While I present my ideas in a direct manner, they are meant to be only suggestions. It is my intent not to be dogmatic but rather to bring comparative generalizations before the scholarly community.

This main focus of this chapter is comparative frontier change and continuity, with emphasis on the processes involved in the production of either condition. In addition, I am interested in classifying frontiers in terms of whether their historical development was directed primarily by factors intrinsic or extrinsic to them. The frontier was a natural laboratory for this approach because it represented a stage of historical development usually associated with the new and unknown, providing an actual or conceived test for established notions and practices brought to it.

The analysis of change in any historical context involves disassembling the many woven threads that produce historical development. This is a difficult job at best because the relationships among the threads fluctuate or vary in relation to each other. For my purposes frontier variables fall into two broad categories: those inherent to the demands of the frontier environment and those associated with prefrontier experiences. Frontier change and continuity were both contests between the demands of the environment and the mind set of those entering its confines. The relationship between the two components was determined by how compelling and obvious environmental demands were for change and how deeply rooted were prefrontier principles and practices.

This approach is not meant to be a rigid examination of man's adaptation to differing environments such as cultural ecologists in geography and anthropology employ. Such an emphasis is generally inadequate for the historian.[1] Few historians study history in time frames broad enough to allow the evolutionary contest between man and environment to work out completely. For example, Great Plains agriculture is viewed as a victory of technology over an otherwise hostile environment. But since this phenomenon is only approximately one hundred years old, man's so-called victory may represent only a dysfunctional stage of adaptation.

The historian interested in frontier change must be aware not only of the rate of change but also of the kinds of change. Some changes in American history may represent fundamental alterations in human thinking; other are more modal in nature. For example, the ideological alteration in American history up to the nineteenth century certainly cannot be considered in the same context as the adaptation of agricultural techniques to the Great Plains of North America. Therefore, in comparing American frontiers it is necessary to be aware of different levels of change. Change might be classified as either modal or fundamental. Modal change usually represented an altered overt manifestation of a practice or belief whose conceptual foundation remained essentially the same. Fundamental change involved the replacement or significant alteration of the very assumption upon which practices were based.

Given these suppositions, the comparative study of American frontier development could help determine not only what variables or combinations of variables caused different kinds of change but whether the variables were intrinsic or extrinsic to the frontier environment. I am suggesting that there is a direct relation between the degree of insularity and the level of change experienced on any given frontier. Insularity, in turn, can be precisely determined by analyzing the nature and number of interacting links between a given frontier and its parent culture. If the insulating links were few in number or nonexistent, the frontier was insulated to a significant degree from its parent culture, and the indigenous environment was therefore an important causative for change. Thus frontiers with inherent environments that called for change and with few interacting links were more likely to experience fundamental change. And, of course, the reverse was true for those frontiers that possessed many interacting links with their parent cultures.

Interacting links are associated with questions that western scholars easily recognize. The most obvious relate to the level of technology and its ability to connect frontier regions with the main body of "civilization." This factor is related to other links associated with key economic questions. Was economic activity specialized or nonspecialized? Did local or national and international economic conditions determine economic success? Time might also constitute an interacting link. For an individual exposed to frontier conditions for only brief periods of time, memory served as an interacting link, because the connection between the frontiersman and his problem-solving reference base was not severed. Once the interacting links have been clearly defined and outlined, the scholar then needs to juxtapose them in a comparative manner to frontier environments with an eye toward how compelling their respective demands were for change.

Given this perspective, one could suggest that American frontier experiences fell into two broad categories, cosmopolitan and insular. Cosmopolitan frontiers were associated only with modal change or change caused by factors not found exclusively within the confines of the frontier. Insular frontiers were associated with fundamental change primarily caused by factors exclusive to the frontier experience.

Insular Frontiers

Based on this hypothesis trans-Appalachian agricultural settlement was the only insular frontier in American historical development, because the number of interacting links between it and the main body of American civilization were few. The agricultural frontier is synonomous with self-sufficiency, or that stage when the settler was family-oriented in determining his needs for future crop production. Self-sufficiency, of course, was not self-imposed but resulted from the high cost of transporting goods. The pioneer agriculturalist was usually initially concerned with establishing a capital base by clearing land to improve the value of his property and by his need to construct implements to make his operation more efficient. Energies expended on these activities could not produce goods for market even if one was available.

Another variable associated with frontier agriculture was the scarcity and consequential high cost of labor. The family had to act as their own labor complex, utilizing as many members as possible. Two English agricultural speculators, Morris Birkbeck and George Flower, went to Illinois in the early nineteenth century with hopes of establishing a large-scale farming operation complete with large numbers of hired laborers. Unable to satisfy their labor needs, they turned to importing laborers, but they soon lost the services of these individuals because the laborers were able to make enough money to enter into farming on their own. Birkbeck and Flower eventually abandoned their enterprise as they had conceived it.[2] One English traveler in Illinois speculated that a laborer who was diligent in saving his wages could earn enough in two years to buy a quarter section of land along with some livestock and enough implements to begin operations.[3]

With the expansion of internal improvements the market displaced the family as the determinant of the quantities and types of crops to be grown. At this point the agriculturalist ceases being a part of a subfrontier process and enters the purview of a modernization process affecting the nation as a whole. The evolution of commercial agriculture and the erosion of the frontier stage was an uneven process, advancing faster in some regions than in others. Percy Bidwell and John Falconer, two early and still important historians of American agriculture, suggest that eastern regions of cis-Mississippi agriculture had reached the commercial stage by 1830, while the western regions of the cis-Mississippi did not experience commercial agriculture until 1850. Self-sufficient agriculture and the high cost of labor are but two examples of economic variables that, when considered along with social, political, and intellectual variables in the context of their insulation from the parent culture, produce more precise understanding of the frontier process. Employing just one of these variables, self-sufficiency, one could think in terms of the number of interacting links that this condition prevented.

For example, national economic programs that affected agriculture had little immediate direct bearing on the pioneer agriculturalist. Agricultural societies, county fairs, and other institutions for disseminating new agricultural techniques, while well developed in the East, had had little growth in the trans-Appalachian West by the early nineteenth century. Even in the East, where agriculture was more commercially oriented, conceptions of self-sufficient farming lingered. As late as 1821 the New York Board of Agriculture, the supposed seat of enlightened agricultural practices, said that the farmer should "produce everything necessary to sustain life in a comfortable and respectable manner: and he should surround himself with everything that he wants by his own industry." It was twenty years before that body realistically advised the farmer of the specialized economic characteristics of commercial agriculture.[4]

On the federal level, the United States House of Representatives in 1820 and the United States Senate in 1825 established permanent committees on agriculture. The federal government largely confined its role to adjusting tariffs and gathering and reporting statistics that affected farmers. The impact of national policies affected the pioneer agriculturalist little because his surplus sales were minimal, and the needs of his family or, at best, the local economic picture directed his economic decisions.[5]

The amount of settlement that occurred in the trans-Appalachian West up to the mid-nineteenth century was much exaggerated. Land speculators, and some guides to emigrants, claimed that the West was a beehive of activity and produced startling growth figures. Even John Peck's more responsible guides fostered this impression. After listing population statistics for Missouri, Arkansas and Indiana, Peck concluded that "the advancement in business and improvements has been equal to the increase of population." He went on to state that "this region of the country will continue to advance in the production of property, equal to its progress in numbers. . . ."[6]

Any study of cis-Mississippi agricultural frontiers must also consider the work of Frederick Jackson Turner. Beginning in 1893, Turner made historians aware of the significance of the frontier as a vehicle for change. In Turner's view "the existence of an area of free land, its continuous recession and the advance of American settlement explain American development."[7]

Turner did more than merely describe the role of the frontier. He demonstrated, albeit vaguely, how it worked as a process. He simply stated that the presence of free land attracted to the frontier individuals of varying backgrounds and nationalities. The isolation encountered there prompted the erosion of tradition and promoted new practices and ideas, which, in turn, were the product of the homogenization of the diverse mixture of individuals who shared the frontier experience. The frontier also affected more civilized areas by serving as a safety valve or avenue of escape for society's malcontents.

In the past western historians have had a tendency to use Turner rigidly in viewing the frontier as the sole causative for the pervasive changes associated with American history up to the early nineteenth century. In my judgment their instincts were correct, but their focus was incorrect. By narrowly concentrating on pioneer agricultural settlement, they have missed the point that this frontier experience was merely one part of a larger frontier process. That process involved more dimensions than agriculture and related to more than the geographical boundaries of the United States. Therefore, while the cis-Mississippi agricultural frontier experience did serve as a causative for fundamental change, it was a subfrontier acting simultaneously within the purview of a larger frontier process, namely America as a frontier of Europe. Walter Prescott Webb, in *The Great Frontier,* suggested this perspective, but he like Turner never really analyzed the process.[8]

Cosmopolitan Frontiers

Cosmopolitan frontiers were lacking in fundamental economic, political, or social change. Many of the factors that served to minimize the number of interacting links in the cis-Mississippi agricultural frontier were absent in the fur-trading, ranching and mining frontiers. As a result, these frontiers possessed a low degree of insulation from the main body of American civilization and consequently experienced little indigenous development and the fundamental change that usually accompanied it.

Furtrading, for example, did not involve any fundamental changes from previous practices and attitudes already well established when first brought to the New World from Europe. Continuity in American fur trading frontier can be established by undertaking a macroview of the American and European trading establishments as they related to national imperial designs of their respective countries. In addition, it would be useful to comparatively view inherent environmental problems faced by both European and American traders and how their similar business structures reflected similar solutions to these problems. Finally it is necessary to address the fur frontier as a process, specifically the homogenization process implied in the Turner thesis. The diversity of nationalities, personalities, and backgrounds on the fur-trading frontier presents an interesting laboratory for determining whether diversity became homogeneity as a result of exposure to a frontier setting. If the frontiersmen were not visibly changed by the experience, then perhaps an explanation for the lack of change is in store.

American fur trading was part of the commercial revolution and national mercantilism prominent from the thirteenth century until the eighteenth century. The ideological infrastructure of mercantilism launched the mercantile capitalist as a vital factor in the history of rising central states and the accompanying struggle for world empires. Global struggles placed severe strain on national treasuries, making the individual mercantile capitalist's economic goals exceedingly compatible with national goals, which attempted to create greater self-sufficiency through the accumulation of precious metal in an orderly colonial-trade network. From the perspective of national policy makers, the needs of individual traders and the nation-state were best served by the elimination of wasteful competition in the private sector of the economy. As a result, mercantilism on a national scale placed a premium on trade regulation in order to eliminate harmful competition within a nation's own trading community.[9] Hence the merchant trader was closely aligned with the nation-state in a symbiotic relationship. the nation-state offered the mercantile capitalist order and regulation through monopolistic grants and military protection wherever feasible, while the mercantile capitalist assisted the nation-state by exploring potential imperial acquisitions and directly, or in some cases unwittingly, assisting in colonization.[10]

The American fur-trading establishment was part of the same national empire-building milieu as their European counterparts and consequently faced many of the same environmental obstacles. Understandably, American national policy makers and the trading fraternity faced these same problems. The United States as an emerging nation had to face the realities of survival in the international community of nations, survival that, just as with any European power, depended upon the harmonious relationship between domestic economic components and successful competition for empires. American policy makers emerging from a colonial status within the British mercantile scheme therefore reasonably applied the same formula for maintenance and survival.

This development can be illustrated by concentrating merely on the role of the American fur trader in the trans-Mississippi West after the Louisiana Purchase in 1803. After the initial exploration of the Louisiana Purchase, the far Northwest became a competitive trading ground between the United States and Great Britain; Spain and Russia were no longer serious contenders by the time of the American arrival. The environment of the far Northwest trade constituted nothing short of an all-out economic war, a war in which nations competed for empires and traders competed for individual wealth, each serving the other's purpose. Mercantilism-inspired imperial designs were on the minds of even the first explorers, Lewis and Clark. William Clark's comments on the economic implications of the region to American national interests are indeed telling:

I consider this tract across the continent of immense advantage to the fur trade, as all the furs collected in $9/10$ parts of the most valuable fur country in America may be conveyed to the mouth of the Columbia and shipped thence to the East Indies by the 1 of August in each year and will of course reach Canton earlyer (*sic*) than the furs which are annually exported from Montreal to Great Britain.[11]

Since the trader was to be the soldier in this North American imperial struggle, then mercantilist policy, if it was to conform to the Old World, would dictate order through monopolistic grants and regulations. The British followed the ideology of mercantilism to the letter, as their efforts to eliminate competition among their traders clearly demonstrates. When the Hudson's Bay Company and the North West Company, two of Great Britain's most powerful soldiers in the war for imperial acquisition, began to destroy each other, efforts were made in 1821 to consolidate the two into one giant company, which then had a complete monopoly in the far Northwest.[12]

The American response to the challenge of imperial acquisition in the far Northwest, unlike the British response, was not classic mercantilism, which to the less discerning eye might seem to be a major departure. Upon closer scrutiny however, it can be suggested that it was certainly mercantilist-inspired. The American response to these suggested problems was not classical mercantilism for three simple reasons. First, American colonial possessions were propinquitous to areas already incorporated into the nation as states. Second, as a result, certain considerations involving the competing interests of permanent settlement had to be considered. Third, if eventual permanent settlement was going to take place, the native inhabitants of the land in question had to be dealt with. This last factor was not a concern to the British, for traders only minimally disturbed the regional ecosystem of people and environments.[13]

Thomas Jefferson's Indian and colonial policy perhaps best illustrates how American national policy hoped to serve two goals—imperial acquisition and permanent settlement. Jefferson, in neoclassical mercantilist fashion, was fearful of the harmful effects of private traders and consequently attempted to revive the factory system and extend it all the way to the Pacific coast. Jefferson's intention to expand the factory system was prompted not by the domestic pressures but by the imperial contest with Great Britain.[14] The goal, then, was simply to maintain the allegiance of the native inhabitants with an eye toward creating stability and security in American colonial possessions.

A comparison of American and British trading practices can also be made in a more specialized manner by focusing on how their similar business structures were dictated by similar economic environmental pressures. As with national colonial policy, the form and structure of the American fur-trading establishment had its origins in earlier European business practices. American fur trading, albeit on a much smaller scale, and in some cases at a more primitive stage, began where the great joint-stock ventures of Europe left off. One should see the Missouri Fur Company, the American Fur Company, the Columbia Fur Company, the Rocky Mountain Fur Company, and countless other partnerships and joint-stock agreements as extensions of such Old World organizations as the Dutch East India Company, the English East India Company, and the Virginia Company, to name but a few.

The major obstacle to successful trading was waste and inefficiency in organization and the high risk of loss through unforseen "acts of God" or through theft and piracy. The high-risk problem was met by European traders through the use of the regulated company and the joint-stock associations. The joint-stock company represented a pooling of capital and investors in order to assemble necessary funds to carry out a costly business venture, as well as a method of distributing the losses in the event that the undertaking did not succeed. The usual practice involved businessmen issuing shares of stock to the public but retaining the controlling number of stocks. Theoretically, once the venture was completed, the association was to be dissolved, the shareholders dividing the profits acquired from the sale of the company's assets. In reality, the larger joint-stock association went on to have a life of its own resembling a modern corporate structure. The joint-stock association was the primary business structure for traders during the period of exploration and discovery, just as it was the primary structure for its counterpart in the New World, the American fur-trading community.[15]

The mercantile capitalist was the key figure in national and individual economic aspiration during the Age of Discovery. Mercantile capitalists were sedentary merchants who sought to control their economic fortune through diversification of function and efficient administration. Ideally, he wanted simultaneous command of the full range of activities connected with trading transactions: wholesaling, retailing, banking, warehousing, and shipping. The mercantile capitalist, unlike his predecessor, did not travel about but concentrated on efficient administration of all these variables from one place of operation. Hence success to a mercantile capitalist was determined by how skillfully he could use managerial skills to coordinate an army of clerks, craftsmen, laborers, ships, captains, and sailors. Control was the paramount factor for effective decision making and was dependent on an efficient information-gathering network that determined how orders were carried out.[16] As in Europe these factors were prominent in the American fur-trading business structure.

The acquisition of the Louisiana Territory in 1803 set the stage for large-scale mercantile activity in the far Northwest. St. Louis became the center for most of the far western trade expeditions, and, like the great trade centers of Europe, it became a mercantile hub complete with banking houses, mercantile firms to outfit expeditions, and a network of warehouses for storage of the goods. St. Louis had been a trade center before the American purchase of Loisiana. Reflecting its European influence, trade at the time of the Americans' arrival was regulated by a Spanish system of granting trading monopolies to trade with individual tribes.

When the Americans arrived, trade was theoretically opened to anyone who wished to compete in it, but the economic environment of the trans-Mississippi West trade did not allow entrepreneurs acting individually to prosper. American, French, and Spanish traders faced the same environmental obstacles in the New World as their predecessors had faced in the Old World. The potential for profit was high, as was the risk. As in Europe, these environmental obstacles were met with partnerships and joint-stock arrangements that served to accumulate a sufficient capital base for large-scale operations to distribute the risk among the investors.

The final selective comparison that should be undertaken is that of the frontier as a process, specifically, a process that according to the Turner hyopthesis should foster homogenization among the diverse collection of traders assembled and exposed to the frontier environment. If the inherent environmental demands of a given frontier setting remained constant, then the response elicited by these pressures should be similar. This premise can be pointed to empirically with respect to technological adaptation. In fur trading, for example, scholars can observe the evolution of watercraft to suit the environmental needs of shallow western rivers. On an institutional level scholars can point to the rendezvous system as man's adaptation of an Idian technique to supply raw materials more efficiently. But what of social behavior or individual world views?

In the discussion of the cis-Mississippi agricultural frontier it was pointed out that pervasive fundamental change occurred in American history, culminating in the early nineteenth century. Does this same process occur on the fur-trading frontier? It is my contention that it does not. Or, put more specifically, it does not appear that fur traders were fundamentally changed from their previous world view because of their frontier experiences; or, if alteration did occur, it was not precipitated by the frontier but was rather a part of a national alteration regardless of setting, frontier or nonfrontier.

Biographers of fur traders should look anew at their subjects with an eye on the impact of the frontier on behavior. I am convinced that a prosopographic survey of fur traders would indicate not only that they did not change from their previous world views but that as a body of individuals they shared only one common role, namely, that of mercantile capitalist. If the associations between trading establishments and national imperial designs are compared and if the structures of trading associations are compared, they all suggest the same dynamic—continuity and inertia on the fundamental level of human activity. A recognition of this fact is only the beginning, because the emphasis of study now shifts to the search for the causatives of this continuity.

As I suggested in my introductory comments, the answer might be provided by categorizing the variables present in respective

American frontier settings before comparing frontiers for the presence or absence of these variables. For example, when comparing fur trading to the cis-Mississippi agricultural frontier, it can be seen that several variables absent from fur trading are present in the agricultural frontier setting. First, the fur trader was not exposed to the environment of the fur-trading frontier for any great length of time. Most traders were separated from the influence of their parent cultures for no more than two years at a time.[17] As a result, memory was a reference for their problem-solving needs. Second, the fur traders visited trading regions, completed their transaction, and left without significantly affecting the area (except for the eventual depletion of fur-bearing animals). As a result, they had little need or desire to interact with the demands of their immediate environment. Most traders were not interested in seeing the Native American become assimilated. The two cultures met, transacted business, and separated without any conscious acculturation taking place. Finally, one can point to the economic specialization of fur trading as an interacting link that reinforced existent beliefs and practices. Furs as a commodity of trade had to be sold or traded to individuals in a central location, whether it was St. Louis, New York, Montreal, London, or Canton, and as a result economic conditions in these distant places affected their economic well-being. the cumulative effect of these factors never jeopardized the links between the traders and their parent cultures.

It must be emphasized again that the evidence presented here to show strong ties between the Old World and the New World trading communities is only selective and certainly only suggestive. It is for western historians in the future to reexamine closely the American fur-trading frontier and to scrutinize comparatively its history through either case study or broad synthesis. for example, while I have looked only selectively at entrepreneurial behavior patterns, the whole range of human activity should be comparatively explored in terms of its prefrontier and postfrontier experiences.

A comparison of the ranching and cis-Mississippi agricultural frontiers suggests that the former was another example of a frontier that experienced little fundamental change. Western scholars usually associate the ranching frontier with the trans-Mississippi manifestation of the industry. If one examines this arena of the ranching industry in terms of its interaction with national affairs, its business practices, and the frontier's impact on individuals exposed to it, it should become obvious that its historical process was similar to that of the fur-trading frontier and dissimilar to cis-Mississippi agriculture. This is so perhaps because the two frontiers were similar in that their respective environmental settings served as interacting links that reinforced existing beliefs and practices. In ranching, methods of grazing, identifying, and marketing cattle all had their precedent in the colonial American and Spanish cattle industries.[18] In addition to the continuity of business practices, one is struck by the lack of homogeneity among the early cattlemen, with the exception of entrepreneurial behavior patterns, which were similar in most of their careers and carried over from earlier experiences. A prosopographic review of early cattlemen would illustrate this point. Such a study is sorely needed, because the existing literature on early cattlemen invariably views them as great men in conscious control of their destinies. Supposedly not bound by external forces, their strong and intelligent free wills determined their success. Western scholarship would be better served if studies of these individuals, like all frontier dwellers, concentrated on the relationship between established patterns of behavior and different environments that may or may not have demanded change from them. Cattlemen should be viewed as problem solvers acting within a limited range of options placed before them by external frontier circumstance and internal prefrontier intellectual preparation.

Early cattlemen viewed in this manner demonstrate shared patterns of behavior, patterns that depict them not as community builders but as mercantile capitalists engaged in financial ventures.[19] The number of early cattlemen who demonstrated previous trading and swapping behavior is so significant that it constitutes a trend that cannot be ignored. To date only Lewis Atherton, in *The Cattle Kings*, has paid any attention to these entrepreneurial patterns. He perceptively concluded that

if any one word explains or offers a universal key to how so many men started without inherited money and became cattle kings, that word would be "trader." Instead of relying simply on the natural increase from a small herd of cattle to make them wealthy, such men traded in cattle, in mines, in beef, in store goods—in anything that came to hand and yielded a profit by being passed on to someone else in the channels of trade.

He went on to say: "By such means they obtained the capital resources that they concentrated in herds of cattle. Many gained most of their wealth from ranching, it is true, but they acquired their basic capital for foundation herds through trading enterprises."[20]

Besides the compatibility of the environment, another significant interacting link between the ranching frontier and the main body of American civilization was the commodity of exchange itself, cattle. In order to realize the true profit potential of cattle, the ranchers had to trade or sell them to other individuals, usually living in different sections of the country. This transaction, in effect, created an economic symbiosis between the seller and the buyer. This relationship in turn served to cast local affairs into a broader perspective, thus preventing true indigenous development and consequently preventing fundamental change.

The history of the post–Civil War ranching period would be benefited immeasurably if western scholars compared the business practices of cattlemen with those of the eastern industrialists.[21] Alfred D. Chandler has succinctly outlined the controlling process involved in the rise of eastern big business. the thrust of Chandler's argument is that "costs, rather than interfirm competition, began to determine prices."[22] In the context of the later ranching period, might not the increased emphasis on sound management techniques represent a different manifestation of the same trend? By the same token, might not the increased use of fencing be viewed partly as a cost-cutting device because it diminished the number of labor units needed and made more efficient use of available pasture lands?

Chandler also states that eastern businesses attempted to stabilize prices not only by integrating marketing procedures but also by creating interfirm organizations. Trade associations were formed in all the major industries to eliminate harmful competition and to promote the general welfare of the member firms. Could cattlemen's associations be seen as the ranchers' response to the same external factors that stimulated the growth of trade associations in the East? Cattlemen's associations mediated disputes, kept brand books, organized *de facto* law-enforcement units, all as responses to factors that tended to produce instability or otherwise adversely affect the general welfare of the ranching industry. Perhaps the histories of such great cattlemen's associations, the Wyoming Stock Growers Association, the Colorado Stock Growers Association, and others, should be rewritten with this perspective in mind.[23]

Control and consolidation for greater efficiency were very much a part of the later ranching era. Perhaps the histories of such ranching empires as the XIT and the JA and of such organizations as the Matador Land and Cattle Company and the Swan Land and Cattle Company should be rewritten incorporating the forces and responses associated with eastern industrial consolidation and growth.[24] This perspective, it seems, would add dimension to the premise of existing studies, which suggests that large profits brought big investors, which meant consolidation at the expense of small ranches. The underlying impulse of such an interpretation leaves human greed as the only causative. this premise is much the same as the one that until recently influenced studies of industrial growth during the Gilded Age. Recently scholars like Chandler have shown this period to be more dimensional by revealing a business logic in the growth process. Unfortunately, the subject of ranching has had to date no Chandler to reveal cattlemen as problem solvers and to explain the logic they employed to operate more efficiently. Somewhat ironically, therefore, western historians may learn more about the range of the cattle industry by reading the histories of industrial growth in the East than by reading existing works on the subject.

Much like the ranching and fur-trading frontier, the mining frontier and its scenario of events and cast of characters have been neatly stereotyped. The mere mention of western mining trips into consciousness an image complete with bearded prospector smitten with gold fever and his trusty burro heavily laden with supplies. The prospector followed his wanderlust to a setting complete with bustling tent cities, boom towns, gambling dens, dance halls, and prostitutes. Episodic accounts containing these stereotypical ingredients are in no short supply.

On a scholarly level, mining-frontier history has been closely associated with the Turner thesis and its contentions concerning the furtherance of democratic political procedures and social equality.[25] It is difficult to turn one's back on these themes, for they are ever present in the literature of the mining frontier. Mining codes, vigilance committees, and *de facto* courts seem to serve as illustrations that the American West did indeed spawn or at least amplified democratic political and social development.

A noted mining scholar, Duane Smith, states the proposition directly: ". . . democracy, under the leveling influence of poverty and a fresh start in a strange land reached a zenith."[26] A casual view of these mining developments could suggest that Turner's thesis might have a valid application to the mining frontier. In fact, they only represent an endorsement of the fact that institutions had to be re-created where there were none before. For the Turner thesis to be truly applicable, democratic assumptions must have been born on the mining frontier or must have evolved as a radical departure from previous practices and assumptions. Few historians would suggest that the conceptual foundations of American history were not already democratic by 1848. the mining frontier was not the originator in a Turnerian sense but a setting that reinforced existing notions. Ironically, therefore, a better perspective of political and social behavior on the mining frontier can be gained if they are couched in terms of national trends that occurred in the decades before the initial rush to California.

American mining scholarship should also broaden its time-place perspective to view mining as a universal phenomenon and concentrate on the historical process at work on mining frontiers regardless of time and place. This point can be simply illustrated by drawing a comparison between the Georgia gold rush in the early 1830s and the trans-Mississippi West gold rush that began several decades later. More specifically, one might list nine characteristics commonly recognized as part of the trans-Mississippi mining-frontier scene and then suggest that each of the characteristics was also a part of the Georgia gold-rush scene. The shared characteristics are the following:

1. Stories of chance discoveries.
2. The rapid influx of a diverse group of people.
3. A social leveling process.
4. High prices and little credit.
5. A high rate of itinerancy.
6. A "den of iniquity" image juxtaposed to concerted efforts by the people to ensure a stable community.
7. Bizarre or unusual characters that are easily transformed into legendary ones.
8. With the desertion of miners, merchants, and professional people, the appearance of a ghost town or a shift in the premise of the community's existence.
9. With the end of placer-stage mining, takeover of the next stages of mining by outside pools of capital.

The discovery of gold in 1799 in the Piedmont region of North Carolina preceded the little-known Georgia gold rush. The trail led from there south to northern Georgia, where, in 1814, prospectors began invading mineral areas then inhabited by the Cherokees. The main rush, however, did not occur until 1828, when a hunter accidentally kicked over a rock only to discover gold beneath it. Although that is the incident that most point to as setting off the rush, there are other tales of chance discoveries. There is the story of the slave who presented his master with a peculiar-looking rock he had found in the woods, which had gold ore imbedded in it.[27]

Once the news of gold spread, north Georgia was flooded with eager gold seekers. Since the ore was on Cherokee land, federal troops were sent in to keep the miners out. These efforts, however, were to no avail. Succumbing to the pressures brought on by the sudden influx of people, the state of Georgia created a county out of the region, bringing it under white jurisdiction. That marked the beginning of the unimpeded gold rush.[28]

Mining activities in Georgia became centered on two communities, Auraria and Dahlonega. As in the far-western mining communities, growth was sudden and dramatic. Auraria in 1832, a year after its founding, had between twelve and fifteen law offices, twenty stores, and five taverns. The number of law offices might indicate, just as in the far West, that claims disputes made the mining frontier a lawyer's paradise. At its peak Auraria had 1,000 permanent residents and 10,000 itinerants. But as the gold boom faded, so too did Auraria. In 1854, auraria had only five merchants, and today it is a ghost town.[29]

Dahlonega, the other mining community, was laid out in 1833 and went through much the same boom cycle. From its inception to 1848, Dahlonega's population rose from 800 to 5,000. As in Auraria and many far-western mining communities, merchants, lawyers, bankers, barbers, doctors, and artisans of all kinds moved to Dahlonega to make money off the miners. When news of the California gold strike reached Georgia, however, Dahlonega's population dramatically shrank to just a few hundred people in less than a week. Unlike Auraria, Dahlonega did not become a ghost town; it had earlier been named the county seat and hence had some local importance.[30] This boom-bust pattern should be a familiar one to most western-mining scholars.

Inflation was another characteristic that the Georgia gold rush shared with the far-western gold rush. In Auraria in 1834 corn sold for $0.75 to $0.875 a bushel. Flour sold for $10.00 a barrel, while butter cost $0.25 a pound.[31] In comparison, in Virginia at the same time a barrel of flour cost $4.81. Two years earlier in the New York City market flour had cost $6.00 a barrel. These figures, although merely exemplary, indicate that there is merit in calling for a more thorough study of questions concerning capital, credit, and inflationary patterns in the Georgia gold regions.[32]

As in the far-western mining communities, newspapers played an important role in creating the outside world's image of the Georgia gold rush, as well as stimulating more immigration. Special correspondents were sent to the area by regional newspapers, and the mining communities spawned seven newspapers of their own.[33] It was through these newspapers that a stereotypical boom-town image was created. The outside world learned that all manner of vice and crime was rampant in the gold region.

Gambling, drinking, and fraternizing with prostitutes were the order of the day.

Also as in the far West many colorful tales of bizarre characters emanated from the gold fields. For example the noted southern novelist William Gilmore Simms created the legendary Guy Rivers. Guy Rivers supposedly inhabited a cave ten miles from Auraria and spent most of his waking hours terrorizing the community. Although Rivers was ficticious, his legend grew until it became indistinguishable from reality.[35] Later tours of the region included a stop at the cave in which Rivers supposedly had lived. Simms certainly was imbued with the spirit of the phenomenon when he wrote: "It is a tale of Georgia—a tale of the miners—of a frontier and wild people, and the events are precisely such as may occur among a people & in a region of that character."[35]

Thus the image of the Georgia gold rush was created in much the same likeness as that of the far West. To be sure, these communities were not stable. Boom-town environments whether gold, oil or tourist, produced a high rate of itinerancy and with it irresponsible behavior that was not in the best interest of the permanent population. Indeed, within the communities the pressure of population fostered a concerted effort to deal with crime and sanitation problems. In Georgia committees were appointed to devise plans to ensure stability within the community.[36]

Also like the far-western mining frontier, the Georgia gold scene was viewed as an arena where class lines were obliterated. Contemporary observers of the Georgia gold rush suggested that even the slaves employed in the mines were treated like white hired labor. This equalizing tendency, as well as the image of the "den of iniquity," is captured nicely in a poem inspired by Auraria:

> Wend you to the Cherokee?
>   Where the Indian girls are prattling;
> Where everyone is conscience free,
>   And "chuck-luck" boxes loud are rattling;
> Where gin by the barrel full is drank,—
>   And whites and blacks are all the same;
> Where no respect is paid to rank,
>   But every one's of equal fame.[37]

The poem, of course, is a sarcastic response to what was conceived to be dangerous democratic trends in Auraria. In fact, part of the fear of crime stemmed from the influx of slaves who were used in the mines.

The economic trends and demographic patterns of the Georgia gold rush were also quite similar to those of the far West. News of strikes caused sudden and feverish migrations from one location to another. Once the surface placer deposits disappeared, prospectors, lacking the capital to continue to mine the remaining deposits, moved on to places where gold could be mined with little capital. Not only was there considerable movement within the Georgia gold fields but with the California strike in 1848 many Georgians took their experience and ambitions west to seek fortunes. One can picture the Dahlonega assayer pleading with miners not to leave for California: "Why go to California? There's gold in them thar hills. In that ridge lies more gold than man ever dreamed of. There's millions in it."[38] The miners left, however, and with their departure the frontier stage ended, and the next stage of Georgia mining began.

By the 1870s most mining in Georgia was conducted by corporations capitalized mostly by northerners and Europeans. As in the far West, hydraulic and deep-rock mining required more capital, and the corporate structure was the logical response. By the dawn of the twentieth century the largest gold-mining operations in the East were the Dahlonega Mining Company, capitalized at five million dollars, and the British-Georgia Gold Mining Company.[39] Historians might profit from a comparative investigation of outside investment in the Georgia gold fields and the more frequently studied investment patterns in the far western mines.[40]

This cursory comparison between Georgia mining and far-western mining illustrates that western-mining history may be too involved with its own sense of uniqueness. Historians must be concerned as much with universal historical processes as with occurrences in specific places at specific times.

In the fur-trading and ranching chapters prosopographies were presented to suggest a behavioral continuity between profrontier and frontier experiences. These sketches concentrated on entrepreneurial behavior patterns to demonstrate a mercantile-captialistic, opportunity-oriented mind cast. the mining frontier can be studied with the same techniques, with some qualifications. On the fur-trading and ranching frontiers the initial migration was selective, partly because of the economic nature of these frontiers. Large profits could not be anticipated without considerable capital investment that was usually beyond the capability of single individuals. In addition, considerable skill was required to manage all the economic variables associated with acquiring and disposing of the raw product.

Migration to the mining frontier, however, was not as selective. No doubt it attracted a more diverse group of people than did any other frontier. Despite the diversity, the attracting force was the same—economic betterment with little expenditure. The entrepreneurial skills on the mining frontier were not as demanding as they were on other frontiers. Unlike fur traders and cattlemen, miners did not have to worry about the timing involved in securing and disposing of the raw product. Theirs was merely a question of finding it.

A reexamination of the mining prospector is needed. Most studies have concentrated on the exploits of individual miners with little attention to the miners as a group phenomenon. The prospector image has been fixed much as that of the mountain man was until William Goetzmann made strides toward giving the latter some logical behavioral pattern. At present the prospector's behavior is explained only in such vague terms as ''wanderlust'' and the compulsive drive to find the big strike. Such characteristics did exist in prospectors, and they have been chronicled in episodic descriptions of countless bizarre figures, but was the directionless, wandering prospector actually representative of those who went to the mining fields? an examination of miners' diaries and journals may in fact reveal just the opposite pattern both for those who struck it rich and for those who realized only small or modest returns.

The mining frontier, like the ranching and fur-trading frontiers, possessed many characteristics that served as interacting links. Economic specialization, geographic mobility, and technological advances all served as links between the frontier and the main body of American civilization. Miners more than any other frontier dwellers were dependent on others for goods and services, and hence more than any other frontiersmen they were linked to national political, economic, and social development.

Furthermore, the very pursuit of precious metals by prospectors in camps and boom towns prevented all but the most temporary commitment to local affairs. When they did become involved, national trends or memory of how things had been done before most likely dictated their actions. Like cattlemen and fur traders, prospectors, claims promoters, and locators should be comparatively studied for shared economic and social-behavior patterns to determine whether their frontier experiences had any effect on previously learned behavior. In my judgment such a prosopographic review would show a pattern of continuity in their behavior, albeit amplified in instances where individuals suddenly became wealthy. Al; these factors, when combined, served to link the mining frontier with national development in many ways and thus never allowed the high degree of indigenous development necessary for fundamental change to occur.

Whether western historians view their subject in comparative or noncomparative terms, their role as active members of the historical profession would be greatly enhanced if they simply recognized that the ingredients of the western historical process were not fundamentally different from those associated with historical process of other times and places. Western history, like all other history, involves the study of people as problem solvers who attempted to gain maximum political and economic success while maintaining intellectual and social stability. If these perspectives are incorporated into western history, perhaps a dialogue between western historians and the rest of the historical profession can be reestablished.

Notes

1. The contest between man and environment is not, of course, a new research endeavor. Anthropologists and geographers have been concerned with this interaction since the inception of their disciplines. Even historians, and Frederick Jackson Turner certainly is an example, have been aware of the process.

Cultural ecology, a developing field of interest in geography and anthropology, has a direct interest in cultural and environmental interaction. For a good overview of this field and an extensive bibliography as well, see Robert McC. Netting, "The Ecological Approach in Cultural Study," *Addison-Wesley Modular Publication,* no. 6 (1971). Cultural ecology invariably has an evolutionary perspective, of which there are three distinct schools. The Unilinear school proceeds from the assumption that all societies evolve through similar and detectable stages. This school is best represented by Leslie White, *The Science of Culture* (New York, 1949). The Cultural Relativist school views each society as a separate entity and hence is concerned with uniqueness. This view is usually associated with Ruth Benedict, *Patterns of Culture* (New York, 1934). Finally, the Multilinear school assumes that basic culture types may develop similarly under similar circumstances. This school rejects the rigidity of stages and looks to similar culture types as manifesting themselves at different rates and in different ways. The best representative study of the school is Julian Steward, *Theory of Culture Change: The Methodology of Multilinear Evolution* (Urbana, Ill., 1955). There are some scholars of course who reject evolution entirely as a method of studying culture. Bronislaw Malinowski, *A Scientific Theory of Culture* (Chapel Hill, N.C., 1944), studies culture as a static phenomenon, almost totally rejecting regularities and patterns in cultural developments.

Cultural ecology as a subfield of geography shares most of its methodological concerns with anthropology. For a good overview of cultural ecology in geography see the introduction in Marvin W. Mikesell and Philip L. Wagner, eds., *Readings in Cultural Geography* (Chicago, 1962). Also in the same volume see an essay by Derwent Whittlesey, "Major Agricultural Regions of the Earth," and Max Sorre's essay, "The Concept of *Genre de Vie."* Another volume which should be useful to the frontier scholar is William L. Thomas, Jr., ed., *Man's Role in Changing the Face of the Earth* (Chicago, 1956). Several of the essays in this volume are methodologically if not topically useful to the American historian. A classic essay in this volume is Alexander Spoehr, "Cultural Differences in the Interpretations of Natural Resources"; see also E. Estyn Evans, "The Ecology of Peasant Life in Western Europe"; and Gottfried Pfiefer, "The Quality of Land Use of Tropical Cultivators." There are geographers directly concerned with comparative American frontier studies. Most historians are familiar with Marvin Mikesell's "Comparative Studies in Frontier History," *Annals of the Association of American Geographers* 51 (1961): 62–74. For a good overview of geographical models for frontier study see John Hudson, "Theory and Methodology in Comparative Frontier Studies," in David H. Miller and Jerome O. Steffen, eds., *Frontiers: A Comparative Approach* (Norman, 1977).

2. Percy W. Bidwell and John I. Falconer, *History of Agriculture in the Northern United States, 1620–1860* (Washington, 1925), p. 164. See also Morris Birkbeck, *Letters from Illinois,* introd. Robert M. Sutton (New York, De Capo Press reprint edition, 1970); and George Flower, *History of the English Settlement in Edwards County, Illinois . . .* (Chicago, 1882).

3. Bidwell and Falconer, *History of Agriculture,* p. 163.

4. Ibid., p. 255.

5. Paul W. Gates, *The Farmer's Age: Agriculture 1815–1860* (New York, 1960), pp. 312–27.

6. John Peck, *A Guide for Emigrants, Containing Sketches of Illinois, Missouri, and the Adjacent Parts* (Boston, 1831; reprint ed., New York, 1975).

7. Frederick Jackson Turner, "The Significance of the Frontier in American History," *American Historical Association Annual Report for the Year 1893,* p. 199.

8. Walter Prescott Webb, *The Great Frontier* (Cambridge, Mass., 1951).

9. The most nearly complete and most highly respected work on mercantilism is Eli heckscher, *Mercantilism,* trans. Mendel Shapiro, ed. E. F. Soderlind II (rev. ed., New York, 1955); see also G. Schmoller, *The Mercantile System and Its Historical Significance* (New York, 1958); Charles H. Wilson, *Mercantilism* (London, 1958); and Peter King, *The Development of the English Economy to 1750* (London, 1971). For a reliable review of the historiographical development of the subject see D. C. Coleman, ed., *Revisions in Mercantilism* (London, 1969). Some insight can be gained into the relationship between national policy and trading practices in Barry Supple, *Commercial Crisis and Change in England, 1600–1642* (London, 1964); C. H. Wilson, *England's Apprenticeship, 1603–1763* (New York, 1965); and Murray Lawson, *Fur: A Study in English Mercantilism, 1700–1775,* Toronto University Studies: History and Economics, vol. 9 (Toronto, 1943).

10. N. S. B. Gras, *Business and Capitalism: An Introduction to Business History* (New York, 1939), pp. 74–90.

11. William Clark to George Rogers Clark, September 24, 1806, in Reuben Gold Thwaites, ed., *Original Journals of the Lewis and Clark Expedition, 1804–1806* (New York, 1959), vol. 7, pp. 338–39.

12. The best treatment of the Hudson's Bay Company is E. E. Rich, *The History of the Hudson's Bay Company, 1607–1807,* 2 vols. (London, 1958–62). See also H. A. Innis, *The Fur Trade in Canada* (New Haven, 1930); Federick Merk, ed., *Fur Trade and Empire: George L. Simpson's Journal,* 2d ed. (Cambridge, 1968); introduction, Richard Glover, *David Thompson's Narrative, 1784–1812* (Toronto, 1962); John S. Galbraith, "British American Competition in the Border Fur Trade of the 1820's," *Minnesota History* 40 (Winter 1966); and K. G. Davis, "From Competition to Union," *Minnesota History,* 40 (Winter, 1966).

13. Some insight into the competition between agrarian settlers and fur traders for the attention of federal policy makers can be found in Jack Eblen, *The First and Second United States Empires* (Pittsburgh, 1968); and William A. Williams, "The Age of Mercantilism: An Interpretation of the American Political Economy, 1763–1828," *William and Mary Quarterly* 15 (October, 1958).

14. The standard text on the factory system is Ora Peake, *The American Factory System, 1796–1822* (Denver, 1954). Also useful is Edgar Wesley, "The Government Factory System Among the Indians, 1795–1822," *Journal of Economics and Business History* 4 (May, 1932); and Larry A. McFarlane, "Economic Theories Significant in the Rise of the United States Indian Factory System, 1795–1817" (Master's thesis, University of Missouri, 1955).

15. Gras, *Business and Capitalism,* pp. 81–88, 103–14.

16. *Ibid.,* 83–103.

17. The mountain man may seem to be the exception; however, William Goetzmann ably points out, in "The Mountain Man as Jacksonian Man," *American Quarterly* 15 (Fall, 1963): 404–405, that the mountain man was for the most part engaged in trapping as a means of acquiring capital to enter other careers. Goetzmann implies, as I contend, that the traders were affected little by the fur-trading frontier environment. For what in my judgment is an unsuccessful attempt to dispute Goetzmann's findings, see Harvey Lewis Carter and Marcia Carpenter Spencer, "Stereotypes of the Mountain Man," *Western Historical Quarterly* 6 (January, 1975): 17–32. For William Goetzmann's reply to Carter and Spencer see the communications sections of *Western Historical Quarterly* 6 (July 1975): 295–300. There is a reply by Carter

to Goetzmann in the same issue, pp. 301–302.

18. For a discussion of the Spanish influence on American ranching see Odie B. Faulk, "Ranching in Spanish Texas," *Hispanic American Historical Review* 45 (May, 1965): 257–66; Sandra L. Myers, "The Ranching Frontier: Spanish Institutional Backgrounds of the Plains Cattle Industry," in Harold M. Hollingsworth, ed., *Essays on the American West* (Austin 1959); William H. Dusenberry, *The Mexican Mesta: The Administration of Ranching in Colonial Mexico* (Urbana, 1963); Terry G. Jordan, "The Origin of Anglo-American Cattle Ranching in Texas: A Documentation of Diffusion from the Lower South," *Economic Geography* 45 (January, 1969): 63–87; and Terry G. Jordan, "The Origin and Distribution of Open Range Cattle Ranching, *Social Science Quarterly* 53 (June, 1972): 103–21.

The best general works on the development of the range-cattle industry are Lewis Atherton, *The Cattle Kings* (Bloomington, 1961); Lewis Pelzer, *The Cattlemen's Frontier: A Record of the Trans-Mississippi Cattle Industry, 1850–1890* (Glendale, Calif., 1936); and Ernest Osgood, *The Day of the Cattleman* (Minneapolis, 1929). These works should be supplemented with Edward Everett Dale, *The Range Cattle Industry: Ranching on the Great Plains from 1865 to 1925* (Norman, 1930); and Joseph G. McCoy, *Historic Sketches of the Cattle Trade of the West and Southwest* (Kansas City, Mo., 1874). The most useful existing works on cattle trailing are Jimmy M. Skaggs, *The Cattle Trailing Industry: Between Supply and Demand, 1866–1890* (lawrence, Kans., 1973); and Wayne Gard, *The Chisholm Trail* (Norman, 1954). On cattle towns by far the best study is Robert R. Dykstra, *The Cattle Towns* (New York, 1968).

It is impossible to cover all the sources on the northward spread of the cattle industry; however, a few of the most useful are Orin J. Oliphant, *On the Cattle Ranges of the Oregon Country* (Seattle, 1968); Harold E. Briggs, *Frontiers of the Northwest* (New York, 1940); and Harold E. Briggs, "The Development and Decline of Open Range Ranching in the Northwest", *Mississippi Valley Historical Review* 20 (March, 1934); Robert G. Athearn, *High Country Empire: The High Plains and the Rockies* (New York, 1960); O. B. Peak, *The Colorado Range Cattle Industry* (Glendale, Calif., 1939); T. A. Larson, *History of Wyoming* (Lincoln, 1965); Robert H. Fletcher, *From Grass to Fences: The Montana Range Cattle Story* (New York, 1960); Bob Lee and Dick Williams, *Last Grass Frontier: The South Dakota Stock Grower Heritage* (Sturgis, S. Dak., 1964).

19. Existing information on some of the early cattlemen can be found in Tom Lea, *The King Ranch*, 2 vols. (Boston, 1957); J. Evetts Haley,

Charles Goodnight: Cowman and Plainsman (New York, 1934); and J.
Evetts Haley, *George Littlefield, Texan* (Norman, 1943), more
scholarly treatments of Littlefield are David B. Gracy, "George
Washington Littlefield: Portrait of a Cattleman," *Southwestern Histori-
cal Quarterly* 68 (October, 1964): 237–58; and David B. Gracy,
"George W. Littlefield: From Cattle to Colonization, 1871–1920," in
John A. Carroll, ed., *Reflections of Western Historians* (Tuscon, Ariz.,
1969).

20. Atherton, *The Cattle Kings,* p. 219.

21. There are several good accounts that cover foreign and domestic
investment patterns in the later ranching era. See Gene M. Gressley,
Bankers and Cattlemen (New York, 1966); and Gene M. Gressley,
"Broker to the British: Francis Smith and Company," *Southwestern
Historical Quarterly* 71 (July, 1967): 7–25; W. Turrentine Jackson, *The
Enterprising Scot: Investors in the American West after 1873* (Edinburgh, 1968); Murice Frink et. al., *When grass Was King: Contributions to the Western Range Cattle Industry Study* (Boulder, Colo.,
1956); Richard Graham, "The Investment Boom in British-Texan Cattle Companies, 1800–1885," *Business History Review* 34 (Winter,
1960): 421–45; William W. Savage Jr. "Cows and Englishmen: Observations on Investment by British Immigrants in the Western Range
Cattle Industry," *Red River Valley Historical Review* 1 (Spring, 1974):
38–45; and William W. Savage, Jr., "Plunkett of the EK: Irish Notes
on the Wyoming Cattle Industry in the 1880s," *Annals of Wyoming* 43
(Fall, 1971): 205–14.

22. Alfred D. Chandler, "The Beginnings of 'Big Business' in
American Industry," *Business History Review* 33 (Spring, 1959): 1–31;
also Alfred D. Chandler, *Strategy and Structure: Chapters in the His-
tory of the Industrial Enterprise* (Cambridge, 1962). In addition, a
useful conceptual reference can be found in Thomas C. Cochran and
William Miller, *The Age of Enterprise: A Social History of Industrial
America* (New York, 1942); and Thomas C. Cochran, *Business in
American Life* (New York, 1970).

23. Some of the existing histories of the stock growers' associations
are Maurice Frink, *Cow Country Cavalcade: Eighty years of the Wyoming Stock Growers' Association* (Denver, 1954); W. Turrentine Jackson
"The Wyoming Stock Growers' Association: Political Power in Wyoming Territory, 1873–1890," *Mississippi Valley Historical Review*
33 (March, 1947): 571–94; W. Turrentine Jackson, "The Wyoming
Stock Growers' Association: Its Years of Temporary Decline, 1866–
1890," *Agricultural History* 22 (October, 1948): 260–70; and John
R. Burroughs, *Guardian of the Grasslands: the First Hundred Years*

of the Wyoming Stock Growers' Association (Cheyenne, Wyo., 1971). The Colorado Stock Growers Association is covered in Ora Peake, *The Colorado Range Cattle Industry* (Glendale, Calif., 1937). The Montana Stockman's Association is treated in Robert H. Fletcher, *From Grass to Fences: The Montana Range Cattle Story* (Helena, Mont., 1960). The Texas and Southwestern Cattle Raisers Association is covered in Lewis Nordyke, *Great Roundup: The Story of Texas and Southwestern Cattlemen* (New York, 1955).

24. Some existing ranching histories and organizations are Harley T. Burton, *History of the JA Ranch* (Austin, 1928); William C. Holden, *The Spur Ranch* (Boston, 1934); and Lewis Nordyke, *Cattle Empire: The Fabulous History of the 3,000,000 Acre XIT* (New York, 1949). A more useful study of the XIT is David B. Gracy II, *Littlefield Lands: Colonization on the Texas Plains, 1912–1920* (Austin, 1968). See also A. Ray Stephens, *The Taft Ranch: A Texas Principality* (Austin, 1964); and Dulcie Sullivan, *The LS Brand: The Story of a Texas Panhandle Ranch* (Austin, 1968). For land and cattle-company histories see Virginia H. Taylor, *The Franco-Texan Land Company* (Austin, 1969); and W. M. Pearce, *The Matador Land and Cattle Company* (Norman, 1971).

25. The most widely accepted definition of the frontier stage of mining is presented by Rodman Paul in *Mining Frontiers of the Far West, 1848–1880* (New York, 1963). Paul associated the mining frontier with the placer stage of gold mining. Paul's succinct study is an excellent beginning point for students of the far-western mining frontier. Another usable general study is William S. Greever, *The Bonanza West: The Story of the Western Rushes, 1848–1900* (Norman, 1963). Of note in western mining history, especially eastern and European mining techniques and social organizations, are Otis E. Young, Jr., *Western Mining: An Informal Account of Precious-Metals Prospecting, Placering, Lode Mining, and Milling on the American Frontier from Spanish Times to 1893* (Norman, 1970), and Otis E. Young, Jr., *Black Powder and Hand Steel: Miners and Machines on the Old Western Frontier* (Norman, 1976).

26. Duane A. Smith, *Rocky Mountain Mining Camps: The Urban Frontier* (Bloomington, Indiana, 1967), p. 47.

27. Fletcher Green, "Georgia's Forgotten Industry: Gold," *Georgia Historical Quarterly* 19 (June, 1935): 98–100; T. Conn Bryan, "The Gold Rush in Goergia," *Georgia Review* 9 (Winter, 1955): 398–99.

28. Green, "Georgia's Forgotten Industry," 101–106.

29. E. Merton Coulter, *Auraria: The Story of a Georgia Gold-Mining Town* (Athens, Ga., 1956), 17–31.

30. Green, ''Georgia's Forgotten Industry,'' p. 109.

31. Coulter, *Auraria*, p. 20.

32. Lewis Gray, *History of Agriculture in the Southern Unaited States to 1800* (Washington, D.C., 1933), 2: 1039; *DeBows Review: The Commercial Review of the South and West . . .* 1 (1864): 44.

33. Coulter, *Auraria*, pp. 33–46.

34. William Gilmore Simms, *Guy Rivers: A Tale of Georgia . . .*, 2 vols. (New York, 1834).

35. Coulter, *Auraria*, p. 55; taken from Mary C. Simms Oliphant et al., eds., *The Letters of William Gilmore Simms* (Columbia, S.C., 1955), 1: 55.

36. Coulter, *Auraria,* pp. 73–93. For a comparative treatment of far-western mining law and order see Duane A. Smith, *Rocky Mountain Mining Camps: The Urban Frontier* (Bloomington, 1976). See also Charles Shinn, *Mining Camps: A Study in American Frontier Government* (New York, 1884); and Wayne Gard, *Frontier Justice* (Norman, 1949). For local and regional treatments of this question see the bibliographies in Rodman Paul, *Mining Frontiers of the Far West, 1848–1880* (New York, 1963); and Ray Allen Billington, *Western Expansion: A History of the American Frontier,* 4th ed. (New York, 1974).

37. Coulter, *Auraria,* p. 58.

38. Bryan, ''Gold Rush in Georgia,'' p. 400.

39. Green, ''Georgia's Forgotten Industry,'' pp. 224–26; Bryan, ''Gold Rush in Georgia,'' p. 402.

40. For a discussion of investment in far-western mining see Clark Spence, *British Investment and the American Mining Frontier, 1860–1901* (Ithaca, N.Y., 1958); and W. Turrentine Jackson, *The Enterprising Scot: Investors in the American West After 1873* (Edinburgh, Scotland, 1968).

5. RECENT TRENDS AND NEW DIRECTIONS IN NATIVE AMERICAN HISTORY

Reginald Horsman

Interest in Native American history has never been greater. Books, articles, anthologies, documentary collections, reprints pour from the presses. No general American history conference is complete without its "Indian" session, and even journals short of space have been willing to devote entire issues to Native American subjects. The publication of Native American history has probably been helped rather than hindered by the general problems of scholarly publication. Publishers looking for "in" subjects have been quick to see the commercial possibilities in Indian history. This flaring of interst has led to some potboilers contrived to cash in on a favorable market, but the results have generally been favorable. Major gaps have been filled, traditional assumptions have been questioned, and there are clear signs that when the flurry of enthusiasm dies down there will still be a steady production of far more sophisticated works than would have been possible twenty years ago.

There are, of course, continuing problems in the writing of Native American history. A major difficulty is that three different groups, historians, Native Americans, and anthropologists, are approaching Indian history in different ways that have not yet been particularly well integrated. Clearly these three groups overlap. There are Native American historians and anthropologists, historians versed in anthropology, and anthropologists versed in history. Yet, as groups, there are marked distinctions. Most historians are still bound by the frame of white history. Even when

they are writing on Native Americans rather than on white attitudes, they are still primarily interested in white-Indian relationships. there are many reasons for this: The chronological frame of
Puritan New England, Revolution, Re-construction, New Deal,
and the rest is more familiar; the written sources are to most
historians more manageable; and the political, economic, and social units of white society present fewer conceptual problems for
the historian than such units in an Indian-centered history. It is not
that most historians are unsympathetic to an Indian point of view,
it is simply that internal Indian history presents problems in sources
and method that most historians are not trained to handle. As a
result, much of the best work by historians is on the shaping of
white attitudes and policies toward the Indians. here the historian
is on familiar ground.

Native Americans are now frequently looking to their history
for a usable past. Familiar to anyone who has attended conferences on Native American history is the sight of Native American
spokesmen rising from the audience to tell those who have read
papers that what they have been talking about is white, not Indian, America. Many Native Americans feel that their past has
been stolen from them by white historians, who ask questions
relevant only to themselves, not to Native Americans. In recent
years tribal and other groups have begun to commission or pub-
lish works with the specific object of presenting a Native American point of view. Frequently these works do not deal with historical materials in a way that is acceptable to many historians. They
represent a conscious effort to retain a cultural heritage and to
regain the past. It is clear that anthropologists feel far more at
home with these materials than most historians do.

When ethnohistory developed as a separate, organized entity in
the early 1950s, there was clearly a feeling that the techniques of
anthropology and history should be welded together to produce
effective histories of Native American societies. The necessity
for such a welding is as apparent now as it was then. In reality,
however, most ethnohistorians are anthropologists by training,
and though many ethnohistorians still think too much as anthropologists for most historians, they have in general more successfully taken techniques from history than historians have from

anthropology. Yet this is not a large branch of anthropology, and most anthropologists simply have not considered the historical problems posed by their materials.

The different focus of those interested in the Native American past has produced a somewhat strange division of labor in writing on the American Indian. Anthropologist-ethnohistorians dominate the period before white contact as they dominate the contemporary Indian scene. Historians feel at home from the coming of the Europeans to the recent past and tend to resent the broad sweep and generalizations that anthropologists bring to that historical period. Native American spokesmen often feel that the anthropologists are patronizing, that historians simply are not writing about Indians but are writing about white history and that Indian tradition needs much more attention. Fortunately, the enthusiasm for Native Americans studies in recent years has given the opportunities for interaction both at conferences and in print, and there are signs that the mistrust and misunderstanding between those interested in the Native American past are diminishing.

An obvious development in the recent past has been a rapidly increasing popular and professional sympathy for the Native American and an increasing willingness to condemn the manner in which the white Europeans and their successive governments treated the Indians. In the 1960s it became commonplace to condemn the historical record of the United States in its relations with the Indians, so much so that those historians who find praiseworthy aspects in the policies of the United States have come in for considerable criticism. On a popular level this widespread interest in the Indian was clearly connected with the whole course of contemporary protest movements and the new awareness of those in America who had not shared in the American dream. On a historical level it became linked to a general interest in the ''underside'' of American history. The degree to which the new criticism encouraged a national propensity for self-flagellation was strikingly demonstrated by the popular success of Dee Brown's *Bury My Heart at Wounded Knee* and Vine Deloria's *Custer Died for Your Sins*. Brown's recital of white maltreatment of the Indians was viewed as imperfect history by most specialists but was received enthusiastically by Native Americans, by the general public, and by students. Vine Deloria's contribution represented a far more significant departure in that it presaged a more active role for Native Americans in discussing American society and their place in it. It also marked the beginning of a highly successful career as author and lecturer for Deloria, a Standing Rock Sioux.[1]

Within the historical profession the new sympathy for the Indian brought, by the late 1960s, both a rethinking of how Native American history should be written and a major controversy between those who wished to condemn the historical record of the United States in its dealings with the Indians and those who viewed white attitudes and policies more favorably. The latter controversy was in many ways unfortunate, for, at a time when Native American history was being broadened beyond the history of white-Indian relations, it concentrated considerable effort and argument on the question of whether historians were "pro-white" or "pro-Indian," rather than on whether they were writing sound history. In miniature it re-created the situation that had arisen in the history of westward expansion earlier in the century, when most writing was judged as "pro-Turner" or "anti-Turner." More significant for the future of Native American studies was the rethinking of how the subject should be written.

There were, of course, writings sympathetic to the Indian long before the surge of public interest in the 1960s. Since the time of Helen Hunt Jackson's *Century of Dishonor* in 1881, writer after writer has written of the sufferings of the Indian tribesmen.[2] Throughout American history there has been a body of American opinion that has condemned the immorality of private attitudes and public policies toward the American Indian. It was never a majority viewpoint, but it was at times extremely influential. The most dominant view throughout American history was that the Indian was an obstacle in the path of American progress. In the historical profession this view was institutionalized by the writings of Frederick Jackson Turner; in popular culture it was revealed in a host of dime novels, westerns, and movies. Even here one might at times find sympathy for the Indian, but it was a sympathy based on the assumption that "an untutored savage" knew no better than to resist the progress represented by white farmers, cattlemen, the telegraph, and the railroad.

Historians of the first half of the twentieth century, like those of the nineteenth century, were for the most part unabashadly ethnocentric. For most it was as though Franz Boas had never written and that cultural relativity was an unknown concept. They were willing to point out examples of injustice—violated treaties, corrupt Indian agents, meaningless negotiations—but their assumptions were cast within a framework of white values and white history. In this view Indians by the very fact of European invasion had irrevocably lost one way of life; the only question left was whether they could assume a totally different culture, that of the Europeans. The time frame of white history was for historians the time frame of Indian history. Before contact Indians existed only in the writings of anthropologists. Even historians who thought of themselves as sympathetic to the sufferings of the Indians wrote in terms of savage Sioux attacks against intrepid pioneers, of crafty Apaches murdering innocent women and children, of bloodthirsty Comanches roaming the southern plains.

The most obvious result of the widespread sympathy for the Indian that arose in the 1960s was to bring a greatly increased sensitivity among historians to ethnocentric value judgments. Historians sympathetic to the Indians were quick to point out that the whites were the savages and aggressors, that government agents were the crafty deceivers, that the pioneers and the soldiers were the bloodthirsty villains disrupting peaceful Indian villages. the history of Native Americans was still thought of by many in a white time frame, actions were still judged by white values, but traditional moral judgments were often reversed. This has led to a vigorous debate about the nature of white attitudes and policies. It has also led to criticism from those who believe that this particular quarrel is not the decisive question in the writing of Native American history.

The most persuasive and influential historian who questions the effectiveness of both old approaches and the new surge of sympathy for the Indian is Robert F. Berkhofer. Since the 1960s, Berkhofer has been asking for a new sophistication in Native

American history. He emphasizes that historical understanding is not helped by an approach that, while reversing traditional moral judgments and emphasizing white rather than Indian villainy, continues to regard Native American history as merely a history of white-Indian relations. In his *Salvation and the Savage,* published in 1965, Berkhofer suggested that modern scholars who find a disparity between American ideals and the treatment of the Indian fail to realize that

earlier Americans acted as they did for the same reason that the Indians reacted as they did. Both groups behaved according to their own cultural systems. Any contradiction that the scholar finds between professed ideals and actual behavior is more a reflection of the ambivalence in past cultural assumptions than deliberate hypocrisy, unless proved otherwise, and even then the incongruity may be explained by reference to conflicting values. Thus current indictments of past American conduct are on the same plane as earlier American condemnations of savage society.

What Berkhofer called the " 'Century of Dishonor' approach" results, he argued, in a distortion of the historical past.[3]

In an essay on Native Americans and United States history published in 1973, Berkhofer suggested the weaknesses of histories that attempt to give more praise to the Indian by stressing Indian contributions to white society, emphasizing the contribution of Indian heroes, depicting the fraudulent nature of white treaties, writing of white rather than Indian barbarities, and stressing the importance of Indian values to contemporary American society. Although Berkhofer understands that these are ways of building cultural and ethnic pride and of redressing the balance of past accounts, he emphasizes that histories that consider the Indian past only in this manner are simply allowing the Native American past to be dominated by white concepts, values, and standards. While trying to be fair to the Indian, such histories simply increase the belief that Indian acts and beliefs only have value in so much as they contribute to the white framework of history or are judged by white standards.[4]

Berkhofer's answer to the dilemma of Indian escape from a

white straitjacket is "a new Indian-centered history." This history

focuses on Indian actors and Indian-Indian relations and relegates white-Indian relations and white actors to the periphery of the main arena of action. Rather than assuming inevitable unilinear progress toward assimilation, Indian-centered history presents Indians as individuals in their cultures and tribes coping with Indian-introduced as well as white innovations to older ways of life. Indian-centered history follows Indian peoples from before white contact to their present lives on reservations, in urban ghettoes, and on rural farms.[5]

To achieve this new history, Berkhofer argues, historians need to make use of the work of anthropologists and anthropological techniques. By concentrating on the internal dynamics of Indian societies, historians will be freed from their emphasis on the collapse of Indian societies under white pressure and will see that Indians, like all other peoples, have changed in time under various pressures and influences. Berkhofer argues that "political anthropology," with its broader definitions of politics as embracing all struggles over the distribution of power, might well provide the central theme for the reconstruction of the Indian past in its true complexity.[6]

To achieve the shift of emphasis asked for by Berkhofer, it is clear that historians will have to move beyond their traditional sources and methods to achieve a new understanding of Indian societies. The kind of knowledge that is needed is well expressed in a brief introduction by anthropologist John C. Ewers to a recent bibliography on Native American history. "The archaeologist's spade and the folklorist's tape recorder," writes Ewers, "yield data quite as important to an understanding of Indian history as the archivist's shelves of manuscripts. Dated artifacts, maps, drawings, paintings, and photographs are as revealing as written words." Ewers lays particular stress on the importance to historians of the archaeologists' work on Indian history before white contact: "The evidence literally uncovered by archaeologists in field excavations is uniquely valuable to historians. It provides the background necessary for an appreciation of antiquity, especially the dynamics of Indian experience in the various environments of North America before the coming of Europeans.'' Such work, argues Ewers, apprizes historians of the rise and fall of Indian communities before Columbus, allows them to perceive continuity into the historical period, and informs them of the rich variety of Native American life. In a similar way observations of contemporary Indian societies by anthropologists and others allow historians to perceive the persistence of basic values.[7]

In a 1974 article P. Richard Metcalf argued that Berkhofer's plea for an Indian-centered history, with Indian political behavior as a central theme, is at last emerging. Metcalf himself accepts the premises of ''political anthropology'' as the most useful unifying theme for the Native American past. He briefly suggests the deep factionalism within Indian societies at the time of white contact and emphasizes the extent to which Indian leaders were often more worried about the power struggle within their own individual communities than they were about responding directly to the white invaders.[8]

In spite of Metcalf's hopes for a new Indian-centered history, and in spite of a number of historical studies that demonstrate a new richness in source material and a new sensitivity to the complexities and continuities of Indian societies, most of the writing by historians on the Native American past continues to be dominated by the history of white-Indian relations. This writing, although now generally richer and more informed than in former years, continues to be bedeviled by the controversy about moral judgments of past white behavior. This is particularly the case for those historians writing of white-Indian contacts from colonial days to the Civil War. In the 1960s a wide gulf appeared between those historians who wished to condemn the historical record of the United States and of whites in general and those who were prepared to view white and government policies toward the Indians more favorably. One difficulty is that expressed by Berkhofer when he writes that it needs to be remembered that the whites who were advancing across the American continent were acting as much within the framework of their own cultural systems as were the Indians who were being overrun. Presumably historians who can understand why Indians were attacking white settlements can also understand why white settlers were attacking Indian villages. It has long been a cliché of historical training that the values of the present should not be injected into the past, and to some there has seemed a danger that widespread sympathy for the Indian has produced such presentism.

The dangers of injecting present moral values into the past is, however, only part of the problem. There is also a genuine disagreement about the motives and morality of past policies of Europeans, Americans, and their governments on the North American continent. Some historians, like most Native Americans, believe that the historical record demonstrates a history of aggression, brutality, and hypocrisy by the whites toward the Native Americans. Others believe that that is a false or incomplete picture; they are prepared to defend white attitudes and policies in North America or wish to depict a mixture of motives, aggressive and philanthropic, that inspired white actions. In the 1960s and early 1970s the popular mood was clearly most sympathetic to those who were highly critical of the past performance of whites in their relations with the Native Americans. As a result those historians who either were prepared to defend white policies or were unwilling to join the general condemnation of all aspects of past attitudes and policies came in for a good deal of criticism. They in turn were critical of historians who they thought were substituting sympathy for scholarship. The disagreements were sharp, and for a time the protagonists were driven by controversy into more extreme statements of their arguments than they probably otherwise would have made. There are now indications that the gulf in interpretations is not unbridgeable.

The best known of those historians who have become known for seeing merit in the white historical record are Alden Vaughan, Douglas Leach, Francis P. Prucha, and Bernard Sheehan. Alden Vaughan in his *New England Frontier* presents an interpretation of the Puritans and the Indians that is far more favorable to the Puritans than is acceptable to many critics. ''What emerges from my investigation of the sources,'' he writes, ''is a conviction that the New England Puritans followed a remarkably humane, considerate, and just policy in their dealings with the Indians. In matters of commerce, religious conversion, and judicial procedure, the Puritans had surprisingly high regard for the interests of a people who were less powerful, less civilized, less sophisticated, and—in the eyes of the New England colonists—less godly.'' Vaughan characterizes the Puritan society as ''unified, visionary, disciplined, and dynamic,'' the Indian as ''divided, self-satisfied, undisciplined, and static.'' Leach by no means defends the Puritans with the vigor of Vaughan, but he writes of ''the complex, dynamic culture of western Europe'' imposing itself upon ''the simple, static culture of aboriginal New England.''[9]

To those who are highly critical of white attitudes and policies toward the Indians, Prucha and Sheehan are for the early national period what Vaughan is for the seventeenth century. Since the early 1960s Prucha has most consistently challenged what he views as simplistic interpretations of American Indian policy in the first decades of the nineteenth century. Although Prucha is generally cautious in his conclusions, the tendency of his work has been to place American government policies in a more favorable light than that shown by most historians. Because Prucha bases his work on a meticulous study of the sources, he presents a formidable challenge to those who find nothing of merit in federal Indian policy. In his book *American Indian Policy in the Formative Years,* published in 1962, he pointed out that Indian removal was effected not merely out of greed for land but also to facilitate the civilization and preservation of the Indians. Prucha argued that, although Jackson and his administration failed to enforce the decision of John Marshall regarding the Cherokees, ''it is unfair... to charge them with cynical expediency and complete disregard for Indian rights and feelings, despite the later miseries of the Trail of Tears.' '' He stressed that removal was supported not only by land-hungry frontiersmen but also by such ''highminded'' men as Lewis Cass, Thomas McKenney, and William Clark.[10]

In subsequent articles Prucha has emphasized the weaknesses in blanket condemnations of the removal policy. He has pointed out that the Indians were removed to generally favorable wooded, prairie country rather than to the middle of the ''Great American Desert,''[11] and in a far more controversial article has attempted a revision of the traditional view of Andrew Jackson. Prucha maintains that Jackson's "outlook was essentially Jeffersonian" and that he "looked upon removal as a means of protecting the process of civilization, as well as of providing land for white settlers, security from foreign invasion, and a quieting of the clamors of Goergia against the federal government."[12] Although this article caused a sharp reaction from those historians who wished to see unqualified condemnation of Jackson, Prucha emphasized that in writing the article he was attempting to rebut the simplistic "devil theory" of American Indian policy in which moralistic condemnations of American policy are substituted for historical analysis. Moreover, in other writings Prucha has asked for a balanced viewpoint, not for an uncritical acceptance of white values. In the introduction to his *Americanizing the American Indians,* a collection of writings by "friends of the Indian" in the 1880–1900 period, he writes that, though they were "sincere and humane in their outlook, the reformers were entrapped in a mold of patriotic Americanism that was too narrow to allow them to appreciate the Indian cultures. Their all-out attack on Indianness must be judged a disaster for the Indians, and therefore for the nation."[13]

Prucha has received most support in the writings of Sheehan, and it is clear that, while critics think that Sheehan's writing is too much imbued with white values, Sheehan, like Prucha, perceives his own work as combating simplistic views of the white-Indian relationship. In a review article published in 1969, Sheehan's comments on method are reminiscent of those of Robert F. Berkhofer. "The issue of right or wrong," he writes, "must give way to an understanding of the process of cultural conflict that characterized the meeting of European and Indian in the New World."[14] In his book *Seeds of Extinction,* on attitudes toward the American Indian from the Revolution to the 1830's, Sheehan says that writers have assumed that whites of the early nineteenth century "saw Indians in the same manner that the modern historian sees them, and hence the treatment of the native population has been judged as reprehensible." Sheehan's emphasis on the philanthropic intentions of government policy and his endorsement of some of Prucha's research have brought sharp reactions from government critics. Sheehan argues that the philanthropic commitment to incorporate the Indians within American society did not change from the Revolution to 1830 and that the purpose of Indian removal was to preserve the theoretical structure of this commitment rather than to negate it.[15]

Prucha's and Sheehan's meticulous stress on sources has been healthy, but their interpretations are open to challenge on the grounds that they underestimate or ignore the political pressures that brought about the removal decisions and ignore the extent to which the federal government itself allowed conditions to develop that made removal seem necessary even to some friends of the Indian. There is considerable evidence to show that removal was a pragmatic decision in which the interests of the Indians were completely subordinated to internal political pressures and that general Indian removal occurred because the southern states, with sizable Indian populations and landholdings, rejected the Jeffersonian ideal of Indian civilization and incorporation and persuaded the federal government to comply with their wishes in the years 1817 to 1830. The conflict between the ideal and reality, which had always been implicit in Jeffersonian Indian policy, became explicit in the era of removal.

The most sweeping indictment of the point of view expressed by Vaughan, Leach, Prucha, and Sheehan is that of Francis Jennings in *The Invasion of America.* In building a theoretical framework for analysis of the meeting of Native Americans and Puritans in New England, Jennings argues that all these historians either overtly or implicitly have accepted the civilization-savagery dichotomy in their writings and that contemporary writers have inherited the ideology that European invaders developed to justify their actions in the New World. Jennings rejects Vaughan's interpretation of the meeting of Puritans and Indians in the seventeenth century and launches a vigorous attack on Puritan motives and actions, as well as on those historians who have defended them.[16]

For Jennings the answer to the proper study of the European–Native American interaction in the seventeenth century is the technique of ethnohistory. ''In the lexicon of the ethnohistorian,'' he writes, ''the opposing absolutes of evil savagery and good civilization become morally neutral and relatively campara-

ble as 'societies' and 'cultures.' " Jennings argues that "modern
American society is the product not only of interaction between
colonists and natives but of contributions from both."[17] Rather
than viewing the seventeenth century from the perspective of the
European invaders, Jennings attempts to bring an Indian perspective to the material and to survey the changing cultures of both
Indians and Europeans.

Although Jennings provides a healthy corrective to markedly
pro-Puritan views, a problem with his approach is that he hardly
treats the Puritans with that dispassionate ethnohistorical method
he urges others to use in comparing societies and cultures. "I
have recognized in myself a strong aversion toward the Puritan
gentry," he writes, "and have tried to compensate for it by
documenting heavily from their own writings whenever possible.
It may be well to notice that I have tried to practice restraint but
not concealment of my distaste, and to say further that it was
acquired in the course of my research."[18] It seems unlikely that
Jennings would have been gentle in his response if a "pro-
Puritan" author had written a similar statement asserting an aversion toward Indians.

Jennings' argument that American society represents a welding
of European and Native American influences is helped by certain
aspects of the writings of James Axtell. Axtell is interested in
education in colonial America, and he considers education in a
broad context. He stresses that it was not simply a question of
missionaries and others attempting to educate Indians in colonial
America; often Indians were more successful in educating whites
in their way of life than whites were in educating Indians.[19]

The question of Puritan attitudes toward the Indians is constantly being reexamined by historians. G. E. Thomas, like Jennings, expresses disagreement with Vaughan's interpretation.
After lumping Vaughan with Prucha and Sheehan as leaders in
the school of historians who emphasize "humanitarian" aspects
of white policy toward the Indians, Thomas attacks the Puritans
as harsh, brutal, and ethnocentric. He sees in Puritan attitudes
toward the Indians a foreshadowing of later racism in that, "no
matter how hard the Puritan tried to transform the Indian or how
completely the Indian conformed, the cause was ultimately hope-

less because the Indian could never become white.''[20] James Muldoon differs from Thomas in that he emphasizes the importance of attitudes toward the ''Wild Irish'' in the formation of Puritan attitudes toward the Indians, but even if the Puritans did not think of the Indians as a distinct race, Muldoon argues that by the end of the seventeenth century they viewed them as irredeemably sunk in savagery.[21] Richard Slotkin, in his *Regeneration through Violence,* goes beyond the Puritan-Indian experience to examine the darker side of American attitudes from the seventeenth century to the Civil War. American violence, Slotkin argues, is not peripheral but rather at the very core of American character. For Slotkin the frontier mythology that shaped American literature was at the heart of the national character.[22]

In the 1960s, Wilcomb E. Washburn took the lead in challenging Prucha's interpretations of the white-Indian relationship in the early national period. Washburn, particularly in his earlier writings, challenged Prucha's interpretations of government policy, arguing that Prucha had too readily accepted the good faith of the American government. Washburn has condemned what he perceives as a continual pattern of unjust government actions toward the Native Americans. Like Prucha, however, he appears to be modifying his viewpoint in his recent writings.[23] In his volume *The Indian in America,* published in 1975 in the New American Nation series, Washburn is ambiguous on the subject of Indian removal. After pointing out that it is possible either to condemn removal or to argue, ''as Paul Prucha does, that those advocating removal were concerned with the Indian's good rather than his harm,'' Washburn reaches the conclusion that, ''considering the practical alternatives faced by those concerned with Indian policy at the time ... and accepting the limitations imposed by those alternatives, it is possible to understand, and possible to sympathize with, the policy that emerged.''[24] Although Washburn is clearly attempting a balanced viewpoint, possibly because of the nature of the series in which he is writing, his position represents a shift in emphasis from ten years before.

Whereas Prucha's and Sheehan's interpretations emphasize the efforts of government to protect and help the Indian, other historians have placed more emphasis on the greed and the practical politics of American Indian policy. In my *Expansion and American Indian Policy,* (1967) I emphasized that the greater order that the government brought to Indian affairs in these years was a means of facilitating rapid expansion rather than curbing it, and in articles I have stressed the extent to which Indian removal was a political rather than a philanthropic decision and the extent to which racist assumptions were beginning to permeate attitudes toward the Indian in the 1830s and 1840s.[25] Ronald N. Satz, in his study of Jacksonian Indian policy, carefully delineates the mixture of motives that inspired the Jacksonian administration and shows some of the practical realities of the policy.[26]

Far more controversial and unusual is Michael Paul Rogin's study of Andrew Jackson and the Indians, *Fathers and Children.* Rogin, a political scientist, uses the techniques of psychohistory to explain Jackson's attitudes and policies toward the Indians. His study of Jackson is a useful corrective to those historians who have attempted to explain Jacksonianism without regard to Indian policy, but the book is badly flawed. Rogin sees whites in general, and Jackson in particular, indulging primitive longings in their attitudes toward the Indians—seeking to regain the infant-mother connection from a position of domination rather than dependence. Jackson, according to Rogin, acted toward the Indians with infantile rage. In some ways the study is traditional in its view of Jackson the Indian hater, but it attempts far more in claiming that Jackson "forged American national identity in westward expansion and Indian removal." Even those who could agree in general with the condemnation of Jackson's Indian policy find major flaws in Rogin's interpretation. "*Fathers and Children* is a failure," writes Edward Pessen, "neither because of its purpose nor its approach but because of its fatal weakness in its author's historical imagination, his conceptualization, his documentation, his use of language, and his lapses from good sense."[27]

The most vigorous historical controversies in the interpretations of white-Indian relations are from the seventeenth century through Indian removal. After removal, although there are disagreements, the main need has been for basic monographs rather than refinements of existing interpretations. Traditionally, the most abundant historical writing on white-Indian contact after removal has been on the Indian wars of the 1850s to 1890s. An interest in the details of warfare and campaigns has continued, more as a branch of military and local history than Indian history, but in the general area of military-Indian relations a new sophistication has developed. Robert M. Utley, in his *Frontiersmen in Blue* (1967) and *Frontier Regulars* (1973), gives a general interpretation of the army and the Indian from the end of the Mexican War to the beginning of the 1890s. Rather than simply reciting the detailed history of campaigns and incidents, Utley relates the army on the frontier to the broader aspects of military history and Indian policy.[28]

A more unusual development in recent years has been the number of historians who have begun to provide basic monographs on nonmilitary aspects of American Indian policy in the second half of the nineteenth century. Robert A. Trennert, in a detailed work on the years from 1846 to 1851, emphasizes the importance of these years for the emergence of a reservation system as an alternative to extinction.[29] The 1850s has had less full treatment in recent years, but the evolving reservation system is the focus of Edmund J. Danziger's work on the Civil War era. Danziger surveys the general reservation policy throughout the country and criticizes the general federal goal of assimilation.[30] There is a need for still more intensive work on the middle decades of the nineteenth century, work that will show how the increasingly common scientific and popular view of the Indian as inferior and expendable entwined with the continuing philanthropic vision of Indian improvability and how both affected political realities. There is also a need for additional research on the practical realities of Indian policy in the 1880's and 1890's. The best work has been on the reformers,[31] but the complex interrelationships of reformers, western exploiters, and political figures still needs fuller delineation. An indication of the lack of recent detailed analysis of the Dawes Act is that in 1973 the University of Oklahoma Press reprinted the account of the allotment policy written for the Bureau of Indian Affairs by D. S. Otis in the early 1930s.[32]

Historians are only beginning to touch the rich sources for

white-Indian relations and Native American history of the twentieth century. Hazel W. Hertzberg's *The Search for an American Indian Identity* is a pioneering work on the development of Pan-Indian movements in the first decades of the twentieth century. In the work she devotes considerable space to the Society of American Indians. Far more work remains to be done on these years.[33] Even in such a traditional historical area as biography it has been dynamic military leaders rather than Indian politicians and reformers who have attracted most attention. The mass of white society has heard of Pontiac, Tecumseh, or Crazy Horse but ignores Charles A. Eastman, Arthur C. Parker, or Carlos Montezuma.

The only aspect of twentieth-century white-Indian relations that has drawn enough historical interest to produce much variety in historical interpretation is that of the evolution of the New Deal philosophy in regard to the American Indian. Kenneth Philp takes a generally favorable approach to the work of John Collier, but Lawrence C. Kelly is more critical of Collier's role, and he points out the shortcomings of the Indian Reorganization Act. Margaret Szasz's *Education and the American Indian,* which deals with the years 1928 to 1973, is more limited in its scope than its title suggests. The main focus of the book is the educational mission of the Bureau of Indian Affairs. The book, however, provides more evidence for the limitations of the Collier reforms.[34]

The flurry of books on the traditional field of white-Indian contact has not been matched by a similar mass of material on new areas or on areas traditionally assigned to anthropologists. This reluctance to enter into such subjects is demonstrated by the paucity of works by historians on the basic demographic history of Native Americans. This is surprising in a profession that is increasingly attempting to make use of quantitative techniques. Until recently the commonly accepted population total for indigines north of Mexico at the time of the coming of the Americans was about one million.[35] In a 1966 article anthropologist Henry F. Dobyns suggested that a more likely figure was 9.8 million or more.[36] Although Dobyns' article has generated considerable interest, it has not produced comprehensive new research and analysis. Without new research the results are what might be expected. There is a tendency for those historians who are most critical of European attitudes and policies to accept the new Dobyns figures, while others remain doubtful.[37] It is an obvious area of interest for those historians with an expertise in quantitative techniques, as is the whole field of Indian depopulation and recovery.

Physiologist Sherburne F. Cook has shown the possibilities for this kind of research in two articles on the impact of disease and of warfare respectively on the New England Indians in the century after European contact. In his article on disease Cook points out that the New England Native American population suffered both from lethal epidemics of plague and smallpox and from debilitating chronic maladies such as tuberculosis and dysentery. The disastrous effect of these diseases was compounded by warfare with the whites; Cook estimates that in one hundred years a quarter of the aboriginal Indian population died in armed conflict with the Eurpoeans.[38] Calvin Martin has suggested a new area of interest in an article pointing out that wildlife diseases (zoonoses) have previously been overlooked in the depopulation of the North American Indian. He points out that little is known on this subject and suggests possible avenues of research.[39] This whole demographic area needs work; even Indian removal has not attracted the detailed quantitative work that is needed to supplement the analysis of attitudes and policies. Unless such work is undertaken, there will be an expansion of the tendency by which those who wish to be most critical of white policies accept the larger population figures (to increase the guilt) and those who see more merit in white policies accept lower estimates (to diminish the responsibility).

The possibilities of basic demographic work on the Indians is interconnected with another new area of interest that is as yet relatively untouched: the whole subject of the Indians and their environment. In gathering a collection of his articles and essays into a book in 1972, Wilbur F. Jacobs suggested the necessity of realizing that for the Indians the coming of the white man's frontier was an ecological calamity, and he argued that the primary purpose of his book was to throw more light on the ecology of the frontier and early Indian-white relations.[40] Jacobs has tried to stimulate an interest in ecological history, and in recent years several authors have suggested possible points of departure for studies of Native Americans in their environment. This is clearly an area that demands the use of anthropological and ethnohistorical techniques. Richard White, in a study of Island County, Washington, shows how the Salish tribes were able to alter their natural environment to create and maintain an effective ecosystem.[41] More ambitious is an article by Calvin Martin, who, by using the methods of cultural ecology, demonstrates how the European impact changed the ecosystem among the Micmacs in the northeastern United States. Martin suggests that Native American history can be seen as a type of environmental history.[42]

The approach that links Indians firmly with their environment is one that finds much favor among the Native Americans themselves. Until recent years historians of the American Indians, with some notable exceptions, such as D'Arcy McNickle, have been white, and even oral tradition has usually been filtered through white anthropologists. Yet the development of an Indian power movement and the search for a usable Indian past have produced a renewed interest in Native Americans' own depictions of their past. Tribal and other groups have recently begun issuing their own books on their history and traditions or have cooperated with non-Indians to produce what amount to authorized tribal histories. In many ways this material plays a more important part in developing ethnic consciousness than it does in shaping or modifying traditional professional histories, but such material will inevitably affect those interested in the Native Americans in the twentieth century.[43]

Indian oral traditions have also been perpetuated in recent years by large-scale projects, often leading to at least microfilm publication, of interviews with Native Americans. Notable among the new sources of oral history are those produced under grants from the Doris Duke Foundation of New York. Beginning in the late 1960s oral-history projects were sponsored by the Duke Foundation at the Universities of Arizona, Illinois, New Mexico, South Dakota, and Utah. Although these projects have resulted in the collection of large amounts of material, there has as yet been little perceptible impact on the historical profession.[44] An example of the kind of research made possible by this material is an article by William W. Savage, Jr., who uses Oklahoma data to study white racial attitudes and the Indian reaction in two southern-plains communities.[45]

The problem of writing Native American history that will be satisfactory to activist Native Americans, anthropologists, and historians has not yet been solved. Indeed, none of these three groups, has, or even wants, internal agreement regarding the components of such history. Native Americans frequently ask for an Indian-centered history that will show both the extent of their mistreatment by the whites and the extent of their contribution to the general American past. Both aims frequently lead to history that conforms to a white structure rather than to an Indian-oriented study of the Native American past. Also there is a danger that requests for history written from a Native American point of view can lead to ethnic propaganda rather than sophisticated analyses of the total Native American past.

Anthropologists also have severe problems in dealing with the Native American past. The best ethnohistorians have tended to be anthropologists. Ethnohistorians such as Nancy Lurie, Anthony F. C. Wallace, Joseph G. Jorgensen, and Harold Hickerson have done much to give a historical dimension to anthropology.[46] Yet ethnohistorians have had difficulty establishing a major role for themselves within the general discipline of anthropology, and most anthropologists appear to have as little respect for the archival methods of history as most historians have for the fieldwork of the anthropologists. Anthropologists have often had most success with ethnohistory in that period of early white contact when archival sources have to be used even for ethnological material. Where there has been less success in using ethnohistorical techniques is where they are most needed—the twentieth century. Effective histories of the white–Native American reaction in the twentieth century require sophistication in working with both archival and oral materials, but, in working on twentieth-century history, anthropologists and historians have usually pursued separate paths.

In the minds of most historians of the American Indian, white-

Indian relationships continue to dominate. Moreover, historians, whether of the American Indian or of any other subject, clearly find certain periods in North American history both of more professional interest and of greater accessibility than others, and even the mass of writing in recent years has left certain periods barren of general interpretations, while producing considerable argument on others. North American history before white contact is still the domain of the anthropologist, and for the most part historians have not integrated archaeological, linguistic, and oral materials into their work. Berkhofer's request for an Indian-centered history deeply grounded in the prewhite past has for the most part not been answered by historians. Only a rare work, such as Warren L. Cook's *The Flood Tide of Empire,* dealing with Spain in the Northwest from 1543 to 1819, demonstrates the rare combination of history and anthropology, with the major concentration history rather than anthropology.[47]

What has come out of the flurry of interest in Native American history has been far more extensive research in basic aspects of the white-Indian relationship. This analysis has usually been far stronger in areas of white attitudes and policies than in the Indian response. Also, for all the arguments on whether historians are "pro-white" or "pro-Indian," there is in general a greatly increased sensitivity among historians to the values of different societies and cultures. A professional historian of today would have to be remarkably cloistered to write of ferocious savages wreaking havoc on innocent white pioneers, but a casual glance through the frontier histories of twenty or thirty years ago would produce many examples of such writing. There may not be general agreement among historians about the merits or faults of specific government policies, but there is at least an awareness of the problems of cultural relativity that was long absent from western history. The parochial assumptions of white progress and Indian savagery inherent in the whole Turner tradition are now no longer the norm.

Where the historians of the American Indian often remain parochial is in the lack of work on the total context of the white-Indian relationship in North America. Relationships between Europeans and aboriginals can be viewed on a world as well as an

American scene. These relationships are part of the history of European thought, or colonialism and imperialism, as well as of the American frontier. Attitudes toward the American Indian to the end of the eighteenth century are discussed by intellectual historians as part of the whole subject of European views of non-European peoples, but for the nineteenth and twentieth centuries American historians turn inward, as though political independence automatically brought cultural and intellectual independence. Even comparative studies are exceedingly rare, although Jacobs has suggested possible points of comparison with Australian and New Guinea frontiers,[48] and American thought and attitudes, which in the eighteenth century are linked to a trans-atlantic culture, are for the nineteen and twentieth centuries often viewed as something unique. the bitter fights over the extent or nature of white American guilt might be given a more effective perspective if seen in the light of the contact between European and non-European peoples.

Notes

1. Dee Brown, *Bury My Heart at Wounded Knee: An Indian History of the American West* (New York, 1970); and Vine Deloria, *Custer Died for Your Sins: An Indian Manifesto* (New York, 1969). Among Deloria's other works are *We Talk, You Listen: New Tribes, New Turf* (New York, 1970); *Of Utmost Good Faith* (San Francisco, 1971); *God Is Red* (New York, 1973); and *Behind the Trail of Broken Treaties: An Indian Declaration of Independence* (New York, 1974).

2. Helen Hunt Jackson, *A Century of Dishonor: A Sketch of the United States Government's Dealings with Some of the Indian Tribes* (New York, 1881).

3. Robert F. Berkhofer, Jr., *Salvation and the Savage: An Analysis of Protestant Missions and American Indian Response, 1787–1862* (Lexington, Ky., 1965), pp. ix–x.

4. Robert F. Berkhofer, "Native Americans and United States History," in William H. Cartwright and Richard L. Watson, Jr., eds., *The Reinterpretation of American History and Culture* (Washington, D.C., 1973), pp. 37–52.

5. Ibid., pp. 47–48.

6. Robert F. Berkhofer, "The Political Context of a New Indian History," *Pacific Historical Review* 40 (August 1971): 357–82.

7. John C. Ewers, Introduction to *Indians of the United States and Canada: A Bibliography,* ed. Dwight L. Smith (Santa Barbara, Calif., 1974), pp. xiii–xvi. See also John C. Ewers, "When White and Red Men Met," *Western Historical Quarterly* 2 (April 1971): 133–50.

8. P. Richard Metcalf, "Who Should Rule at Home? Native American Politics and Indian-White Relations," *Journal of American History* 61 (December 1974): 651–65.

9. Alden T. Vaughan, *New England Frontier: Puritans and Indians, 1620–1675* (Boston, 1965), pp. vii, 323; and Douglas E. Leach, *The Northern Colonial Frontier, 1607–1763* (New York, 1966), p. 55.

10. Francis Paul Prucha, *American Indian Policy in the Formative Years: The Indian Trade and Intercourse Acts, 1790–1834* (Cambridge, Mass., 1962), pp. 224–25, 245.

11. Francis Paul Prucha, "Indian Removal and the Great American Desert," *Indiana Magazine of History* 59 (December 1963): 299–322.

12. Francis Paul Prucha, "Andrew Jackson's Indian Policy: A Reassessment," *Journal of American History* 56 (December 1969): 534.

13. Francis Paul Prucha, ed., *Americanizing the American Indian: Writings by the "Friends of the Indian" 1880–1900* (Cambridge, Mass., 1973), p. 10.

14. Bernard Sheehan, ''Indian-White Relations in Early America: A Review Essay,'' *William and Mary Quarterly,* 3d ser. 26 (April 1969): 270.

15. Bernard Sheehan, *Seeds of Extinction: Jeffersonian Philanthropy and the American Indian* (Chapel Hill, N.C., 1973), pp. ix, 11.

16. Francis Jennings, *The Invasion of America: Indians, Colonialism, and the Cant of Conquest* (Chapel Hill, N.C., 1975), pp. 8–12. See also Frank Jennings, ''Goals and Functions of Puritan Missions to the Indians,'' *Ethnohistory* 18 (Summer 1971): 197–212; Frank Jennings, ''Virgin Land and Savage People,'' *American Quarterly* 23 (October 1971): 519–41; and Neal Salisbury, ''Red Puritans: The ''Praying Indians'' of Massachusetts Bay and John Eliot,'' *William and Mary Quarterly,* 3d ser. 31 (January 1974): 27–54.

17. Jennings, *Invasion of America,* pp. viii–ix, 13.

18. Ibid., p. 185.

19. James Axtell, *The School upon a Hill: Education and Society in Colonial New England* (New Haven, 1974); James Axtell, ''The Scholastic Theory of the Wilderness,'' *William and Mary Quarterly,* 3d ser. 29 (July 1972): 355–66; and James Axtell, ''The White Indians of Colonial America,'' ibid., 32 (January 1975): 55–88.

20. G. E. Thomas, ''Puritans, Indians, and the Concept of Race,'' *New England Quarterly* 48 (March 1975): 4, 27.

21. James Muldoon, ''The Indian as Irishman,'' *Essex Institute Historical Collections* 111 (October 1975): 267–89.

22. Richard Slotkin, *Regeneration Through Violence: The Mythology of the American Frontier, 1600–1860* (Middleton, Conn., 1973). The white image of the Indian has attracted considerable interest of late. See Elémire Zolla, *The Writer and the Shaman: A Morphology of the American Indian,* tr. Raymond Rosenthal (New York, 1973); Gary B. Nash, ''The Image of the Indian in the Southern Colonial Mind,'' *William and Mary Quarterly,* 3d ser. 29 (April 1972): 197–230; Robert Shulman, ''Parkman's Indians and American Violence,'' *Massachusetts Review* 12 (Spring 1971): 221–39; Roy Harvey Pearce, ''From the History of Ideas to Ethnohistory,'' *Journal of Ethnic Studies* 2 (Spring 1974): 86–92; and Ellwood Parry, *The Image of the Indian and the Black Man in American Art* (New York, 1974).

23. Wilcomb E. Washburn, ''Indian Removal Policy: Administrative, Historical and Moral Criteria for Judging Its Failure,'' *Ethnohistory* 12 (Summer 1965): 274–78; Wilcomb E. Washburn, ''The Writing of Indian History: A Status Report,'' *Pacific Historical Review* 40 (August 1971): 261–81; Wilcomb E. Washburn, ''American Indian Studies: A Status Report,'' *American Quarterly* 27 (August 1975): 263–74; and

24. Wilcomb E. Washburn, *The Indian in America* (New York, 1975), p. 167.

25. Reginald Horsman, *Expansion and American Indian Policy, 1783–1812* (East Lansing, Mich., 1967); Reginald Horsman, "American Indian Policy and the Origins of Manifest Destiny," *University of Birmingham* (England) *Historical Journal* 11 (1968): 128–40; and Reginald Horsman, "Scientific Racism and the American Indian in the Mid-Nineteenth Century," *American Quarterly* 27 (May 1975): 152–68. The Revolutionary era still needs additional work, although James H. O'Donnell, *Southern Indians in the American Revolution* (Knoxville, Tenn., 1973), presents an overview of one aspect, and Barbara Graymont, *The Iroquois in the American Revolution* (Syracuse, N.Y., 1972), ably depicts Iroquois as well as white society.

26. Ronald N. Satz, *American Indian Policy in the Jacksonian Era* (Lincoln, Nebr., 1975). Herman J. Viola, *Thomas L. McKenney: Architect of America's Early Indian Policy, 1816–1830* (Chicago, 1974), looks upon McKenney in a favorable light. See also Linda K. Kerber, "The Abolitionist Perception of the Indian," *Journal of American History* 62 (September 1975): 271–95; and Arthur H. DeRosier, Jr., *The Removal of the Choctaw Indians* (Knoxville, Tenn., 1970).

27. Michael Paul Rogin, *Fathers and Children: Andrew Jackson and the Subjugation of the American Indian* (New York, 1975), p. 167; see also Michael Paul Rogin, "Liberal Society and the Indian Question," *Politics and Society* 1 (May 1971): 269–312; and Michael Paul Rogin, "Indian Extinction, American Regeneration," *Journal of Ethnic Studies* 2 (Spring 1974): 93–104; and review by Edwards in *New York History* 57 (January 1976): 110–11.

28. Robert M. Utley, *Frontiersmen in Blue: The United States Army and the Indian, 1848–1865* (New York, 1967); Robert M. Utley, *Frontier Regulars: The United States Army and the Indian, 1866–1891* (New York, 1973). See also Richard N. Ellis, *General Pope and U.S. Indian Policy* (Albuquerque, N. Mex., 1970). The army on the frontier in the early national period is dealt with (in the Macmillan series the Wars of the United States) by Francis P. Prucha, *The Sword of the Republic: The United States Army on the Frontier, 1783–1846* (New York, 1969).

29. Robert A. Trennert, *Alternative to Extinction: Federal Indian Policy and the Beginnings of the Reservation System, 1846–1851* (Philadelphia, 1975).

30. Edmund J. Danziger, *Indians and Bureaucrats: Administering the Reservation Policy During the Civil War* (Urbana, Ill., 1974). M. Thomas Bailey's *Reconstruction in Indian Territory: A Story of Av-*

arice, Discrimination, and Opportunism (Port Washington, N.Y., 1972) was severely criticized for the nature of its research in *American Historical Review* 79 (June 1974): 876. The author answered in ibid., pp. 916–17.

31. A good example is Robert W. Mardock, *Reformers and the American Indian* (Columbia, Mo., 1971).

32. D. S. Otis, *The Dawes Act and the Allotment of Indian Lands,* ed. Francis P. Prucha (Norman, Okla., 1973). See also H. Craig Miner, *The Corporation and the Indian: Tribal Sovereignty and Industrial Civilization in Indian Territory,* 1865–1907 (Columbia, Mo., 1976); William T. Hagan, "Kiowas, Comanches, and Cattlemen, 1867–1906: A Case Study of the Failure of U.S. Reservation Policy," *Pacific Historical Review* 40 (August 1971): 333–55; and Donald J. Berthrong, "Cattlemen on the Cheyenne-Arapaho Reservation, 1883–1885," *Arizona and the West* 13 (Spring 1971): 5–32.

33. Hazel W. Hertzberg, *The Search for an American Indian Identity: Modern Pan-Indian Movements* (Syracuse, N.Y., 1971).

34. Kenneth Philp, "John Collier and the Crusade to Protect Indian Religious Freedom, 1920–1926," *Journal of Ethnic Studies* 1 (Spring 1973): 22–38; Lawrence C. Kelly, "The Indian Reorganization Act: The Dream and the Reality," *Pacific Historical Review* (August 1975): 291–312; and Margaret Szasz, *Education and the American Indian: The Road to Self-Determination, 1928–1973* (Albuquerque, N. Mex., 1974). See also Stephen J. Kunitz, "The Social Philosophy of John Collier," *Ethnohistory* 18 (Summer 1971): 213–29.

35. This was based on the suggestions by James Mooney, "The Aboriginal Population of America North of Mexico," *Smithsonian Miscellaneous Collections,* vol. 80, no. 7 (Washington, D.C., 1928); and Alfred L. Kroeber, *Cultural and Natural Areas of North America* (Berkeley, Calif., 1939).

36. Henry F. Dobyns, "Estimating Aboriginal American Population: An Appraisal of Techniques with a New Hemisphere Estimate," *Current Anthropology* 7 (October 1966): 395–416; see also Harold E. Driver, "On the Population Nadir of the Indians of the United States," ibid., 9 (October 1968): 330. Geographer Michael F. Doran has indicated what can be done with a specific area at a later date in "Population Statistics of Nineteenth Century Indian Territory," *Chronicles of Oklahoma* 53 (Winter 1975–76): 492–515.

37. See, for example, Wilbur F. Jacobs, "The Tip of an Iceberg: Pre-Columbian Indian Demography and Some Implications for Revisionism," *William and Mary Quarterly,* 3d ser. 31 (January 1974):

123–32; and Jennings, *Invasion of America,* pp. 15–31.

38. Sherburne F. Cook, "The Significance of Disease in the Extinction of the New England Indians," *Human Biology* 45 (September 1973): 485–508; Sherburne F. Cook, "Inter-racial Warfare and Population Decline Among the New England Indians," *Ethnohistory* 20 (Winter 1973): 1–24.

39. Calvin Martin, "Wildlife Diseases as a Factor in the Depopulation of the North American Indian," *Western Historical Quarterly* 7 (January 1976): 47–62. See also Mark V. Barrow, Jerry D. Niswander, and Robert Fortune, comps., *Health and Disease of American Indians North of Mexico: A Bibliography, 1800–1969* (Gainesville, Fla., 1972).

40. Wilbur F. Jacobs, *Dispossessing the American Indian: Indians and White on the Colonial Frontier* (New York, 1972), p. xii. There are some stimulating ideas on this whole subject in Alfred W. Crosby, Jr., *The Columbian Exchange: Biological and Cultural Consequences of 1492* (Westport, Conn., 1972). See also Wilbur F. Jacobs, "The Indian and the Frontier in American History: A Need for Revision," *Western Historical Quarterly* 4 (January 1973): 43–56; and Wilbur F. Jacobs, "Native American History: How It Illuminates Our Past," *American Historical Review* 80 (June 1975): 595–609.

41. Richard White, "Indian Land Use and Environmental Change: Island County, Washington. A Case Study," *Arizona and the West* 17 (Winter 1975): 327–38; see also Carl L. Johannessen, William A. Davenport, Artimus Miller, and Steven McWilliams, "The Vegetation of the Willamette Valley," *Annals of the Association of American Geographers* 61 (June 1971): 286–302.

42. Calvin Martin, "The European Impact on the Culture of a Northeastern Algonquian Tribe: An Ecological Interpretation," *William and Mary Quarterly,* 3d ser. 31 (January 1974): 3–26.

43. This work has been discussed in a number of recent articles. See Henry F. Dobyns, "Native American Publications of Cultural History," *Current Anthropology* 15 (September 1974): 304–306; Herman J. Viola, "Some Recent Writings on the American Indian," *American Archivist* 37 (January 1974): 51–54; and Washburn, "American Indian Studies," pp. 263–74. Recent examples are James Jefferson, Robert W. Delaney, and Greogy C. Thompson, *The Southern Utes: A Tribal History,* ed. Floyd A. O'Neil (Ignacio, Colo., 1972); and Allen P. Slickpoo, Sr., and Deward E. Walker, Jr., *Noon Nee-Me-Poo (We, the Nez Perces(: Culture and History of the Nez Perces,* vol. 1 (Lapwai, Idaho, 1973). Tribal histories in a more traditional white historical form have often gained a new breadth in recent years; examples are Arrell M.

Gibson, *The Chickasaws* (Norman, Okla., 1971); and C. A. Weslager, *The Delaware Indians: A History* (New Brunswick, N.J., 1972).

44. The project at Oklahoma is discussed in Julia A. Jordan, "Oklahoma's Oral History Collections: New Source for Indian History," *Chronicles of Oklahoma* 49 (Summer 1971): 150–72. Material from the South Dakota American Indian Research project is used in Joseph H. Cash and Herbert T. Hoover, eds., *To Be an Indian: An Oral History* (New York, 1971). Examples of oral history published with greater tribal involvement are Zuni People, *The Zunis: Self-Portrayals*, tr. Alvina Quam (Albuquerque, 1972); and Allen Slickpoo, Sr., Leroy L. Seth, and Deward E. Walker, Jr., *Nu Mee Poom Tit Wah Tit* (Nez Percé legends) (Lapwai, Idaho, 1972).

45. William W. Savage, Jr., "Monologues in Red and White: Contemporary Racial Attitudes in Two Southern Plains Communities," *Journal of Ethnic Studies* 2 (Fall 1974): 24–31.

46. See, for example, Elenor Burke Leacock and Nancy Oestreich Lurie, *North American Indians in Historical Perspective* (New York, 1971): Nancy Oestreich Lurie, "The World's Longest On-Going Protest Demonstration: North American Indian Drinking Patterns," *Pacific Historical Review* 40 (August 1971): 311–32; Anthony F. C. Wallace, *The Death and Rebirth of the Seneca* (New York, 1970); Joseph G. Jorgensen, *The Sun Dance Religion: Power for the Powerless* (Chicago, 1972); Harold Hickerson, "Fur Trade Colonialism and the North American Indians," *Journal of Ethnic Studies* 1 (Summer, 1973): 15–44.

47. Warren L. Cook, *Flood Tide of Empire: Spain and the Pacific Northwest, 1543–1819* (New Haven, 1973).

48. Wilbur Jacobs, "The Fatal Confrontation: Early Native-White Relations on the Frontiers of Australia, New Guinea, and America—A Comparative Study," *Pacific Historical Review* 40 (August 1971): 283–309. The issue in which this article appeared was devoted to the Native Americans, and it has been reprinted as *The American Indian,* ed. Norris Hundley, Jr., fwd. Vine Deloria, Jr. (Santa Barbara, Calif., 1974).

6. WESTERN FICTION AND HISTORY: A RECONSIDERATION*

Richard W. Etulain

Serious study of western American literature is of recent origin. Not until the 1960s did scholars organize a group devoted to the examination of the literature of the American West. Such well-known authorities as Franklin Walker, Bernard DeVoto, and Henry Nash Smith had published significant works on western writing, but few scholars followed the trails they blazed.

But in the 1960s and 1970s a new interest in western literature has arisen. The Western Literature Association was organized in 1965 and began sponsoring the journal *Western American Literature*. Five years later the Southwestern Literature Association was organized and launched its journal, *Southwestern American Literature*. Meanwhile, a national group, the Popular Culture Association, commenced in 1967 and founded the *Journal of Popular Culture*. These three associations and their magazines have provided a powerful impetus for students and scholars interested in doing research on western authors and their works. Although scholarly study of western literature still lags behind serious historical research on the West, literary studies have increased appreciably in number—and in merit—since the 1960s. For the first time one can speak of western American literature as

*I am indebted to the Idaho State Research Committee and the American Philosophical Society for grants that made possible the research for this chapter.

a subject that is attracting a large number of competent scholars.[1]

Some of these interpreters have begun to discuss such large questions as, What is the nature of the literary West? Is there a single outlook that unifies western literature, or are there several dominant themes? The first answers to these and other significant questions indicate no unanimity of approach or findings. In fact, the plethora of research methods and the variety of opinions about western literature demonstrate that scholars have not come to similar conclusions about the subject. Nonetheless, without over-emphasizing agreement, one can distinguish a few points of view that dominate research about western writing.

The oldest thesis has its roots in early American history and reflects a conflict that arose between seaboard and backcountry areas of the first colonies. Frontiersmen were convinced that their eastern brethren dismissed them as illiterate barbarians innocent of any cultural attainments. Whether that conviction was accurate is still being debated, but many westerners considered it to be correct.

The idea of the frontier or the West as a colonial culture has continued into the present era. During the first thirty years of this century the southwestern novelist Eugene Manlove Rhodes argued heatedly against considering the West as culturally inferior. Near the end of Rhodes's life the western historian-novelist-essayist and general disturber of the peace Bernard DeVoto took up the battle for the West, sometimes from Harvard Yard and sometimes from the editorial offices of *Saturday Review* and *Harper's*. DeVoto spoke of the West as a "plundered province" and implied in several of his works that the East too often dominated the culture of the West and tended to emasculate the freshness and uniqueness of its literature. Robert Edson Lee argued the same point in his stimulating book *From West to East: Studies in the Literature of the American West* (1966). Others have championed this view—for example, Vardis Fisher, the best of Idaho's authors, and several leading interpreters of western American literature.[2]

A second approach to western literature follows closely the ideas and research methods in Henry Nash Smith's pathbreaking book *Virgin Land: The American West as Symbol and Myth*

(1950). Smith emphasized the importance of understanding the myths about the West that many Americans came to believe in the nineteenth century. He argued that students must scrutinize these patterns of thought as they clustered around three themes: "A Passage to India," "The Sons of Leatherstocking," and "The Garden of the World." In the years since its publication *Virgin Land* has had more impact than any other study upon students of the literary West, especially those who received their training in departments of American studies or popular culture. Scholars have been particularly drawn to his discussions of Cooper's fiction, the heroes and heroines of the dime novel, and imaginative writings about western agriculture.[3]

A third thesis has become increasingly popular since 1960. Proponents of this view contend that the literature of the American West is primarily a land-oriented and nonrational literature, that it is akin to the philosophies of many Native Americans, that it is Jungian rather than Freudian, and that its books are (to use the terminology of critic Richard Chase) more often mythic *romances* than realistic *novels*. If one centers his attention on the work of such western writers as Frank Waters, Walter Van Tilburg Clark, and John Steinbeck and the western poet Gary Snyder, he finds a good deal to support this point of view. If one reads much recent commentary on western American literature, he will realize how pervasive this thesis is. Among others, the editors of the two most important scholarly journals dealing with the American literary West, *South Dakota Review* and *Western American Literature,* are advocates for this view.[4]

A fourth group of interpreters stresses the importance of viewing the West as an arid and spacious environment. Wallace Stegner, for example, argues that in the interior West aridity and openness are the major forces shaping writers and their work. As he points out, the westerner has difficulty finding himself "in any formed or coherent society. . . . His confrontations are therefore likely to be with landscape, which seems to define the West and its meaning better than any of its forming cultures, or with himself in the context of that landscape."[5] Several other scholars have noted that on occasion western writers have been so enthralled with their awesome environment that they have fallen into overly romantic descriptions of setting or have limited their plots to conflicts between men and nature.[6]

These four theses are important for a broad understanding of western literature. They augment our comprehension of a new and intriguing subject. But I should like to point to another significant emphasis in western fiction, one that has not received sufficient attention. This is the noticeable tendency among many western novelists to search for a useful or usable past. In common parlance, western writers have a hangup on history. At the center of their work is a concern for understanding the western past and for communicating the connections or continuities between past and present. It would be incorrect to argue that this is *the* most important theme of western literature; it is equally mistaken to omit its importance in a discussion of the major themes of western writing. To judge from the attention paid to history by several western novelists, historians should reexamine their assumptions about the relation of western fiction and history.[7]

In this chapter I shall discuss three ways in which western writers have used history. Vardis Fisher illustrates those who have thoroughly researched their historical subjects in order to write stirring narratives. A. B. Guthrie, Jr., who is also interested in the use of history in fiction, moves beyond Fisher in his desire to interpret as well as narrate his historical materials. Finally, Wallace Stegner takes the giant step. I treat his *Angle of Repose* at length because he has produced a western novel that is more than *about* history; he has written a first-rate fictional interpretation *of* the historical development of the West. I am convinced that an examination of the significant relationship between western history and the western novel will open new vistas of research for historians and literary scholars.[8]

Some students of the life and works of Vardis Fisher are convinced that he was born with a cocklebur in his diaper. They describe his life as one spent either trying to rid himself of the irritant or attempting to understand why he was not chosen one of the elect. It is true that few western writers have been as emotionally involved as he in searching out his own past and that of other persons. From his first novels, published in the late 1920s and early 1930s, until his last novel, *Mountain Man* (1965), Fisher was on a lifelong quest to narrate man's movement through history. During his productive career Fisher dedicated himself to the fruitful union of history and literature in an attempt to recount the past.[9]

For Fisher, first of all, the story was a personal one. His first seven novels (including the Vridar Hunter tetralogy), published between 1928 and 1937, were regional novels dealing with frontier life in the Antelope Hills area of Idaho. They were autobiographical works that dealt with fisher's tortured feelings about his early life in the region. The son of pioneer Mormon parents, Fisher battled throughout his early years with his ambiguous responses to his backgrounds. He was not sympathetic to the teachings of the Mormons, and he thought them often bigoted and self-righteous. Yet he praised the leadership of Brigham Young and the loyalty and perseverance he inspired among his followers. Similar tensions are evident in Fisher's feelings about his father. He frequently pictured his father as epitomizing the worst kind of religious fundamentalism. On some occasions his father figures are unfeeling men, introverted and blindly idealistic. But Fisher also admired his father's individualism and his hard work; these were qualities that Fisher tried to emulate in his own life.

In his tension-filled, love-hate reactions to his formative years Fisher displayed his inordinate interest in reporting his past. Some have suggested that his earliest novels were primarily excursions toward self-understanding. What is apparent is that he found some satisfactory answers for comprehending his life, and thus he was able to move back to Idaho—"to come home again"—and to carve out his ranch and build a home in Hagerman Valley. Other questions, however, still vexed him: What about the nature of man? Had people changed through the centuries? What were the forces that had the largest impact on history?

To deal with these questions, Fisher set out on one of the most ambitious projects in American literary history. His ten-volume Testament of Man series (1943–1960) is a monument to Fisher's tenacity, to his unwillingness to let go of the past until it had yielded up at least partial answers to some of its mysteries. The series, which chronicled man from his prehistoric origins to the modern era, was, in one sense, a continuation of his earliest work, although now the issues raised were less personal and more universal. Anyone who has plowed through the series—or even part of it—must admire the prodigious amount of research involved in the project. Fisher the historian-novelist shines through in every volume.[10]

Most of Fisher's western historical fiction also illustrates his thirst for narrating the past. In his most controversial book, *Children of God* (1939), Fisher sought to record how by 1900 the Mormons had evolved into a powerful institution. He had little sympathy for the doctrines and religious practices of the Church, but he exhibited a great deal of interest in the humanity of several of the early Mormon leaders. His own unsatisfying experience with the Latter-day Saints colored his interpretations, but it is noteworthy that, while devout Mormons at first harshly criticized the novel, some have recently recommended it with reservations.

Fisher's search for the historical West led him to the Donner party (*The Mothers,* 1943), the beaver wars of the Northwest (*Pemmican,* 1956), Lewis and Clark (*Tale of Valor,* 1958), and finally the western fur trappers (*Mountain Man,* 1965). His final novel illustrates several of the techniques that he used repeatedly in historical fiction. *Mountain Man* is based on wide research in original sources dealing with the trappers. Fisher seldom wrote about a subject that he had not researched as if he were writing a doctoral dissertation (he received a doctorate in English literature with high honors from the University of Chicago in 1925). At the same time the novel betrays the strong feelings Fisher had about contemporary issues rooted in the freedom, the spontaneity, and the perseverance that the lives of the mountain men illustrated. He also celebrated, through his hero Sam Minard, the strong feelings for nature that he shared with mountain men. In short, Fisher's final novel was a combination of his desire for historical veracity and his goal of demonstrating how the past is related to the present.

A. B. Guthrie, Jr., the Montana novelist, shares Fisher's strong interest in the historical novel. In accounting for his late arrival as a writer of historical fiction (Guthrie was forty-six when

The Big Sky was published), he says that early in life he fell in love with the West and wanted to explain in fiction the artifacts he found and the men he encountered in diaries and journals. But he kept putting off rounding up his ideas. Then in 1944, on the strength of a Nieman Fellowship to Harvard, he was able to spend a vigorous year reading, researching, and reflecting upon the era of the mountain man. Three years later *The Big Sky* illustrated Guthrie's extensive work in historical documents.[11]

Guthrie's subsequent novels seem less and less based on factual research. As one moves from *The Big Sky* to *The Way West* (1949), to *These Thousand Hills* (1955), to *Arfive* (1970), and on to *The Last Valley* (1975), the last of his five-volume fictional history of the West, one moves gradually across the frontier of fact into the region of Guthrie's remembrances of the West. Each of the first four novels deals with a crucial era in the historical development of the West: the years of the mountain men, the coming of the overlanders,, the rise of the cattle ranchers, and the beginnings of town building. The final book in the series treats several themes of the era 1920 to 1945.

In writing *The Big Sky,* Guthrie used many of the standard historical sources dealing with the 1830s and 1840s. He ransacked the works of travelers like Nathaniel J. Wyeth and Washington Irving, as well as the writings of later historians, such as Hubert Howe Bancroft and Hiram H. Chittenden. The writer he seems to have followed most was George Frederick Ruxton, an Englishman who traveled extensively throughout the frontier West. Guthrie may have borrowed much of his trapper talk and perhaps some of his characters from Ruxton's semifact, semifictional work, *Life in the Far West.*[12]

But *The Big Sky* is much more than the scissors-and-paste product of Guthrie's reading and research in western history. He shapes incidents, scenery, and characterizations to fit his thematic concerns. Guthrie once remarked, after finishing his first two novels, that his major thesis was that man kills or destroys the things he loves most. *The Big Sky* illustrates this theme in several ways. Boone Caudill, the major character in the novel, kills his best friend and destroys his marriage to an Indian girl because he mistakenly thinks they have been sleeping together. Besides specific incidents that epitomize Guthrie's thesis, the entire novel deals with the seeds of destruction the trappers bring to the mountains. They love the out-of-doors and sense a new freedom and exhilaration in their occupation. At the same time they strip the Rocky Mountains of its beaver, kill more meat than they are able to use, and exhibit wanton wastefulness in their yearly rendezvous. Boone realizes the destructiveness of his life, as well as that of his companions, when near the end of the novel he tells a friend that they have "spiled" the mountains and that he does not want to return.[13]

In *Arfive,* the penultimate novel of Guthrie's series, he deals with what historian C. Vann Woodward has called the twilight zone of man's experience—that shadowy era in which history and memory overlap. The novel describes a Montana town in the period of Guthrie's boyhood, the years around the opening of World War I. The emphasis is on a small community and its citizens' efforts to adjust their frontier backgrounds to changes thrust upon them. The two major characters have to realize that the past is gone, that new ideas and problems have arisen, and that they too must change if they are to adapt to a fluctuating environment. *Arfive* is a persuasive picture of an important era in our past—when the West ceased to be a frontier and gradually began to take on the appearance of a settled region.[14]

The Last Valley, which Guthrie claims is the last of his fictive treatments of the West, illustrates his absorbing interest in history, his preoccupation with the ideas of change and progress, and some of the similarities in method of historians and novelists. Guthrie uses the central figures of *Arfive*—Benton Collingswood and Mort Ewing—in *The Last Valley.* They are employed as Dick Summers, the mountain man and overland guide, was in *The Big Sky* and *The Way West;* they function as bridges from the past to the present and as commentators on the dangers and benefits of change and progress. And they serve another important purpose. Novelists and historians face analogous tasks of selection and omission when they try to produce a book that portrays a twenty-five-year period without drowning the reader in a deluge of facts.[15] Guthrie attempts to solve this problem by selecting specific events in the 1920s, 1930s, and 1940s and allowing his major characters to react to these occurrences. Their diverse reactions—which Guthrie deals with repeatedly—are similar to what historians call historiography, that is, varying interpretations of a single happening. The technique of probing several reactions to one event or idea allows historians and novelists to broaden the perspectives of their works and to demonstrate the complexity of the past.

Guthrie's most recent novel is also a first-rate treatment of the fluidity of time, of the shadowy boundaries between past, present, and future. Collingswood, Ewing, and Ben Tate, a journalist and Collingswood's son-in-law, are reflective persons, and on several occasions, as they ponder their present circumstances, remembrances of past experiences flood in and condition their thoughts and actions. By uniting past and present—sometimes jamming them together—Guthrie shows how much human history is a flow, an ongoing current rather than a series of separate, isolated eras. The painting on the dust jacket of *The Last Valley* further illustrates Guthrie's method and message. In the background verdant mountains loom above the rest of the setting, but a town, with its streets, buildings, and smoking chimneys, occupies the center of the painting. In the immediate foreground a single horseman rides away from the town. He is not in headlong flight, but he is leaving. The mountains, the town, and the horseman are not distinctly separated; they are merged. Like the novel, the painting hints at some of the tensions between nature and civilization, between past and present. Alongside the evidences of tension and conflict are emphases on juxtaposition and continuity. In fact, the major themes portrayed in the painting and treated in *The Last Valley* are the key ideas dealt with in all of Guthrie's western historical novels. In a speech he summed up his ambiguous response to the inevitable movement of history and to change: "I accept the fact that progress leaves us no retreat. We can only insist *no undue haste*. We can only try to guide it. We can't stay it. Neither should we."[16]

The interest in history, so evident in the work of Fisher and Guthrie, is even more prominent in the recent work of Wallace Stegner, whom many commentators have come to consider our best contemporary western writer. Norman Cousins, in a review in *Saturday Review/World* of Stegner's superb biography of Bernard DeVoto, has even higher praise for Stegner, calling him the leading man of American letters. Throughout his distinguished career as historian, biographer, and novelist, Stegner has been profoundly interested in western history. Nowhere is this concern better demonstrated than in his novel *Angle of Repose* (1971), which won the Pulitzer Prize for fiction in 1972.[17]

On one level the novel is the story of an eastern woman, Susan Burling, who marries another easterner, Oliver Ward, goes west, and tries to acclimate herself to western ways. On another level the book is about Susan's grandson, Lyman Ward, a retired history professor, who is an amputee and alienated from his world of 1970. By shifting back and forth between the late nineteenth century and events and ideas of the 1960s, Stegner deals with a full century of western history. It is a huge task and one that Stegner accomplishes through two major themes of western history: (1) What is the relationship between East and West? Should the emphases be placed on continuities or on differences? and (2) What comparisons and contrasts can be made between the frontier West and the New West of the 1960s? Because it deals with the major questions involved in a discussion of the nature of western history, Stegner's work is a paradigm for the western novel as history.[18]

The first theme of eastern influence upon the West is developed primarily through the character of Susan Burling Ward. She lives most of her life in the West as she follows her husband to the mining camps of California and Colorado, to the new community of Boise, and finally to Grass Valley, California. Unlike her husband, she never becomes a westerner. Throughout her life she holds on to her eastern, genteel symbols. Her clothing, her maid, and governess (probably the one household in Boise in the 1880s to have both), her eastern literary friends, and her allusions to the East and the classics—all these illustrate her connections with the East.

Through adroit use of symbolic action Stegner represents how much Susan is a stranger to western ways. On one occasion, while standing on an elevated porch and speaking to a Mexican worker, she drops her handkerchief. The laborer quickly retrieves it and hands it up to her. She reaches down for the handkerchief but quickly withdraws her hand when she realizes what she is doing. She cannot—in fact will not—take the handkerchief from his hand; finally she calls her maid to get it back. Another night, while she and Oliver are returning to Leadville—Colorado's rip-roaring mining town—they are forced to bed down in a flophouse. Oliver hesitates, for he realizes that his wife is horrified by the prospect of sleeping in a curtained-off section of a room no more than snoring and belching distance from rough miners and dirty vagabonds. Susan is queasy about the situation, and she lies awake most of the night—first in fear and then, true to her character, in dreaming about how she will picture this "rough" West for eastern magazines. Obviously much of the truth will be brushed away and large doses of romanticism applied before the "dreamed up" West will be publishable in *Century* and *Scribner's*.

A third scene—from which Stegner wrings multiple meanings—is the most revealing incident about Susan's attachment to a nonwestern perspective. Before this scene Oliver and Susan have argued about the suitability of an eastern man who has come west. Susan, overcome by her respect for his reading and his obvious exposure to eastern culture, declares him a cultivated gentleman. She is amazed and upset when Oliver says that the man is worthless in the West—in fact a hazard because he knows so little about mining and engineering. Susan does not see that his lack of experience in these professions should be held against him. One night soon after this discussion Susan and Oliver sit down to dinner, and she mentally criticizes Oliver for not washing before eating—there appears to be smudge on his thumb. Later a third person tells of the day's happenings (the account does not come from Oliver, for, as Susan says, he does not like talkee, talkee). Oliver, the eastern engineer, and others were in the mines when someone shouted a warning. The easterner froze in his tracks, and had it not been for Oliver's quick thinking and fast reactions the gentleman might have lost his life. The smudge on Oliver's thumb is an ugly bruise suffered by aiding a man whom he does not respect. At the end of the scene the reader realizes—and so does Susan—how much her perspective prevents her from understanding the West and what it demands from its residents.

Susan's life in Boise—her longest stay in one place in the West before the family moves to Grass Valley—epitomizes the tensions that eat at her even after she has lived in the West for more than a decade. Stegner catches her dilemmas in one ironic sentence of description: "There sat Susan Burling Ward, tired-eyed after a day's drawing, dragged-out after a day's heat, and tightening her drowning-woman's grip on culture, literature, civilization, by trying to read *War and Peace*" (p. 421). Like the local colorist she is, Susan loves the scenery, the wild and picturesque part of the Boise Valley; but once she faces the problems of living "in" the Boise area, she finds its remoteness and crassness repugnant and is stifled by the boosterism of its residents. Life in Boise seems acceptable only when she withdraws from it—when she and Oliver move up a river canyon and when she tries to establish a western miniature of Brook Farm.

Yet she becomes attached to the West, despite her reluctance to do so. Near the end of the Wards' stay in Boise, disappointments, failures, and tragedies seem to engulf them. Oliver's irrigation schemes will not hold water, their youngest child drowns (ironically, in an irrigation ditch), Oliver takes to the bottle, and a young engineering friend complicates Susan's problems by declaring his love for her. Susan almost gives up on the West; she leaves Oliver, ships her oldest son to an eastern boarding school, and thinks of remaining in the East. But she cannot remain in the East; something draws her west again—back to Oliver, back to disappointments, back to the dreadful West. She realizes, in spite of herself, that she has become attached to things in the West—even if she is not yet a westerner.

It would be a mistake to picture Oliver as the archetypal westerner—as the exact opposite of Susan. But he does take on characteristics ascribed to many westerners. His dreams are expansive—and expensive—but he is a diligent worker. Because he realizes the need for help in achieving his dreams, he is less class-conscious than Susan and evaluates a person more by his abilities than by his cultural achievements. Though he is overly protective of his wife, he does not allow an excessive gentility to blind him to the realities of a region that demands a ruggedness unknown to Susan's eastern friends.

He is not a local colorist caught up in the picturesque, picnic West. For him the region is a place where his dreams can be put to work; it is a place to be conquered. He finds Susan's classical allusions to miners and their arduous work "about used up" (p. 139), and he bluntly tells her that the cultured gentleman who claims to be an engineer is worthless in the West. At times Susan realizes that Oliver is different: "It was his physical readiness, his unflustered way of doing what was needed in a crisis, that she most respected in him; it made him different from the men she had known" (p. 234).

Oliver's dreams are pregnant with promise, although most of them eventually miscarry. He invents devices to save time and money. He discovers the necessary ingredients to make cement. He lays out a usable scheme to irrigate an entire western valley. But he cannot bring his dreams to fruition, and a major reason for his lack of success is a problem that plagued many western dreamers: he is dependent upon eastern capital, and too often sources of eastern capital are as untrustworthy as Lady Fortuna. All of Oliver's dreams prove workable—but only after he has left the scene. Like many westerners, his schemes and partial successes are destroyed by his inability to control sources of financing.

Stegner, sometimes through his narrator and sometimes as omniscient author, also comments on the relationship between East and West. Early in the novel Lyman Ward says: "I am impressed with how much of my grandparents' life depended on continuities, contacts, connections, friendships, and blood relationships. Contrary to the myth, the West was not made entirely by pioneers who had thrown everything away but an ax and a gun" (p. 41). On other occasions Stegner contrasts Susan's romantic perceptions with what the West was really like.[19] By depicting these two kinds of Wests, Stegner makes clear how much eastern visions defined what the West was to Americans. Most of these foreign interpreters overstressed the uniqueness of western life and underplayed the continuities between East and West. The point Stegner argues is the central thesis of Henry Nash Smith's brilliant book *Virgin Land* and among the major contentions in the writings of the western historian Earl Pomeroy.[20]

The second theme in Stegner's novel is his depiction of the West as it moves from frontier to settled community and finally on to the Bay Area counterculture of the 1960s. By keeping two eras of western life before the reader and by commenting on the transitions between the two periods, Stegner continually narrates and interprets the historical development of the West. Susan's life, as it moves from raw Leadville to semisettled Boise and finally to the security of Grass Valley, illustrates the flow of western history that Stegner is narrating. Throughout the novel the life and mores of the Wards are placed alongside the Berkeley fever of Lyman's young neighbor, Shelley Rasmussen, and his son, Rodman. And Lyman is the link. As he says, "I really would like to talk to somebody about my grandparents, their past, their part in the West's becoming, their struggle toward ambiguous ends." He likes the idea of seeing how "a fourth-generation Trevithick should help me organize the lives of the first-generation Wards" (p. 50). What Lyman notes is the irony of Shelley, who is a descendant of a Cornish miner, helping him interpret the meaning of the lives of a family who "ruled" her ancestors. And more to the point: It is a Trevithick (Shelley's mother) who, more than any of his kin, keeps Lyman moving physically. Stegner implies that the social and cultural history of the West has leveled some mountains, elevated some valleys, and bridged several chasms.

Stegner also suggests that if contemporary westerners paid more attention to their past they could learn from their history. Shelley is excited about the commune that her husband is planning, and she is disappointed that Lyman does not share her enthusiasm. Her problem, Lyman says, is that she could learn from Susan's experiences in trying to set up a psuedo Brook Farm in the Boise Canyon and from other historical precedents. What Lyman preaches (and one hears Stegner in the background at this point) is that if one knows the past one can better manage the present and plot the future.

It is from Lyman Ward, who acts as narrator, as commentator, as synthesizer, that one receives the most explicit comments about history, especially on the frontier becoming the New West. From the opening pages of the novel Stegner establishes a fluidity of time for his narrator. This fluidity is important, for Lyman switches from present to past and to present again as he searches for an understanding of his life. As he tries to seize hold of his present circumstances, he perceives the paradoxical truth that as soon as he defines the present it has become the past. And he realizes, too, that his life is cumulative: he is *in* and *of* the past just as he is tied to a complicated present. Both periods impinge upon him; he can escape neither. In his attempt to comprehend fully the relationship between the Old and the New Wests, Lyman utilizes two geological terms. The first is ''angle of repose,'' the incline at which rocks cease to roll. He wishes to study his grandparents to discover how they achieved an angle of repose in their lives. The second term, the Doppler Effect, defines the way in which he wishes to undertake his study. It is not enough, he thinks, to stand in 1970, look back to the late nineteenth century, and write about his ancestors. Instead, he must place himself alongside his grandparents and, in a sense, live their lives with them. Like the good historian, he wishes to be past-minded, to climb into their shoes, and to relive their lives with understanding and objectivity.

But several pressures keep Lyman from producing the kind of history he wishes to write. In the first place, so few of his contemporaries think his subject or his method is correct. Lyman wants his son and the Berkeley generation to understand how much they are tied to the past. The problem is, he says, that they are ''without a sense of history. . . . [To them] it is only an aborted social science.'' His son, Rodman, sums up the view that his father fears: ''The past isn't going to teach us anything about what we've got ahead of us. Maybe it did once, or seemed to. It doesn't any more.'' But Lyman wants to study the past. It is, he argues, ''the only direction we can learn from.'' He continues: ''I believe in Time, as they did, and in the life chronological rather than in the life existential. We live in time and through it, we build out huts in its rivers, or used to, and we cannot afford all these abandonings'' (pp. 15–16, 17, 18). The Berkeley generation has not yet learned this lesson; the youth of the 1960s, he says, are ''by Paul Goodman out of Margaret Mead.''[21]

Nor does Lyman want a distorted meaning of the past once it is scrutinized. Too many readers are like Rodman, who wants the drama and the color of something like the life of Lola Montez. But to Lyman this kind of writing is worthless: ''Every fourth-rate antiquarian in the West has panned Lola's poor little gravel. My grandparents are in a deep vein that has never been dug. They were *people*'' (p. 22).

Most of the time Lyman the historian practices what he preaches. He establishes what the region was like when Susan went west. The reader sees her trip in the context of early trans-continental rail travel and within the tense atmosphere that Americans experienced a few weeks after Custer's defeat in the summer of 1876. Here Lyman utilizes the Doppler Effect when he draws close to his subject, near enough for the reader to discern the sounds of her inner struggles. In addition, he wants to make sure that his readers see the continuities in the time periods he describes. When he summarizes the authoritarianism of mine owners and the ill-treatment of miners in the 1870s, he reminds his listeners that much will change in the next century. The West-ern Federation of Miners, the Industrial Workers of the World, and the United Mine Workers are yet to come. One cannot hurry history; one must study it and write about it as it was, not as he wishes it had been. Nor must he remold it entirely by the outlook of his contemporaries. Lyman implies that presentist historians make these mistakes and thus distort history.

Lyman also realizes that the historian (or even an entire soci-ety) can easily fall in love with the past and use it as a refuge from an oppressive present. In fact, in spite of his vows not to fall victim to an alluring past, Lyman does so. On one occasion when the counterculture seems to be knocking at his door, he muses: ''I am not going to get sucked into this. I'll call the cops in a minute if I have to. And this is all, absolutely all, I am going to think about it. I am going back to Grandmother's nineteenth century, where the problems and the people are less messy'' (p. 170). Or, in another situation, he catches an epiphany-like glimpse of himself: "This is not a story of frontier hardships, though my grandparents went through a few; nor of pioneer hardihood, though they both had it. It is only Lyman Ward, Coe Professor of History, Emeritus, living a day in his grandparents' life to avoid paying too much attention to his own" (p. 409).

It would be a mistake to consider Lyman merely the mouthpiece of Wallace Stegner. Students of literature avoid the error of always identifying the ideas of a character with those of its author, but historians need additional warning about the pitfalls of such comparisons. Yet much of what Lyman talks about, Stegner has spoken for on other occasions. Stegner shares some of Lyman's distaste for the student radicalism of the 1960s. Stegner remarked in 1972 that the student movement "started at Berkeley and we inherited it at Stanford. The kids didn't come to learn, they came angry and with answers—not questions." He added, "I don't know why when you get mad at Mr. Smith, you break Mr. Jones's windows."

Much of this misplaced anger, Stegner argued, would have been avoided if we were better students of our past:

In times of crisis people turn to history. Certainly, as some of the protesters . . . argue, we may be prisoners of the past, but we also are imprisoned in the human species. We have to keep our ties with the past to learn and grow. Cut loose from the past and we become nothing. It doesn't make any difference if there are flaws in the marble or not; that's the marble history must be carved from.[22]

In an interview with John R. Milton, Stegner was even more explicit about some of the ideas contained in his novel: "This is what I would really like to see some western writer manage to do, to put together his past and his present." This statement led to *Angle of Repose,* which Stegner described as

a novel which involves some pretty refined *eastern* characters who are going to have some of the refinement ground out of them. . . . It's a Willa Catherish kind of theme. She keeps pointing out that the frontier breaks the really refined. . . . The frontier was a brutalizing experience, but it also could be, for people who weren't actually broken by it, an experience which changed them in other ways. It could be a coarsening experience but also a strengthening one. So I've got some genteel-tradition folks who are going to have to develop a few callouses.[23]

Not only does Stegner ask the most important questions about the making of the modern West; he seems to give the best answers. A full discussion of his answers would be the subject of another chapter, but allow me to summarize briefly what I think he says about the nature of western experiences. Scratch a westerner deeply enough, and one will find an easterner who has carried along much of his cultural baggage and has had to readjust his thinking and living to fit a new environment. In other words, the westerner is not something entirely new; he is a product of his past as well as his present.

Second, if one wishes to understand the modern West, he ought, Stegner hints, to study and comprehend the meaning of such nineteenth-century activities as the gold rush, labor disputes in the mines, and political malcontents like the Populists. In short, what Lyman seems to learn is that the American West is the product of two angles of repose: it is East *and* West; and it is the frontier *and* the Berkeley generation. The answers that Stegner provides are the products of a probing mind trying to decipher the nature of the American West. He shows that the open marriage of history and literature will lead us to the best fictional treatments of the West. And thus, if I were asked to name the most significant western novel of the last decade, I would nominate *Angle of Repose*. I know of no other novel of the last ten years that says as many meaningful things about the American West as Stegner's book. It is a model for subsequent novels written about the West.

At this point one must ask, If such novelists as Fisher, Guthrie, and especially Stegner have made notable use of history in their western novels, why is it that this tendency has not received much notice? I am convinced that the answer to this worthwhile question is rooted in the current trends of scholarship in history and literature and in the inclinations of western historians.

In the past few years historians have been urged to employ more of the research techniques of the social sciences. They are told that the use of statistics, demography, and social psychology, for example, will enhance the specificity of their studies. Many students of history have heeded this urging, and historical monographs and essays in historical journals evidence an increasing use of social-science methods. This trend has not been detrimental to historians, for these new techniques have broadened their perspectives. At the same time there is a decreasing interest among historians in utilizing literature in their studies; the scrutiny of novels, poems, and plays as a source for historical knowledge seems less and less acceptable to a generation of historians taught to search for exactness in history.

In the field of American literary studies current research continues to move in the direction of myth criticism and the study of linguistics and popular culture. Here too contemporary emphases have widened our viewpoints and added to our understanding of American literature. On the other hand, few critics emphasize literary history or the historical consciousness of novelists. Thus neither historians nor literary critics have recently shown much interest in trying to focus on subjects that cross the disciplines of history and literature.[24]

There are other reasons why the relationship between western history and western literature has not been studied. By and large, western historians have paid scant attention to the literature of the West. The major western-history textbooks contain no extensive discussions of western writing, and there is no published history of western American literature. Western historians, unlike historians of the South, seem unaware either of the historical value of their literature or the historical consciousness evident in the region's fiction.[25] Part of this oversight is due, no doubt, to the widespread but mistaken notion among historians that any novel written about the West is "just another western." It is true that some western writers have chosen to follow the patterned westerns of Zane Grey and his descendants, but to pigeonhole most western authors as writers of westerns—as some historians have done—is to make no distinctions between Zane Grey and A. B. Guthrie, Luke Short and Wallace Stegner, or Frederick Faust (Max Brand) and Vardis Fisher. As we have seen, Guthrie, Fisher, and Stegner have not written Zane Grey westerns.[26]

Other commentators are equally contemptuous of western historical fiction. As one writer has pointed out, the historical novel is treated as if it were " 'a kind of mule-like animal begotten by the ass of fiction on the brood-mare of fact, and hence a sterile monster.' "[27] Here again there is some basis for this negative attitude. For example, James Michener's bestselling novel *Centennial* (1974) illustrates some of the pitfalls of too much popularization in western historical fiction. Michener gives some sense of the vertical (old to new) and horizontal (East and South to West) history of the West, he deals with some ethnic patterns that helped form the mosaic of western society, and he knows how to write appealing narrative history. But the weaknesses of his popular approach limit the historical value of his widely read novel. He conveniently kills off too many of his characters, and he invokes too many chance circumstances to keep his thousand-page novel on the move. He sensationalizes too much of his material. He places too much emphasis on faddish topics: Indians, cowboys, and mountain men. And, on the other hand, he does little with populism, radical farmer groups, or local, state, and federal governmental squabbles, and he generally scants the twentieth century. Michener has "used" (perhaps "abused") western history; he majors on lively and flashy narrative and minors on useful interpretation of the historical materials he utilizes. But to point to Michener or to writers of westerns as the only source of western historical fiction is to distort the evidence, and some historians have been guilty of this distortion.

Now, allow me to snub down my maverick points. The works of several important novelists, as we have seen, evidence a strong interest in history. But current trends in historical and literary scholarship and contemporary predilections among many western historians have kept students from noting this historical consciousness in western fiction. One hopes that western novelists continue to mine the rich lode of western history as well as they have in the past. If they do, literary critics and historians will soon realize that many authors make use of regional history in their western fiction and that this theme merits more attention.

Notes

1. Recent trends in the study of western American literature are summarized in Richard W. Etulain, "The American Literary West and Its Interpreters: The Rise of a New Historiography," *Pacific Historical Review* 45 (August, 1976).

2. For two sources that discuss this point of view, see W. H. Hutchinson, *A Bar Cross Man: The Life and Personal Writings of Eugene Manlove Rhodes* (Norman, 1956); and Wallace Stegner, *The Uneasy Chair: A Biography of Bernard DeVoto* (Garden City, N.Y., 1974). The best treatments of the American West as a colonial culture are Gene Gressley, "Colonialism: A Western Complaint," *Pacific Northwest Quarterly* 54 (January, 1963): 1–8; and the more comprehensive Gerald D. Nash, *The American West in the Twentieth Century: A Short History of an Urban Oasis* (Englewood Cliffs, N.J., 1973).

3. Books and articles that depend heavily on the insights and methods of Smith are discussed in Etulain, "The American Literary West and Its Interpreters."

4. John R. Milton, editor of *South Dakota Review,* expresses this view in "The Western Novel: Sources and Forms," *Chicago Review* 16 (Summer, 1963): 74–100; and in *Interpretive Approaches to Western American Literature* (Pocatello, Idaho, 1972), pp. 7–21. See also Max Westbrook, *Walter Van Tilburg Clark* (New York, 1969). The latest substantiation of the same view is by Thomas Lyon (editor of *Western American Literature*) in *Frank Waters* (New York, 1973).

5. Wallace Stegner, *The Sound of Mountain Water* (Garden City, N.Y., 1969), p. 11.

6. John R. Milton, "The American West: A Challenge to the Literary Imagination," *Western American Literature* 1 (Winter 1967): 267–84; Wilson O. Clough, "Regionalism," in *Rocky Mountain Reader,* ed. Ray B. West, Jr. (New York, 1946), pp. 414–17. Clough enlarges his discussion of this subject in *The Necessary Earth: Nature and Solitude in American Literature* (Austin, 1964).

7. A few authors have dealt briefly with the relationships between western history and literature. For example, see the scattered comments in James K. Folsom, *The American Western Novel* (New Haven, 1966); and in Helen Hitt, "History in Pacific Northwest Novels Written Since 1920," *Oregon Historical Quarterly* 51 (September 1950): 180–206. The best article on the subject is Don Walker, "Can the Western Tell What Happens?" in *Interpretive Approaches to Western American Literature,* pp. 33–47.

8. Although I discuss only three western novelists here, many others

could have been cited for their interest in and use of history in their fiction. For example, in the Middle West, Willa Cather, Ole Rölvaag, and Frederick Manfred; in the Southwest, Conrad Richter, Paul Horgan, and Larry McMurtry; in the Far West, Jack London, John Steinbeck, and H. L. Davis.

9. For Fisher's use of history I am drawing upon Wayne Chatterton, *Vardis Fisher: The Frontier and Regional Works* (Boise, 1972); and Ronald Taber, "Vardis Fisher: New Directions for the Historical Novel," *Western American Literature* 1 (Winter, 1967): 285-96.

10. Fisher's role as historian-novelist is treated in detail in Joseph M. Flora, *Vardis Fisher* (New York, 1965); and Goerge F. Day, "The Uses of History in the Novels of Vardis Fisher" (Ph.D. diss., University of Colorado, 1968).

11. Guthrie discusses his interests in history in his autobiography, *The Blue Hen's Chick* (New York, 1965); and in "The Historical Novel: Tramp or Teacher," *Montana: The Magazine of Western History* 4 (Autumn, 1954): 1-8.

12. Richard H. Cracroft, "*The Big Sky:* A. B. Guthrie's Use of Historical Sources," *Western American Literature* 6 (Fall, 1971): 163-76. A companion article is David C. Stineback, "On History and Its Consequences: A. B. Guthrie's *These Thousand Hills,*" *Western American Literature:* 6 (Fall, 1971): 177-89.

13. These comments on *The Big Sky* are taken from my tape, "The Mountain Man in Literature," Western American Writers Series (Deland, Florida, 1974).

14. See Richard W. Etulain, "The New Western Novel," *Idaho Yesterdays* 15 (Winter, 1972): 12-17, for more on *Arfive*.

15. I am drawing here on the useful comments of Russel Nye, "History and Literature: Branches of the Same Tree," *Essays on History and Literature,* ed. Robert H. Bremner (Columbus, 1966), pp. 123-59.

16. "Author Guthrie—'Going Toward the Sunset,'" *Exponent* [Montana State University], April 2, 1971. Guthrie added to these ideas in his luncheon address at the Montana Historical Conference at Helena in October, 1975.

17. Wallace Stegner, *Angle of Repose* (New York, 1971). Some of the ideas in the previous paragraphs and in the section on Wallace Stegner appeared in different form in my "New Western Novel" and "Frontier and Region in Western Literature," *Southwestern American Literature* 1 (September, 1971): 121-28.

18. I have not dealt here with several other significant themes in *Angle of Repose.* For example, no one yet has studied carefully Stegner's use of the letters and autobiography of Mary Hallock Foote,

the western local-color writer who was the model for Susan Burling Ward. Foote's autobiography has been superbly edited by Rodman W. Paul, *A Victorian Gentlewoman in the Far West: The Reminiscences of Mary Hallock Foote* (San Marino, 1972).

19. Stegner makes these comparisons throughout his novel, but especially notable are those that deal with setting; see pp. 81–82, 84–85, 97–103, 134–35, and 218–36. Near the end Susan is less tied to her perspectives; she begins to see the West in less romantic terms.

20. Earl Pomeroy discusses the ideas of innovation and continuity in western history in his pathbreaking article "Towards a Reorientation of Western History: Continuity and Environment," *Mississippi Valley Historical Review* 41 (March, 1955): 579–600. The same discussions are at the center of his *The Pacific Slope: A History of California, Oregon, Washington, Idaho, Utah, and Nevada* (New York, 1965).

21. Stegner has said: "I am forced to believe in Time. I believe we are Time's prisoners, I believe Time is our safety and strength. I think we build our little huts against it as the latter-day Illyrians built their huts within and against the great palace of Diocletian at Split." *The Sound of Mountain Water,* p. 12.

22. Quoted in *Salt Lake Tribune,* June 11, 1972.

23. John R. Milton, "Conversation with Wallace Stegner," *South Dakota Review* 9 (Spring, 1971): 53, 54.

24. There are, of course, some exceptions. Notable among these are Harry B. Henderson III, *Versions of the Past: The Historical Imagination in American Fiction* (New York, 1974); Nelson Manfred Blake, *Novelists' America: Fiction as History, 1910–1940* (Syracuse, 1969); and David Levin, *In Defense of Historical Literature* (New York, 1967). The outstanding example of a scholar who continues to work the rich relationship of history and literature is Russel Nye; see his extremely useful *The Unembarrassed Muse: The Popular Arts in America* (New York, 1970).

25. A model for western historians is F. Garvin Davenport, Jr., *The Myth of Southern History: Historical Consciousness in Twentieth-Century Southern Literature* (Nashville, 1970). Robert V. Hine's *The American West: An Interpretive History* (Boston, 1973), is notable for its extensive use of literature as a source for history.

26. I have attempted to distinguish between the western and the western novel in "The Historical Development of the Western," *The Popular Western: Essays Toward a Definition,* eds. Richard W. Etulain and Michael T. Marsden (Bowling Green, Ohio, 1974), pp. 74–84.

27. In David e. Whisnant, *James Boyd* (New York, 1972), p. 140.

7. WESTERN URBAN DEVELOPMENT: A CRITICAL ANALYSIS

Ronald L. F. Davis

The history of urban places and life in the American West lacks
an analytical framework. The problem is not in the want of literature or scholarship. A cursory look into the field indicates a
wealth of material that ranges from biographies of cow towns,
mill camps, watering places, mining towns, and major cities to
the more recent attempts by social scientists to view the western
city as part of a network of urbanization that embraces the entire
nation.[1] Much of this material is of lasting value and of important substance. Some of it, such as the work of A. Theodore
Brown on Kansas City, Robert R. Dykstra on Kansas cattle
towns, Robert M. Fogelson on Los Angeles, David G. McComb
on Houston, and Kenneth W. Wheeler on Texas cities, is indeed
significant enough to serve as a basis for the needed analytical
synthesis.[2] But that the synthesis has not yet been made is strong
indication that it will not emerge in the near future.

Although for some time there have been pleas for something
more than urban biography, few historians have attempted to
provide the historical generalizations encompassing the western
cities of the United States. The history of individual cities, to be
sure, had to be written before a synthesis was possible. But what
is lacking now is the proper framework for achieving the synthesis. This is a call not so much for the adoption of a theory of
urban development as for a conceptualization intended to offer
insight into the process of urban development over time as it
occurred in the most recently settled parts of the nation.

The nature of the problem seems to have escaped the historians of the American West. As historians we are interested in describing and explaining change over time in order to have the basis for a critical assessment of the results.[3] Few historians of the American West have attempted to extend their understanding of the frontier as a process to the analysis of western cities. Most of the work instructive for this problem has been done by social scientists. Unfortunately, their models, drawn from contemporary problem-solving situations designed to serve the status quo, have generally failed to comprehend the unique nature of past development or to provide a basis for criticism. Geographers, economists, sociologists, and political scientists equate growth and development with qualitative advances that unnecessarily bias their studies toward a defense of modernization, or at least limit their analysis to an explanation of the process involved. Such neutral objectivity limits the usefulness of their studies.[4]

For example, on the one hand we have a large and significant body of literature documenting the extent to which urban places in the American West fostered and gave impetus to the growth and development of their surrounding hinterlands. Frontier towns and cities, we are told by Richard Wade and Earl Pomeroy, preceded both subsistence and commercial farming settlement.[5] The frontier was an urban frontier with towns functioning as the spearheads of settlement and thus as the generators of development. Although significant for explaining the nature of frontier settlement, this concern with which came first, the farm or the city, is not in itself very revealing about the process of urbanization. It is important to know that California, the most frontier of western states, was also the most urban in its period of settlement, when urban is defined by the concentrations of population in towns and cities. But it tells us very little about what being "urban" meant to the inhabitants.

On the other hand recent work by historical geographers has lucidly and persuasively examined the country's urban places in the context of a network in which (1) the growth and development of each city was and is a function of the entire system of cities to which each belongs; (2) efficiencies and economies, ranging from information flow in and between cities and towns to the multiplier effects of interurban demands for the specialized products of particular urban places, contributed dynamically to the growth of both the individual city and the network; (3) locational factors were less important than the nature of the network for explaining the origin of an urban place; and (4) the peculiar nature and style of urban places reflected their role within the system.[6] Such analysis is helpful because it provides a conceptual framework for the analysis of change over time, but it is one-sided in its applicability for the historian interested in understanding how the system functioned in terms of costs and advantages to the urban population. Concentration upon the growth and development of urban places as an independent structure is conceptually limiting because it implies a qualitative judgment about what is only a quantitative phenomenon. Is the growth of population in a concentrated form, and the spread of its technology to the surrounding hinterland and rural environs, a designation of excellence? If the result of the concentration is a life-style and structural form clearly advanced, then the answer is most certainly yes. If the concentration results in a style and form dependent upon an exploitative technology, politics, and social relationships then the answer is not so clear. Specifically, the above emphasis fails to provide the basis for assessing the costs and benefits of the process. What was the effect of the so-called development upon the people living in urban places? The network model tends to equate the lack of urbanism with a lack of development in a way that suggests lack of change, lack of progress, and lack of well-being for the citizens involved. Qualitative evaluations such as these are rooted in the often unexamined assumption that development is in itself a mark of superiority—clearly a questionable premise reinforcing existing institutions and a status quo geared to increased consumption by the urban population for private gain.

It is not that the above approaches are not helpful, only that they are not adequate for either a study of change over time or a study of the history of urban places in the American West. What is needed is a conceptual framework enabling us objectively to understand the process resulting in a city, the nature of the urbanism created and generated, and its effect upon the social, cultural, and economic well-being of the people involved. Tall orders for any model for understanding, but intentions which should at least provide us with the framework for understanding the past in order to assess the present.

The essential point to understand regarding the process of a city's change over time (its growth and development) is that no structure, which a city is, can be divorced from the reality of its context. What this means is that the form and functioning of cities reflect the forces shaping the economy and society of which they are a part. For our purposes the dominant forces themselves are attributes of the dominant mode of production. This is not to say that institutions and structures may not take on a life of their own capable of enduring and affecting the society and economy long after the forces creating them have passed from the scene. But by starting with this perspective, the scholar has a basis for insight into the history of either a particular city or a network of cities; of urbanism as a factor of human existence and as the historical product of past times and cumulated effects. By relating the structure to the ways in which people made their living, we have a fundamental assumption that allows us to examine the structure and the society that produced it.[7]

Like cities in the eastern part of the United States, urban places in the western United States resulted from and were part of a process of exploitation for private gain: people, land, materials, and institutions. Cities west of the Mississippi River were no different, except that their economies and efficiencies occurred in the context of a national network of urban places. Cities of the American West were forced to grow in the shadow of other, more developed urban places. Their eventual success in the concentration of exploitative powers, instruments, and efficiencies always depended upon their ability to link up to the system. Salt Lake City, San Francisco, San Diego, Los Angeles, Houston, Dallas, St. Louis, and Omaha were, in the early stages of their growth, caught up in an urban rivalry that duplicated the once intensive urban rivalry of eastern towns and cities in their earnest attempt to link up to London and Paris in the colonial and early national periods of United States history. Like their dominant eastern overlords, western cities competed with one another to gain admittance to the establishment. Once admitted, they seldom sought equality, simple security or self-subsistance but aimed for regional and national dominance of the very system itself. Los Angeles competed not only with San Francisco but also with New York and Chicago for preeminence in the system of commerce and information flow.[8] Underlying and propelling this drive for inclusion and dominance was the search for private profit, the desire to protect the status quo once it had become institutionalized, and the nature of the internal dynamic amassed by the city structures—a dynamic that functioned and prospered insofar as it related to the essential mechanism of the modern economy of a developing capitalism. As a result, differences in urban structures and forms, institutions and values were similar differences rather than essential ones, with the rural areas caught up in the process of homogenization that flowed from the nature of an advanced industrial-capitalistic society and its concommitant corporate world.[9]

In this perspective the historical situation of any one city is not determined by the assumptions made above. At any one time in the past the situation in Los Angeles, for example, involved a complex reality of changing components. But it was always a reality reflecting the process described. The outcome was not predetermined by the formula, but once the outcome is at hand, the past will be seen to have conformed to the underlying forces determining the nature and momentum of the economy and its resulting society. For example, urban rivalry is a constant fact in the history of the United States (Boston versus New York, Chicago versus St. Louis, Los Angeles versus San Diego). Those cities that emerged dominant did so through luck, leadership, and location, to be sure, but more importantly through their efficiency in becoming the leading centers in the exploitation of both markets and sources of supply.[10] The outcome was not always the result of locational or resource advantages. San Diego had its natural harbor, whereas Los Angeles was landlocked. But because the powerful San Francisco vested interests failed to view Los Angeles as a rival, rail connections with the Southwest and the South moved to the former city by way of the latter in a deliberate bypassing of San Diego.[11] The small pueblo of Los Angeles responded with a mighty civic effort in building the harbor at San Pedro, an effort that, combined with several others, eventually eclipsed both its northern and its southern urban neighbors.[12] The process itself was complex and can be understood only in terms of the private economy in which it occurred.

In this chapter I suggest that the system of private enterprise functioning under the capitalist mode of production is the perspective needed for understanding the process of urban growth, dominance, and change over time in the American West. Under capitalism institutions and human relationships are determined by their values as defined in the marketplace. The use of products and resources is dictated by such values, thus resulting in urban places that may be unique because of the accidents of time and place but are very similar in the patterns of their development. The tendency is toward a homogeneity of style, form, and structure, because the system of which the urban places are a part demands conformity in the name of efficiency and survival. Although at any one time particular cities within the system may be more or less advanced in similarity, depending on the stage of their development—meaning the degree to which they are colonial or imperial in relationship to other cities—the result will be a similar sociopolitical matrix, as well as a similar urban form. Such factors as the state of technology, the resources available, and the state of productivity certainly determine the particular situation, but not the patterns or the trends involved in the process over time.

More in the way of analysis is possible once this perspective is applied to the history of urban places in the American West. For example, once we accept the basic exploitative nature of the system that produces cities in America, such problems as the nature of urban-rural conflict, the interdependencies of so-called second-rank cities, and the efficiencies involved in urban growth can be confronted. First, it is important to note that the application of this perspective allows for an immediate counter to the biased, uncritical tendencies of alternative approaches. Specifically, the view that emphasizes the generative effect of urban places upon the frontier is essentially correct but nevertheless broadly misleading. To recognize the urban and developmental character of the frontier may be to suggest mistakenly that agrarian antiurbanism rested upon an irrational and mindless search for scapegoats to cover up the inefficiencies of the rural economy. That towns generated growth, development, and eventually the modernization of the countryside is not a sound basis for suggesting that rural inhabitants opposed to urbanism and urban places as disorderly, sinful, and undemocratic failed to recognize the demands of modernization.[13] Progress, growth, development, a higher standard of living, and a better world for all, by implication, were opposed for seemingly nonsensical reasons.

Without ignoring the need to study the antiurbanism of American Jeffersonianism, southern traditionalism, and western populism on grounds other than economic, I would say here only that the exploitative nature of the economic system of which urbanism and individual city places were a part is a perspective that allows us to understand better the true relationship of town and country in the American past. The point to understand is that under capitalism efficiency means a more effective form of exploitation of land, labor, and capital. In this light the urban historian will never lose sight of the fact that, although a city may have been a revolutionary agent of modernization, it was always dependent upon the exploitation of the countryside for its very existence, for the utilization of the surplus by which its concentrated population might survive. As such there is a firm and rational basis for the antiurbanism of rural people: one segment of the population lives off another segment. To imply that cities, because they generated growth and development in the hinterland, were not exploitative is to deny the reality of the system itself.[14]

Too, once the basic exploitative nature of American urbanism is understood, it is possible to evaluate the so-called network of cities in a revealing light. Historical geographer Allan R. Pred correctly notes the generative effect of cities upon one another as they partake in the efficiencies of interdependent market, distributive, and informational utilization.[15] Specialization of labor allows for the generation of input demands having multiplier effects throughout the system. Production centers need service centers. First-stage producers promote and supply second-stage producers. Small centers of concentrated efficiencies and abilities service larger centers of production and processing to the extent that a highly complex network of interdependent urban places blankets the market and resource components of the national, urban economy. In evaluating the outcome of this system, all of which appears to function smoothly, we see that the exploitative nature of the relations relegates some parts of the network to lower-income forms of economic activity. Unable to alter easily their place in the mature network, entire urban places function as colonies of the more dominant urban places with far-reaching effects, many of which have little to do with income. There is substantial evidence, for instance, that the relatively high proportion of the population of western urban places employed in service industries has had wide-ranging impact upon the way of life experienced.[16] Cities historically dominated by service industries and employment may have distinct forms, institutions, and values. The extent to which they are uniquely "western" possibly reflects the extent to which western cities functioned as dumping grounds for eastern manufactured goods.[17]

Finally, it is not at all clear that the emergence of an urban place stemmed from its ability to produce and distribute efficiently the goods and services of its economy. On one level it may be enough to acknowledge that San Diego failed to achieve urban status in the nineteenth century because of the opposition of the San Francisco–based owners of the Southern Pacific Railroad (Charles Crocker, Mark Hopkins, Leland Stanford, and Henry Huntington). But that is hardly a conclusive reason, since other cost efficiencies may have favored San Francisco and Los Angeles. Both places constituted larger urban markets for the disposal of goods shipped west on the transcontinentals.[18] More revealing is the approach that questions the idea that the urban concentrations of population in the American West resulted from and contributed to production, distribution, and information efficiencies. Although economies of scale may be obtainable with the adoption of machinery, it is not at all clear that the cities of the American West (or more precisely the firms in those cities) achieved such economies. Until the research is done, it is mere conjecture to suggest that the firms were either too small or too big (as many were in the East) to achieve economies of scale. That cities existed at all in the American West may have reflected essentially the interests of the owners of the means of industrial production to concentrate and consolidate labor and resources in order to enjoy profits resulting from size. Efficiency, it must be remembered, is a relative statement describing outputs related to inputs; profits are a function of demand and control of the market (for example, size and influence). Firms producing large amounts of goods may have been inefficient but highly profitable because of the size of their production and their control of the market. Efficiency becomes a decisive factor only in a competitive situation.[19]

Even if western firms had achieved economies of scale in the production end of the system, there is no clear reason to move beyond the Company-town arrangement to achieve such economies. Market information dependent upon the close geographic proximity of firms was a declining imperative once the telegraph, the typewriter, and the telephone emerged as the absolute dictators of information flow. The location of stock-market districts and financial centers is largely a function of rent and status rather than the demands of communication in the typical city of the western United States. This fact alone is an important reason why the downtown parts of so many southwestern cities appear to be less than functional or even unnecessary.[20]

It is also less than certain that the concentration of population in an urban place, from the perspective of a concentrated market, is an essential feature of industrialism. Although it is clear that a city concentrates demand, the city may not be necessary for the efficient distribution of the products and services available. That depends, again, on the nature of the system. If the goal of the distribution system is to achieve some common purpose beyond the most profitable mechanism promoting returns to the owners of capital, concentrations of production and demand may not be required. Efficiencies resulting from the concentration (savings associated with low costs of distribution) may be offset by other constraints (costs associated with the environmental impact of high density). In this light the concentration of demand is more directly a result of the level of profits desired by those exploiting the surplus values (worth of the product over costs of production) extracted from the urban and rural labor force.[21]

The whole point of these last few paragraphs is to allow the urban historian to see the process of urbanization for what it was in the American West. Urban forms, structures, and functions are essential manifestation of the mode of production; it is helpful to understand that in the cities of the American West values determined use rather than use values and that the desires and interests of the producers (in contrast to those of the owners) failed to have significant effect upon either the process or the results.

In the sense that a city's form and function reflect basic relationships with the mode of production, urbanism as a way of life is a phenomenon subject to profound changes. Traditionally urbanism was thought to be a style of living characterized by freedom, spontaneity, choice, opportunity, individualism, creativity, and diversity.[22] The idea was most often expressed either in words describing the joy of being "lost in a crowd," having the freedom to experience variety in people, places, and things, or in words describing the deprivation of a valueless society in which the very multitude of moralities produced cynicism and skepticism among the inhabitants, in which the disorder bordered on anarchy, and in which traditional institutions and relationships (family, church, God) were profoundly threatened.[23] This view of urbanism as an internally dynamic structure resulting in a way of life for its participants, regardless of how it was expressed, seldom conforms to the urban experience of the modern city dweller in the American Southwest. Indeed, the modern urban place, if the urban-suburban sprawl is the model, seems to be based upon order, standardization, and structural conformity that promotes a style of living that is postmodern and, according to the characteristics above, posturban, and yet also curiously similar to the preurban structures of a stable community.[24]

The reality of this modification has forced many urban critics to look to the past in hopes of re-creating the traditional character of a "bustling" city. Planning, it is suggested, will enable the modern city to reproduce the spice and variety of the early city places without the more obvious defects of slums and ghettos.[25] The goal should be in the preservation of the layers of history to provide a context and a security from which the residents may face the variety of the urban pace.[26] Too, such planning may be utilized to preserve the competitive nature of the urban scene, a facet of life that once made the city a cauldron of innovation, creativity, and opportunity.[27]

Others, however, fail to see the situation of the modern city in this way. Sam Bass Warner, Jr., a leading historian of American urbanization, suggests that the very sprawl of modern cities, especially those of the American Southwest, allows for a freedom within the suburbanization process that is deep-rooted and growing.[28] The interurban railway system in Los Angeles in the early twentieth century, followed by the automobile and the freeway, provided a life-style for the Angelenos of today and yesterday that is traditionally urban. The easy transportation meant, and still means, that individuals lived within minutes of several distinct ecologies and environments. Variety and adventure were possible with the deposit of the trolley fare or at the turn of the ignition key.

Unfortunately, there is little consensus on the matter. It is not clear, for instance, how planning away the obvious defects of urban living will generate the variety desired, when much of that variety resulted from the so-called defects of the urban place. Much of the romance of the nineteenth-century city depended upon an unplanned density of concentration, which generated the underworlds of the waterfront, the bowery, the French Quarter, New York's "five points," Chinatowns, and back alleys and tangled streets. The romantic was closely related to the tragic.[29] One can carry this view to the extreme, of course, but it seems undeniable that spontaneity, freedom, and true variety were historically a function of high density and randomness.[30] The modern city's attempt to preserve the urban life-style is largely self-defeating because it demands a planned involvement resulting in contrived freedoms. The essential cause is that the nature of the urban economy requires a technology and a motivation for the control of people, places, and things in defiance of freedom and individual choice. The freedom to travel choked freeways to choked beaches and mountains is a planned freedom dependent upon careful programming and preparation to preserve the necessary conformity that the economic system demands, while providing for a semblance of individualism in the process of homogenization: the freeway commuter may choose a tape deck from among thousands for the long stop-and-start journey to a bedroom suburb.

To arrive at an understanding of this process is to arrive at a view of urbanism as a phenomenon reflecting basic relationships in the society. It is not a self-contained phenomenon but one that is defined by the very nature of the economy of which it is a product. The city as a place of freedom, competition, innovation, spontaneous experiences, and meaningful choice is the description of a stage of development rather than a characterization always consistent and applicable. As the economy grows more complex and sophisticated in the control and exploitation of resources for private gain, the opportunity and reality of diverse life-styles and socially challenging mores will be less. Control, standardization, the specialization and division of labor, a reduction of skills, the increased use of machinery, and the coordination of policy are results of the need to increase productivity, to protect profits, and to reduce risks. With this perspective there is little sense in attempting to preserve past characteristics of the urban place within the system of American capitalism. To hope to do so is to fail to comprehend the nature of the process involved and the changing nature of urbanization.

For the student of urbanization the subject of the American West can be investigated only in the context of the private economy and the nature of the urbanization process at work in the country and the world. This is not to say that cities west of the Mississippi River are not different from those of the East. There are vast differences. But the distinctions are the results of the same process. Because most western American cities were born in the era of advancing industrialism, their character is distinct. Never walking cities, they have visually more coordinated form and layouts that are less varied and are imitative rather than original. Few unexpected vistas surprise the traveler or resident of these urban places. Little in the way of new discoveries, unexpected visual experiences, or the confusion of tangled pathways and new byways is possible in cities created to serve land speculators, streetcars, and automobiles. No overwhelming past is present in the cities of the American West—except in the preindustrial-age San Francisco—to give them a character and style similar to those of eastern American urban places. The similarity that does exist is due to the pace at which eastern urban places are rooting out their pasts in duplication of the modernism of the western cities.

This fact of life is especially evident when one looks at the architectural forms of urban places in the cities of the Southwest. It is not that these cities do not have architectural forms different from one another and from those of other places. They, like their eastern counterparts, experienced a rich past of imitation in their buildings and urban structures. San Diego modeled much of its recreational center in Balboa Park, built during the Exposition of 1915, upon a Spanish heritage that included Moorish, Spanish, Mediterranean, and mission influence.[31] Phoenix and Tucson incorporated similar designs into their shopping centers and suburbs. And much of this adaptation involved significant innovations, as expressed in the work of the Greene brothers and their California bungalow and the Spanish colonial style of Irving Gill.[32] But because these places experienced most of their growth in the twentieth century, their form is predominantly functional, standardized, and contrived. Unlike that of the East, the West's favorable land ratio enabled much of the frontier urban architecture to take on the sprawl and low form of the suburban character. In such an environment, where the single passenger car dominates the highways, buildings compete with one another in terms of cost effectiveness and, for those attempting to attract customers, in terms of pop-out displays and signs.[33] The exaggerated façade covering the functional building is standard procedure. Jack-in-the-boxes compete with brown derbys and golden arches in patterns of repetition that turn variety into modified sameness. The result is a regional similarity in urban form that is different from the regional character of eastern cities, especially those dominated by sky-reaching buildings, concentrated impact, and layers of preindustrial historical architectural forms.

Clearly the cities of the American West share an urban form, function, and society that are distinct from those of the preindustrial and industrial cities and yet are basic features and characteristic of urbanism as a way of life. That this way of life is urban and yet homogeneous and standard clearly reveals that the phenomenon of urbanism is itself a changing quality dependent upon fundamental relationships flowing from the nature of the economy. Urbanism and the way of living associated with it, or the lifestyle and values contained in the definition of the term, are functions of the economic mechanism at work and ultimately change as the economy changes. The one is not universal and independent of the other.

What impact or effect did the urban places of the American West have on the well-being of the inhabitants? No conclusive answers are available because the research has not been done. We have no Stephan Thernstrom for Los Angeles.[34] But the adoption of the exploitative model does suggest how we might proceed. The city of the American West, like other urban places, has enjoyed the reputation of being a place of opportunity. Because they were situated in frontier environs and were also urban, the city places of the West were believed to have significant potential for growth, even as young towns. Far from the constraints and closed establishment of the East, yet developmental because they were urban places, the western cities attracted migrants in large numbers. Most newcomers hoped to join in at the beginning of the area's future prosperity. The plan was simple enough. Arriving in the towns and young cities, the urban frontiersmen hoped to become part of the new establishment by linking the settlement or community into the national economy or urban network. In only a few places, such as in Los Angeles and San Diego in the early twentieth century, did incoming settlers hope to preserve the frontier isolation of their new homes.[35] Markets, transportation connections, real estate speculation, and advertising campaigns were the chief ingredients in each success story.

One aspect of the scholarship dealing with this urban-frontier phase of American history has been the degree to which the experience is believed to have been conducive to the institutionalization of democracy. The model is that of a community of equals (incoming settlers) alone in the wilderness and forced to work together for the common good in order to survive.[36] Common problems produced a common effort that served as the foundation for participatory government and shared power. More recently other scholars have suggested that the competitive opportunism of the settlers more likely resulted in conflicts rather than in cooperation as firstcomers clashed with newcomers for positions of power and status. But this opportunism too was conducive to and supportive of democracy as a form of government. According to this view, diverse, often strong-willed individuals struggled with one another in ways that led to a more responsive electorate and majority rule. Normally the crucial ingredients in the process were factionalism and subsequent moves toward compromise as the factions appealed for support to the widest possible franchise.[37]

The implication, of course, is that the urban places of the American frontier, as generators of democracy, contributed to the emergence of the just society. Regardless of the mechanism, spokesmen for both approaches share the conviction that a strengthened democracy resulted from the process. But the important questions for our purposes deal with the nature of the democracy produced. Was the democracy a form dedicated to the creation of the just society in which all enjoyed the maximum opportunities possible? More revealing is the suggestion that the individuals involved in and benefiting from the urban setting were opportunists eager to cooperate or clash among themselves, depending upon which approach better enabled them to exploit the situation. This common character—call it the modern commitment to the exploitative life—is what made the western city of the United States different from the colonial village of America. In the latter the commitment was in the process of developing; in the former the commitment was the chief characteristic of the culture into which the settlers had been born. Unlike Europeans coming to the colonies in America's preindustrial age, migrants to the cities and towns of the far West, living and being part of the industrial age, brought their culture, technology, commitments, and ways of living with them. Western cities were literally modifications and adaptations but were seldom creations resulting from a process of dramatic change.[38]

It is important to understand, moreover, that this so-called modern personality is a function of the possibility for individual advancement and is thus dependent upon the economic forces at work. Where economic growth and development are the characteristics of the setting—whether rural or urban, frontier or heavily settled—the result is likely to be a political economy (usually a middle-class democracy) conducive to innovation, competition, conflicts, and compromise. When the contest is one of economic stability, stagnation, or a single enterprise, the opportunistic personalities and institutions are likely to be few and of little importance. The difference is between life in a community and community building, a society accepting the world as fatalistic and one viewing the universe as manageable.[39]

Again it is in understanding the city as an attribute contingent upon the existing mode of production that we are able to evaluate the democracy of these places. Too, the same model should enable us to gain some insight into the nature of the welfare produced by the urban environment. On the face of it nothing within the capitalism of the nineteenth- or twentieth-century city anywhere in the United States required the institutionalization of a circumstance allowing for the prospects of the least fortunate to be as great as possible. The strictures of the urban society required only that enough of the value produced be redistributed to forstall rebellion and to provide a demand for the products of industrial capitalism. St. Louis, Missouri, held its World Fair in 1904 to promote full employment, business recovery, and the defeat of municipal ownership. San Diego did the same with its Panama Exposition in 1915. But the burdens of regressive property and sales taxation fell upon the lower- and middle-class income groups in a fashion that saddled the cost of urbanization upon those who could least pay while providing the benefits to those who could most afford them.[40] No city west of the Mississippi River eradicated unemployment or poverty. No urban place in the West attempted to make the distinction between a greater opportunity for the consumption of material goods and the quality of the goods consumed.

If western cities are at all distinct from eastern places, the differences are the results of development rather than essential trends. Yet the distinctions may have been of significant consequence for the people involved. Students of the Watts riot in Los Angeles in 1966 noted the surprise it evoked among outsiders, who thought of the Watts district as one of the best-kept ghettos in the country—no tenements, no alleys, no garbage-filled streets. Official explanations for the episode suggest that the violence erupted because of the rising expectations of the black residents, the presence of outside agitators from either the North or the South, or police provocation—all of which focused attention upon the irrational or unusual situation rather than upon the historical nature of the system producing such urban places. That the ghetto dwellers "enjoyed" the suburban, single-family residential sprawl failed to change the fact that it was still a ghetto plagued by massive unemployment and racism.

Also, that cities of the American West were dumping grounds for eastern manufactured goods, as demonstrated by the relatively high proportion of the population employed in service industries, is a fact of far-reaching impact. If being employed in service industries means that you are less subject to a loss of skill because you are not specialized in your job, as is true of workers in manufacturing, then the result is undoubtedly profound. What values holds the man who must know all aspects of a product in order to service that product, in contrast to the bolt tightener at work on the industrial conveyor belt? Is the former more independent in politics? More conservative? Do the many corner shops in the modern suburb produce a shopkeeper different in outlook from the blue-collar worker on the assembly line?[41]

These questions directly relate to the problems of human well-being and welfare. How they are approached depends upon the perspective employed. To assess the extent of social justice in the city of the American West we must understand the reality of which the city is an attribute. For America that reality is the world of private gain in which a city concentrates production and consumption forces and institutions defined by the existing technology, resources, and historical situation (the timing of its link to the national urban network). There is little room for absolute commitment to social justice in such a structure, because the reality upon which it is based requires it in only minimum amounts.

The point of these last few pages has been to suggest that the proper conceptual framework will allow the student of the American West to focus on its system of urban places with the goal of describing the process of their growth, the nature of the urbanism generated, and their impact on human welfare. The view of the western city as an attribute dependent upon the existing and preexisting modes of production in a society provides a basis for seeing the diversity and shared character of western cities. The urban places of the West emerged and survived by virtue of their ability to link to the system of exploitation demanded by the economy of industrial capitalism. Their uniqueness is a result of the time of their appearance and the character of their resources and geography. Some were and still are heavily dependent upon their hinterlands, while others have long ago severed such imperialistic relationships in favor of ones more self-sustaining and generative of hinterland development. Some, like Los Angeles and Houston, are conspicuous in their urban form and consumption, while others, like San Diego and Portland, are less concentrated and intense in both form and spread. Most are postmodern in their suburbanization and in their way of life (which is almost antiurban).

But the very uniqueness of the western city is but a reflection of something held in common with all urban places in the nation, a commonality in which the essential trends are homogenetic and all-compelling. Class lines are perpetuated, the status quo is institutionalized, redistributive justice is blocked, and planning aimed at the creation of an urban place programmed to achieve the common good is an impossibility because the mode of production requires exploitative justice and competitive social relationships. For the historian interested in understanding the process affecting and including the past development and reality of frontier urban places, such a conceptual framework is a good point of departure.

Notes

1. This is not the place to list a complete bibliography of sources. For an introduction to the material see Philip M. Hauser and Leo F. Schnore, eds., *The Study of Urbanization* (New York, 1965); Allan R. Pred, *The Spatial Dynamics of U.S. Urban-Industrial Growth, 1800–1914* (Cambridge, Mass., 1966); Christopher J. Schnell and Patrick e. McLear, "Why the Cities Grew: A Historical Essay on Western Urban Growth, 1850–1880," *Bulletin of the Missouri Historical Society* 27 (April, 1972); Richard C. Wade, "An Agenda for Urban History," in *The State of American History,* ed. Herbert J. Bass (New York, 1970), pp. 43–69; Sam Bass Warner, Jr., *The Urban Wilderness: A History of the American City* (New York, 1972); and David Ward, *Cities and Immigrants: A Geography of Change in Nineteenth Century America* (Fair Lawn, N.J., 1971).

2. See A. Theodore Brown, *Frontier Community: Kansas City to 1870* (Columbia, Mo., 1963); Robert R. Dykstra, *The Cattle Towns: A Social History of the Kansas Cattle Trading Centers Abilene, Ellsworth, Wichita, Dodge City, and Caldwell, 1867 to 1885* (New York, 1970); Robert M. Fogelson, *The Fragmented Metropolis: Los Angeles, 1850–1930* (Cambridge, Mass., 1967); David G. McComb, *Houston: The Bayou City* (Austin, Texas, 1969); and Kenneth W. Wheeler, *To Wear a City's Crown: The Beginnings of Urban Growth in Texas, 1836–1865* (Cambridge, Mass., 1968).

3. The key word in this statement is "critical." Few historians would deny the relevant nature of the profession, but the numbers who feel that the historian's function is to evaluate and to offer informed and opinionated studies are far fewer. For an insightful essay on this subject see Douglas F. Dowd, "The Economic History of the United States in the Twentieth Century," in *The State of American History,* pp. 261–65.

4. The problem lies in the methodology and intentions of the social scientists. Their methodology emphasizes so-called objective analysis, which tends to mean a reliance upon things measurable and quantifiable in contrast to things not measurable. The bias here is that more of something appears to be better than less of something rather than just being different. More important, as scientists of society they generally base their understanding of the past upon their understanding of the present. Indeed, the standard procedure in their work is to use the past as a testing ground for their theories of human behavior—theories formulated in the context of a present situation. Unfortunately, this is not a very reliable way to be objective about the past, because the models so

employed look for specific built-in factors while ignoring those less obvious or less readily measurable. This weakness in the methodology is itself a result of motivations and intentions. Because the social scientist is interested in solutions workable in the existing system, rather than in solutions dependent upon a change in the social construct, such subjective presentism is not just favored but required.

5. Earl Pomeroy, *The Pacific Slope: A History of California, Oregon, Washington, Idaho, Utah, and Nevada* (New York, 1965); Richard Wade, *The Urban Frontier* (Chicago, 1959).

6. See Pred, *Spatial Dynamics;* and E. A. J. Johnson, *The Organization of Space in Developing Countries* (Cambridge, Mass., 1970).

7. The basis for much of the conceptual framework employed herein is David Harvey's *Social Justice and the City* (London, England, 1973).

8. Fogelson, *The Fragmented Metropolis,* pp. 24-63; Wade, "An Agenda For Urban History," pp. 59-61.

9. Dean S. Rugg, *Spatial Foundations of Urbanism* (Dubque, Iowa, 1972), pp. 95-151.

10. See Richard McLeod, "The Development of Superior, Wisconsin, as a Western Transportation Center," *Journal of the West* 13 (July, 1974): 17-28.

11. Richard F. Pourade, *The Glory Years* (San Diego, Calif., 1964).

12. Fogelson, *The Fragmented Metropolis,* pp. 108-34.

13. See Robert Higgs, *The Transformation of the American Economy, 1865-1914* (New York, 1971), pp. 55, 1, 6; Douglass C. North, *Growth and Welfare in the American Past* (Englewood Cliffs, N.J., 1974), pp. 130-39.

14. This process of exploitation in the midst of economic development extends beyond the simple extraction of a surplus food supply. Part of this reality is the extension of the exploitative mechanism to other countries as the farm and rural environment become laborers, managers, or capitalist owners and the modern town-country relationship is extended to the undeveloped countries of the third world. See Dale W. Jorgenson, "The Development of a Dual Economy," *Economic Journal* 71 (June, 1961): 309-44.

15. Allan R. Pred, *Systems of Cities and Information Flows* (Lund, Sweden, 1973).

16. The concept given here is a tentative one in need of much more analysis and substantiation. Suffice it here to note that service industries and the nature of the owner-labor relationship, as well as the more general skills involved, may give rise to styles of living far different from those based upon factory labor.

17. See Ronald L. F. Davis and Harry D. Holmes, eds., "Studies in Western Urbanization," *Journal of the West* 13 (July, 1974): 1-5.

18. Pomeroy, *The Pacific Slope,* pp. 120-64.

19. The implication of this approach is to suggest that it is as likely that diseconomies flowed from the size of the individual firm as that they did not.

20. In addition, the degree to which the downtown parts of western cities are optional parts of the community rather than absolute requirements is a result of the suburban shopping center—itself a product of the postindustrial age.

21. E. J. Mishan, *The Costs of Economic Growth* (Fair Lawn, N.J., 1967).

22. See Harvey Cox, *The Secular City* (New York, 1966); and Louis Wirth, "Urbanism as a Way of Life," *American Journal of Sociology* 46 (July, 1938): 1-24.

23. See John B. Orr and F. Patrick Nichelson, *The Radical Suburb* (Philadelphia, 1970); Morton White and Lucia White, *The Intellectual vs. the City: From Thomas Jefferson to Frank Lloyd Wright* (Cambridge, Mass., 1962).

24. See C. W. Griffin, "The Frontier Heritage of Urban America," in *Perspectives on Urban America,* ed. Melvin I. Urofsky (Garden City, N.Y., 1973), pp. 34-36. The constrained order and community character of the megalopolis are especially evident in Los Angeles, where the pedestrian is not so much a king as a neighbor. All Angelenos love their cars, but when the walker steps off the curbing into the street, all automobiles come to an immediate and friendly stop. It is as if they (the drivers) have reaffirmed the good town feelings in a positive gesture that re related to the store clerk's smile and greeting, "Have a nice day." Not so in New York, where the pedestrian is never sure of anything except that people in cars are not to be trusted.

25. Jane Jacobs, *The Death and Life of Great American Cities* (New York, 1961).

26. Kevin Lynch, *What Time Is This Place* (Cambridge, Mass., 1972).

27. Jane Jacobs, *The Economy of Cities* (New York, 1969).

28. Warner, *The Urban Wilderness,* pp. 113-48.

29. The decision about what is exciting about the urban place is itself a product of class situations, as demonstrated by the white middle class venturing forth for a night out in Harlem in the 1930s and 1940s. See Claude Brown, *Manchild in the Promised Land* (Riverside, N.J., 1965).

30. That this is so is best illustrated by the history of the urban police force in America. The very professionalization of law-and-order-keeping forces resulted from the dangers and unpredictable nature of the high-density towns and cities. See Roger Lane, *Policing the City: Boston, 1822–1885* (New York, 1971).

31. Richard F. Pourade, *Gold in the Sun* (San Diego, Calif., 1965), pp. 97–200.

32. Reyner Banham, *Los Angeles: The Architecture of Four Ecologies* (New York, 1971).

33. Ibid.

34. Stephan Thernstrom, *Poverty and Progress: Social Mobility in a Nineteenth-Century City* (Cambridge, Mass., 1964).

35. Fogelson, *The Fragmented Metropolis,* pp. 63–107.

36. Stanley Elkins and Eric McKittrick, "A Meaning for Turner's Frontier," *Political Science Quarterly* 69 (September, 1954): 321–53.

37. Robert R. Dykstra, *The Cattle Towns* (New York, 1970).

38. See Ronald L. F. Davis, "Conflict, Democracy, and the American Urban Frontier: St. Louis, Missouri, 1803–1830" (paper presented to the Second Oklahoma Symposium on Comparative Frontiers, University of Oklahoma, Norman, March 25–26, 1976.

39. Ibid; see also Barrington Moore, Jr., *Social Origins of Dictatorship and Democracy: Lord and Peasant in the Making of the Modern World* (Boston, 1966).

40. See Harry D. Holmes, "Socioeconomic Patterns of Urban Political Conflict: St. Louis, 1895–1921" (Ph.D. diss., University of Missouri, 1973).

41. See Harry Braverman, *Labor and Monopoly Capital: The Degradation of Work in the Twentieth Century* (New York, 1974), pp. 70–85.

8. REGIONALISM AND THE TWENTIETH-CENTURY WEST

Gene M. Gressley

Edward Abbey, in his pop novel *The Monkey Wrench Gang,*[1] describes the adventures of four characters—a Bronx expatriate, an Albuquerque surgeon, a veteran of Vietnam, and a river runner—uniting for the mission of destroying construction equipment, railroads, strip mines, bridges, and other erstwhile symbols of scenic imperialism. Abbey's message that only a drastically altered life-style will preserve the natural beauty of the West for generations to come has made him a cult hero among would-be "eco-raiders." Abbey's clarion call, "Down with the East, up with the West," is hardly new.

Since the 1890s westerners have loudly protested their colonial status.[2] They have continuously pointed to the domination of their institutions by eastern financial czars, the lack of industrialization, the passage of tariffs unfavorable to their region, and the squandering of their natural resources.

Westerners, imbued with the ideology of progress, have been less introspective about asking the rhetorical questions: Where would the capital for western growth have originated if not in the East and overseas? Was the westerner, on a reduced scale, as speculative as his eastern cousin? And, after all, was not the westerner's "love me or leave me" attitude unrealistic, or at least schizophrenic?[3]

One answer to the impotency of the West is simply that the region has never found or produced an adequate voice.[4] Populist, Silverite, and Progressive protest traditions have left an ineffective political legacy. Furthermore, westerners have become self-mesmerized with the notion that all problems will be erased by economic growth.[5] That sage of Emporia, William Allen White, editorialized with amazing confidence in the 1920s and 1930s that the West, as an inheritor of the Puritan ethic, was the benchmark of American superiority, and its unique environment was obviously a testimony to heavenly philanthropy.[6] White epitomized what Reuel Denny noted years later, that America was never more American than in its adolescence.[7] Nor could White have understood Earl Pomeroy's observation that the West lagged behind the nation politically because the westerner was too busy and too committed elsewhere to care about politics.[8]

There were, of course, other reasons for the westerner's divorce from political matters. The West's temporal and spatial isolation coupled with its rampant individualism did little to foster social or political relationships. In a twist of involuted Madisonianism, the westerner committed himself to an unhealthy skepticism of group political action. Evidence abounds in fiction and the historical imagination about the American West, and one constantly finds it amazing that so little commentary concerns the caste system of the West. The equality of the West might be in evidence at the Buckhorn bar or at the ranch-house dinner table, but inequality triumphed in the state legislature or in the ranch office. Entrepreneurial good fortune meant political and social advancement, West or East. Frequently, bacause of the intensity of personal relationships the class structure appeared even more codified in the West than in the East. Economic individualism, political immobility, and social inequality were all patterns accented by the basic anti-Hegelianism of the westerner.[9] Devoid of a past, the westerner often did not try to discern the slash marks on the path to the future. Prevailing over all else is an inescapable truism.

The West was impotent politically for one elemental reason: The people were not there. Until recent presidential elections the West was largely ignored. The candidates took token trips and mouthed banalities about western scenery and resources. Political power obviously is spelled in numbers. A continuation of the West's population boom and migration, coupled with the region's economic wealth, could conceivably transform, if not reverse, its political role.

To counter its past political impotence, presumably the West might have tried to shake its paralysis by the wholesale adoption of a united regional *vox*.[10] On the contrary, it possessed an innate skepticism about the regional mechanism—a distrust that is instantly in evidence every time a regional banner is waved in a western state election. To many westerners regionalism is essentially administrative regionalism imposed from Washington; or it may be translated as a trumpet call that the West is in economic trouble.

Contemporary westerners define regionalism in terms of multipurpose river-basin developments, soil-conservation districts, and bureaucrats running about the western landscape in the guise of scientists and conservationists, dictating what the West should do about its resources. That most western leaders and their constituencies associate regional planning with depression does little to ease their fears. Regionalism and economic failure are indelibly inscribed on the westerner's mentality. Forgotten are the western Progressives' turn-of-the-century Benthamite campaigns against societal waste. Forgotten are George Norris' speeches and programs, which enshrined regional planning in twentieth-century America. If pressed, the westerner might concede that much of the New Deal's regional projects provided an economic bequest from which the West still benefits.

If the westerner exchanges federally imposed regionalism for the merits of voluntary regionalism,[11] he discovers little to reassure him. Voluntary regionalism to most western states' righters means the surrendering of their state's power, even briefly and with limitations, to a neighboring state to solve some malaise. The Interstate Oil Compact Commission originated with western frustration and inability to deal with the petroleum glut of the east Texas field. The Western Interstate Commission for Higher Education, the Old West Regional Commission, the Western State Governor's Conference, and other regional organizations have been altruistic attempts at remedying tourist, education, and natural-resource problems. Most, however, have remained as vacuous in accomplishment as they are noble in spirit.[12] The vision of western political leaders and their publics extends little farther than the frustrations produced by these abortive attempts at regionalism.

The root of the rebus derives from the simple fact that the westerner, like most other Americans, wants to control his destiny, or at least to think that he does. Furthermore, as a political operative, the westerner cultivates his independence as personified in his states'-rights philosophy.[13] The point on which many of the West's most honorable attempts at regionalism have run aground—state intransigence—is airily dismissed by westerners, if indeed it is comprehended. Westerners see the federal government's push in the 1970s for regional decentralization, exemplified by revenue sharing, as a definite step in the right direction. Even here, however, the westerners remain skeptical about the return to localism as a gossamer trick of federal magic. The westerner insists that the high-sounding sentiments of the current regional euphemism designed to provide him with a feeling of participation and of political input is in reality only political oratory. He has to all intents largely ignored the opportunity that regionalism provides by offering a compromise between state decentralization and federal centralization.[14] The westerner will undoubtedly continue to dismiss nonchalantly the merits of regionalization until he is forced to consider the alternatives.

The 1930s found the westerner more receptive, if no less skeptical, about the merits of a nationally inspired regionalism. Along with the rest of the country the westerner felt powerless to cope with international economic stagnation. In contrast to the South, the West never became convinced that regionalism could serve as a framework for social planning and social action.[15] Nevertheless, the West, pushed by economic holocaust, reached a degree of accommodation to the regional programs of the new Deal that it has not displayed since.

Initially, capitulation to federal projects and bureaucratic leadership could be described as reluctant at best. The pivotal problem, which westerners sometimes sensed only semiconsciously, as Harry N. Scheiber has astutely noted, was the locus of power.[16] With a strong bias for decentralization, inherited from the nineteenth century, western citizens feared any loss of influence as a total abdication of their future. Not only was the West's destiny no longer manifest but tomorrow might not arrive! Western political figures appear to have realized only dimly that much of their leverage in the perpetual joust of states against the nation resided in a revitalization of the state political structure. Not until the 1960s did most western states undertake a revision of their antiquated constitutions, the prime legal base guarding the nineteenth-century status quo. Nor did the state political hierarchies fully comprehend that fiscal centralization that had occurred before the 1930s had been primarily between the local and state governments rather than between the nation and the states. True, even if western states had been fully cognizant of their provincial needs, the belief would have been localized, based on the illusion of fiscal responsibility. That the states had neither the technical expertise nor the financial reserves to cope with the depression became evident all too quickly.[17] Whether or not one judges the property tax as regressive, self-evidently as the mainstay of local fiscal resources it is limiting and inflexible.[18]

Roscoe Martin has observed that 1932 represented a fault-line year in state-urban-federal relations, a primary truth few would deny. Yet the sharpness of that fault line varied widely. The western states made serious, if sporadic, attempts at meeting their social responsibilities.[19] Some states established planning bureaus in a feeble effort to meet welfare needs. State spending, especially in the mountain West, increased, although in some states, as in Colorado, accrued revenue was assigned to balancing the budget. State "Little New Deals" came later in the West and died more quickly than they did in the rest of the nation.

By 1940 the remains of western state progressive measures were minuscule indeed. Only after World War II did state spending in the West begin to catch up proportionally with the rest of the United States. The westerners' innate suspicion of the East, combined with their fervent trust in individualism and their myopic understanding of centralization could not be erased in a decade, not even a decade of disaster.[20]

Perhaps the most consequential bequests of the New Deal in the West, which only ever so slowly permeated its mentality, was a begrudging and partial acceptance of the federal largess. Furthermore, the 1930s provided, in the absence of state political leadership, an aroused opportunity for vested interests to grasp control of the statehouses. This condition served to continue an old western tradition, setting the stage for the private-public power plays of the mid-twentieth century.

If one searches for a scenario setting in which to examine, define, and analyze the twentieth-century West, the development of the West's natural resources—land, minerals, water—provides the theater (often of the absurd).[21] The dramatization would encompass a long litany of western and national visions and despair: states' rights versus federal domination; states' interests versus regional concerns; urban sprawl versus rural shrinkage; private enterprise versus public works; and conservationists versus all.

All of the conflicting drama, as graphic and occasionally as fraudulent as the set of a Hollywood western, reduces to one objective: Who shall guide the western star? On the outcome hinges the control of riches that stagger the imagination. The question is, as it has been for two centuries, What design should be created to exploit most effectively and dispose of the natural wealth of the West? In contrast to the Puritans, who sought to implant a strong sense of order in their world, the Americans' speculative ardor unleashed chaos on the West.

Jack Kratchman, with more than a slight whiff of Toynbeean-Hurstian influence, proposes that the evolution of American law provided the guidelines for natural-resource development.[22] According to the Kratchman thesis, natural-resource growth moved through successive states of maturation and decline. Initially the little legal framework that exists is stimulated or ineffective. Slowly there emerges an elementary but astoundingly influential and perpetual legal principle: first-in-time, first-in-right, a legal maxim to delight the heart of every speculator who ever ventured West.[23]

The transformation from the embryonic everyone-first and nobody-last legal jungle arrived with the second wave of exploiters, who coveted the claims of the first arrivals. Quickly first-in-time became first-in-legal-force. Legislatures rushed to institutionalize what was already established: laissez-faire guarantees of individual action and a maximum access to natural wealth. Besides offering freedom of action and admission, the primary thrust of this legislation was promotional in intention and effect. In the Mining Act of 1866[24] the canonizing of an unrestricted legal right was granted to one and all to explore for minerals on the public domain and to have their claims legitimatized against all rivals. Until the passage of the Mineral Leasing Law of 1920[25] a series of legislative enactments enforced the mineral-development philosophy codified in the 1866 law.

The livestock industry lobbied and secured from the state legislatures rights to grazing on the public domain. Not until the famous Bartlett Richards case did the federal government successfully impose its will on state lassitude. The motive in this singular case appears to have been Theodore Roosevelt's personal pique, rather than any desire to enforce the national sanctity of the public domain.[26]

Inevitably, as hordes of individuals competed for the most valuable elements, and as more sophisticated technology came into play, single-minded natural-resource legislation was altered to reflect a more multipurpose, multiobjective legal philosophy. When western politicians discovered that first-in-time equals first-in-right did not satiate and balance the economic desires of a majority of their constituency, the legislators modified the appropriation water law.[27] The revision of appropriative rights now adjudicated competing interests on the basis of relative rights and claims. The Mineral Leasing Law of 1920, although tortuously drafted and implemented, narrowed the speculative game even further.

Administrative regulation slowly began to dominate natural-resource law, with the inescapable effect of constraining, complicating, and correcting the previous free-wheeling natural-resource acquisitiveness. As an illustration, contrast the Natural Gas Act of 1938, which turned the gas industry into one of the most tightly regulated industries in the nation, with most of the general petroleum legislation grounded on the rule of capture (simply another way of saying first-in-time, first-in-right). The attendant wholesale drilling resulted in a conservation nightmare. Only with the enforcement of the Connally Hot Oil Act prohibiting the interstate shipment of oil, which was overage to state conservation policy, did drilling slow down.

Though we hear dire predictions, buttressed by sophisticated quantification, most natural resources have not moved through the evolutionary stages from elementary exploitation to final exhaustion. We are warned that by 1985 the domestic petroleum industry will have totally drained the oil reserves of the nation. Part of the reluctance to believe the doomsayers derives from the public's absorption of the business philosophy that scarcity can be cured by higher financial rewards. Historically, capital has followed the ups and downs of natural-resource development in a shadow reaction to the price mechanism. The gold industry, in a decline for decades, has had a remarkable resurgence with a startling rise in the world gold market price. Gold mines, forgotten and forgiven, are being reopened with the eternal hope that matches the enthusiasm of a grizzled prospector of forty-nine. Gold and oil are not totally analogous, because no one has forecast the vaporization of gold by 1985. An encouraging omen of the recent legislative, administrative, and conservation imbroglio over coal development on the northern plains is the insistence by all participants on a sense of order, a systematic procedure, or a set of guidelines.

Nowhere has the development of natural-resource regulatory and administrative policies been more vividly portrayed than in the history of the allocation of the public domain.[28] The enormity of the land alone offers unlimited options. The contest for this vast arid frontier beyond the 100th meridian to the Sierras, executed in a thousand settings by thousands of participants, has become one of the legendary experiences of the American people. The emancipation of the frontiersman could be related in a series of oppositive forces—legal opportunism versus legal evolution, aridity versus man, primevalists versus modifiers, Jeffersonians versus Hamiltonians, and localism versus statism.

The legal engineers in the town courtrooms and in the state and national capitals manipulated the rules, defined the future, and provided the verdict. Although perpetually presentist, the laws always lagged behind political and economic events. With the advent of the twentieth century previous public-domain objectives of revenue, philanthropy, and settlement gave way to a revised ordering of goals. From a presumption that the domain was inexhaustible and for private reward arose the commandment that the domain was a national treasure, some of it inviolate and to be guarded, some to be used, and all of it to be strictly supervised for generations to come.

The age-old production-minded philosophy was now reconstructed to announce the premise that legislation of the domain must be oriented to the consumer. The nineteenth-century speculator and the twentieth-century suitcase farmer received the wrath of their neighbors and were roundly condemned by Congress and the bureaucracy. The antispeculator mien remained vibrant in the West. As westerners proceed through the last quarter of the twentieth century, they freely and enthusiastically castigate coal and oil-shale companies, which hedge the future by buying acreage today and developing it tomorrow.

By 1964 the foundation of public-domain legislation appeared antiquated even to the most obtuse observers. Although revision of the public-domain law was essential, pragmatically, little would have occurred had not the executive-legislative relationship reached an impasse. Congress could no longer tolerate the privilege of executive withdrawal and reservation of the domain. The president, just as adamantly, refused to yield this prerogative to Congress. In an effort to resolve this legislative-executive contretemps, to bring public-land objectives into the twentieth century, and, it was hoped, to chart the way for the twenty-first century, on September 19, 1964, Congress passed an act establishing a commission to review the old and recommend the new in public-land laws.[29]

The principal problems facing the commission could be stated with deceptive ease. How should the land resources of the nation be rationed among competing interest groups? Who should establish the standards of the equalization of priorities? And, finally, what judicial or administrative procedures should be established to oversee the domain regulation for the future?

The first recommendation of the commission signaled and systematized a major revolution in public-domain doctrine. Henceforth the future disposal of public lands would occur only after "explicit determination" that the lands involved would produce the "maximum benefit" for the public when removed from nonfederal ownership.[30] Gone was the century-old concept of multipurpose planning. Replacing it was the land symbolism of the dominant use for the dominant public on a specific acreage. Another major reversal of domain polity came with the recommendation that Congress should establish the public-land legislative guidelines and also institute the policies for the executive agencies.[31]

Typically, the commission wavered in adjusting the executive-legislative balance; but in suggesting that congress should assert more authority in the realm of executive withdrawal, it appeared to favor congressional dominance. The commission, after ostensibly consenting to the premise of a strong federalism, reversed itself with the qualification that, in the event of a deadlock between competing agencies and interests, federal supremacy would be recognized (but only after an "overriding" concern was uncovered).

After following the interweaving of the "dominant use" concept through the report, a reader can express only surprise to find in the commentary of the commission's executive director that the basic principle of the commission focused on "the need for statutory goals and objectives for planning with a view to obtaining the maximum number of compatible uses."[32] The statement can provoke only incredulity when one considers that the report itself gives little evidence of balancing competing, economic, and social interests.

This is not to contend that the report ignores the sound and fury of political rationalization. As one observer commented, the report can easily be read as a series of compromises between diverse constituencies: rural and urban, executive and legislative, chairman and staff, economic motivation and environmental desires.[33] Considering the issues to be resolved by vested lobbying and legislative-executive jousting, perhaps the commission's recommendations were inevitable from the first day the commission met. Regardless of motivations, transparent or hidden, the strength of the report was radically lessened by the special boom bias. Few could seriously debate the maxim that dominant use in reality meant the dominant economic power. In recommendation after recommendation the economic use becomes the majority benefit: grazing rights are no longer a privilege but a right; mining is given the highest priority in land utilization; federal regulation replaces state regulation of petroleum; and the inability or unwillingness ever to define the national interest.

In sum, to many westerners the report's orientation brought back memories of their historic colonial complex. Here in bold type, with the federal government's imprimatur, was a renewed license to the eastern populace to hunt and extract western wealth. True, this time a percentage of the West's political leaders (including the commission) participated in its own pillage, but the West has always abetted its exploitation. The report of the Public Land Law Review Commission underscored in black Willard Hurst's well-known thesis that the marketplace dominates legal access.

With the exception of grazing and irrigation, the Commission expended little time or interest on the state of western agriculture.[34] From 1970 the western farmer could more often than not be characterized as an agribusinessman with a belief in long-term prosperity but a wariness of short-term survival. His basic optimism is tempered by the remembrance of droughts and the awareness that he lives in next-year country. He is a rugged individualist who has no desire to be a "ragged" individualist and therefore will quickly modify his individualism when it comes to his neighbors' neglect of soil-conservation practices when it threatens his own livelihood. He is a perpetual speculator, and his omnipresent belief in fundamental agrarianism (that he should pass along to his progeny his farm free of debt) is yielding to a gambler's urge to participate, with a heavier investment, in a boom agrieconomy.[35] Today's farmers reflect little of the Rolvaag-Garland revolt against the soil, if they ever did. It would be difficult not to be reconciled with a land that was at once making you affluent and creating you in your own image of the landed gentry. Besides, the farmer retains a regional consciousness born of both an attachment to land and the age-old belief in a commonality of localism against the foreign marketplace.

Much of the modified fundamental agrarianism of the 1970s had showed up in the 1930s—a time of obvious challenges regardless of one's residence, rural or urban. The drought and the depression exposed the farmer's psyche as dramatically as the wind eroded his fields. The Dust Bowl symbolized the collision between man and nature. Out of an era of choking dust, disastrous drought, and stifling heat arose a folklore and a reality that would alter man's relationship to man and to nature—at least temporarily. From Stein to Steinbeck much has been written about the Model-T migration across the souther plains into Arizona and California.[36] There is less drama, and eventually less history, in investigating those who resolutely refused to move from their homeland.

The emigration from the Dust Bowl was incontestably one of the largest mass movements in twentieth-century America; yet on a comparative basis the numbers who left their dwelling places did not compete with the numbers who left their homes during the drought of the 1890s.[37] Some of the rationale for the "backsliders" readily surfaces, while other motives remain clouded in the psychology of the western farmer and the doctrines of agrarianism. One of the primary reasons to stay put came with the revelation that the western Eden was not the Promised Land. Migrants wrote home from the West Coast that the land of golden hue had become the land of lost opportunity. A second inducement to remain behind may have been uncompounded inertia; leaving family and friends always represents a wrenching experience. Third, and most astonishing, a regional feeling of worth and destiny gave pause to some bent on exodus. Some ranchers commented that their region had to be saved for posterity because of the region's value as a connective link between East and West!

The major influence in retarding migration probably was buried in the elusive character of the Great Plains resident. Willa Cather diagnosed part of this rural perversity when she wrote that the fruit of the land blesses only those who struggle successfully with the land.[38] Even in the late 1970s there remains a fervent emotional contretemps between man and land. Evidently one of the strongest reasons for the refusal of a rancher to sell out to a coal company is the feeling that by so doing he will have conceded that the land has beaten him.[39] Irrational? Certainly; but obviously rational beings frequently surrender to the absurd. Further, the Great Plains farmer has always been a gambler; he was asked in the 1930s to risk more with less until drought became a way of life.

In his now classic study on drought perception, T. F. Saarinen found that the wheat farmer tended to underestimate the frequency of the drought years.[40] The Great Plains resident really believed the hackneyed truism, "Things are not as bad as they seem." Sometimes his sentiments could be summed up in another ghoulish, unstated phrase, "It could be worse; it could be me." Moreover, plains farmers were convinced that they had few economic alternatives, which led to the second strong conviction that luck was the most important ingredient of success (an attitude that hung on long after the 1930s). On the one hand, then, the wheat farmer refused to consider alternatives to his life-style, while on the other hand he objected to being at the mercy of his environment. Success was measured largely in the ability to hold on until the rains came. One wonders at the reaction of the wheat farmer when he read in the Great Plains Committee report, "The land may bloom again if man once more makes his peace with Nature."[41]

It was with and against this unyielding relationship of man to his ecology that the New Deal struggled to find a solution through various conservation programs. One of the men most responsible for the direction of New Deal agricultural policies, Rexford Tugwell, preached one message—institutionalism—in his hurried tours of the drought country.[42] The sermon may have been lost to and on his audiences. According to Tugwell's institutionalism ethic, human nature had not changed in thousands of years, but man had drastically reshaped his environment. The answer to the current debacle was evident: transform man's approach to his environment.

Such a philosophy meshed closely with that of H. H. Bennett and his fellow soil conservationists, who believed that rationalization with nature would arrive only after conservation measures were adopted by the plains residents.[43] What the Great Plains farmers and many historians have missed is that, in implementing the soil conservation program, Washington showed an uncommon hesitation to centralize programs. From the beginning of the formation of soil-conservation districts, Bennett stressed cooperation with the states, continually emphasizing to his staff the value of local, state, and regional participation and planning. Regionalism was given an enormous boost when Bennett insisted that soil-conservation districts should be organized on "natural watershed rather than political divisions."

By avoiding the practice of making direct contracts with individual farmers, Bennett followed the wisdom of the Bureau of Reclamation. Bennett thereby acknowledged that any chance his program of erosion control had would depend on the cooperation of state governments. In retrospect, whether fully realized by either party, the federal soil-conservation program wanted to achieve a balance between centralization and decentralization. Bennett, in effect, aspired to a regional implementation of national objectives.

Did this half-alligator, half-man approach succeed? Yes and no. Roy I. Kimmel's appointed role as "co-ordinator" fell short of the dictatorial powers advocated by some western leaders. He soon encountered hostility, an antagonism that boomeranged responsively with the prosperity of the wheat farmer. The Oklahoma City Chamber of Commerce warned that the New Deal was encroaching on state, county, and local rights. What was the solution? Taking cue from their mineral production friends, the officers of the chamber called for the formation of a dust compact among all the Dust Bowl states.[44] The dust-for-ourselves-and-no-one-else-look-this-way syndrome soon evaporated with successive high winds, depression, and drought, compelling state leaders to face east. Widespread opposition to soil conservation died down, remaining only in the western land-grant universities. Western educators evidently resented federal soil-conservation experts advising their constituents and threatening their federal research funds.

The balance sheet today? The establishment of erosion-control practices had an immediate and long-range impact on the plains farmer. Often, though, like his fundamentalist religion on Sunday morning, the farmer viewed soil conservation as a heavenly theology—telling him what he ought to do but never guaranteeing what he would do. Part of the paradox of the Soil Conservation Service has been the contradictory but highly political policies of campaigning for the inherent values of soil conservation, regardless of who controls the land, while at the same time offering subsidies to farmers whose income does not reach that magical level which has been decreed as the standard for a satisfactory American way of life.

Nothing so clearly demonstrates the inconsistencies of these government strategies as the case of the suitcase farmer. Government financing for acreage control kept the suitcase farmer in business long after 1933.[45] Removed from their neighbors' gaze, suitcase farmers endowed with federal payments and supplementary income prospered in good times and bad. The absentee landowners' cavalier example of ignoring soil-conservation practices, and at the same time profiting from this evasion, reduced the inclination of their neighbors to follow conservation practices.

That the farmer of the 1930s remembers the lessons that the wind taught him or that he has passed on wise soil-conservation practices to his children appears doubtful. John Borchet discovered that in the drought of the 1950s the lessons learned in the 1930s were little remembered.[46] The problem reduces to the fact that soil conservation, as far as the individual farmer is concerned, represents a distant and nebulous economic return. The farmer's attitudes do not reflect a commitment soil conservation to the extent that they should, or one would assume that they should.

Perhaps it is being patently naïve to think that the federal evangelizing of the 1930s should have wrought soil-conservation enthusiasts of the 1950s. After all, the soil-conservation challenge has been with the farmer for centuries. However, as reasonable as Rexford Tugwell's institutionalism sounded in the New Deal, the soil-conservation program belies its effectiveness. Unless human attitudes can be changed, the human habitat is likely to remain the same.

Soil conservation and the rural way of life are analogous to the urban slum-clearance situation. One can place the poor in good housing, but, unless the housing is accompanied by education, fires may be built on the living-room floor. The contemporary agrarian, remembering the years of boom, insists on going his own independent, speculative way, taking his victory from and over the land in his bank account at the county seat. While the wheat farmer of the plains depends on the skies for his salvation, the irrigationist increasingly finds himself at the mercy of political and economic factors that he cannot control.[47] Of the water consumed in the United States, 83 percent goes to irrigation.[48] In an age of exploding metropolitan growth and decreasing rural population the likelihood that the irrigationist can politically or legally maintain the status quo becomes less and less promising.

Since the nineteenth century a persistent inclination in water-resource planning has been the projection of future water use on the basis of sustaining the present requirements. The result has been dreams of astronomical estimates. Historically the rural consumer with the legal foundation of first-in-time, first-in-right has possessed the advantage in water allocation. Added to this legal endowment was the rural nostalgia movement of the early twentieth century, fueled by the missionary work of the disciples of George H. Maxwell, who insisted that America's social problems would be solved by a dispersal of the population across the land through increased irrigation.[49]

The legal, economic, and political complexities of the evolution of western water development are beyond the scope of this chapter. But the outcome and effect on interstate regional water growth is readily perceived. Norris Hundley astutely shows that much of the history of western water law can be written in terms of the Colorado River.[50] Concerning regional water rights, the crucial court case was *Wyoming* v. *Colorado,* in which the Supreme Court handed down its decision on June 5, 1922. Wyoming had objected to Colorado's efforts to divert the Laramie River, while officials in Colorado violently maintained their right to make these diversions. Coloradoans pointed out that Wyoming had been making diversions within their state for years. The Supreme Court ruled that priority prevailed and consequently denied the Colorado claim. However, the Court did agree that water could be transferred from one basin to another.

From the moment that the western populace and their officeholders realized the purport of the *Wyoming* v. *Colorado* decision, the inevitably of the water-compact mechanism was assured.[51] All efforts now bent on resolving differences between contesting basins, whether legal or political, have adopted a regional approach to interstate water problems. The Colorado River Commission Compact of 1922 was filled with so many compromises that it guaranteed future litigation and gave the deceptive appearance of states' rights enshrining regional aspirations.

A western regional society, based on water development, had first captured the imagination of the fertile mind of Francis E. Newlands.[52] When he served as an attorney for his father-in-law, William Sharon, Newlands stated flatly, ''Water is property, and the power granted to water companies to sell water implies, of course, the power to fix the price.''[53] Within a decade Frank Newlands de-emphasized his private-property-rights philosophy to tell Nevadans about his dream for Reno. He envisioned the establishment of an ''enduring civilization.'' The first point in Newlands' master scheme for Nevada was a water plan to assure irrigation and power for all. Such a society would provide the environment for recasting western man (presumably through Social Darwinism) in the image of a European gentleman. This western dandy would then walk along a Paris-style promenade in Reno.

Fanciful and fantastic, yes, but perhaps Newlands' dream of a Paris arising out of the Nevada sagebrush was no more visionary than his goal of western regionalism on a water base. Concurrently with Newlands' advocacy of water regionalism, Senators Warren of Wyoming and Carter of Montana and Congressmen Mondell of Wyoming and Shafroth of Colorado contended that all public lands should be transferred to the states and that any irrigation works built with public funds should become the property of states or private enterprise to operate. Warren and Mondell undoubtedly reflected the western frame of mind more accurately than the quixotic Newlands did. Although Newlands' search for a new western civilization drowned in the practical politics of the silver issue, he did, through the Newlands Act of 1902, bring a regional water scheme to the West. Newlands, in his reclamation legislation, injected the multipurpose concept in resource development, a principle that remains in force to the present day.

The Newlands Act established a reclamation fund to finance

irrigation projects from the sale of public lands and other publicly owned resources on the domain. The fund was restricted to sixteen public-land states west of the 100th meridian. Each reclamation project would be governed by locally organized water-user groups. The Reclamation Townsite Act of 1906, with its authorization to construct hydroelectric plants, was one of the most controversial and significant features of the reclamation program. Five years later Senator Warren quietly pushed through legislation permitting the sale of surplus water to privately owned acreage. The significance of that act, not immediately comprehended, was realized when the bureau ran out of public-domain sites for its projects.

These three pieces of legislation did more than any other enactments in the twentieth century to transform the settlement of the American West. Irrigation and power still dominate much of the West's thinking about its future. Reclamation represents one of the most munificent subsidies that Congress has ever expended on behalf of a region, so much so that today regionalism and reclamation are synonymous terms to the people of the West (and the East) and their congressmen. The Reclamation Fund is jealously guarded by the western bloc in Congress, who share a remarkable unity and fanaticism in the commitment.

Water projects have not been an effective way to induce population redistribution, but regional growth has been stimulated by water development. Regions obviously vary in their response to water projects. Much depends on the alliance of heterogeneous factors, such as the availability of low-cost substitutes, for instance, dry farming; fossil-fuel-generated energy; recreational motivation; demand for water-oriented manufactured goods; regional competitive standing in the national market; and the ability of a region to capitalize on its opportunities.

Aside from economic regionalism, reclamation has nourished a psychological regionalism that is consistently disclosed in congressional debates on the future direction of reclamation. For example, reclamation projects are increasingly coming under attack from both westerners and easterners. The West still clings to the myth of the man with a hoe tilling his 160-acre plot, producing both bountiful farms and ruddy-cheeked children—it is hoped, the farsighted leaders of America's tomorrow. Yet, as

President John F. Kennedy found out in 1961, when he glibly promised a new era to the westerner replete with a list of proposed dams and power grids, congressmen of the region looked the other way.

Kennedy encountered only a few of the many phases of western disillusionment. The conservationists' revolt against dams and the despoilage of the wilderness is the most vocal and visual. Some of the reclamation proposals of the 1960s would have destroyed the multipurpose idea because, for example, some of the projects would have flooded more fruitful acreage than would have been irrigated. Furthermore, the Kennedy administration's advocacy of regulating private utility lines crossing government land bespoke the heavy hand of Washington on western states and private enterprise. The West, with its perpetual preference for paradoxes in the 1960s,—and to some extent at present—is both alarmed at being discredited as a pork-barrel recipient and horrified that its enormous resources may be eventually totally controlled by the federal government.

Other controversies swirling around reclamation concern the disposal of "surplus" products. In 1969, 37 percent of the acreage served by reclamation became eligible for federal price supports. Even the most emotional sponsor of the 160-acre limitation would concede that the concept is out of date in its guarantee of family farms. In fact, the evidence that reclamation has induced cultural patterns different from those of other communities in the West is muddled, to say the least. The antagonists of the 160-acre limitation would gain more legitimacy if the agribusiness combines vacated their ranks.

Joining with the defamers of the reclamation ideology are urban governments facing multiplying water needs and decreasing water stores. The National Water Commission proposes that the obstacles to water-transfer rights should be removed in order to equalize price mechanisms between the high-volume urban water user and the low-volume agricultural consumer.[54] Little imagination is required to realize that before this utopian solution arrives nothing less than a hundred years of water law and legislation would have to be overturned. Nor is reapportionment the answer. One of the major disappointments to political scientists, who foresaw reapportionment as a revolutionary political weapon, is the discovery that reapportioned legislatures do not operate significantly differently from their predecessors. Another solution proposed by the National Water Commission, that of allotting cash payments to the owners of transferred water, is evidently even less popular, unless accomplished under the legal aegis of the police power of the state.

In the long term perhaps the most feasible political, legal, and economic resolution may be the formation of a superregional agency—a court of last resort—responsible for the water management of an entire basin. So far western states have refused to give any regional compact or agency an independent status, thereby condemning most regional efforts to an innocuous never-never land. The Delaware Compact represents a radical departure.[55] Here the federal government was made a signatory polity along with the states. In addition, extremely broad powers were delegated to the commission as the sign of the future.

Realism suggests that such a regional allocatory agency, with czarlike powers, will not come into existence in the West until all other options have been examined, some dissected, and a few implemented. For example, the Western States Water Council has been jeopardized since birth by state jealousies, which have drained the council of even a modicum effectiveness. About all that can be said is that a group of western governors recognized a problem, instituted a council, and reserved all the power to the states.

The West must recognize and live with the knowledge that the nation as a whole views reclamation as a seventy-year-old philosophy of limited application for the future. As with the soil-conservation program, the heart of the matter is whether water policy for the coming decades will be dominated by a rural-agrarian point of view. The answer is far more obvious than is the equation to uncover the solution.

With the possible exception of water, nothing so symbolizes the hazards and the hopes for the West's future as the one word coal.[56] Because of the energy crisis, of all the natural resources coal promises both deliverance and disaster. Depending on the statistics one trusts, there are 1,524 billion tons of coal in sixty-three counties of the northern Great Plains, which represent approximately 50 percent of the nation's coal reserves. Of this total amount the federal government owns about 60 percent, although on much of the federal acreage the nation does not own the surface rights. Already 20 billion tons of the West's coal have been leased to private corporations under the Mineral Leasing Act of 1920 and the Tribal Leasing Act of 1938.

In essence, the coal industry is rapidly moving West, signifying a switch from private reserves to public acreage and from single operators to energy combines. Of the total 35 billion tons of coal mined in this country's history, only 5 percent has come from west of the Mississippi. It is forecast that by the year 2000 222 million tons a year will be mined in seven western states.

The westerner's reaction to an army of corporate lease men knocking on his door is a mixture of chronic uncertainty, downright suspicion, and plain avariciousness.[57] A cloud of forboding has affected the westerner's belief in the future. He is beginning to have a tremendous feeling of powerlessness, a powerlessness that corrupts—sometimes absolutely. The realization that social order will be reorganized and the search for a scapegoat are common attitudes encountered in every western coal community and county.

The westerner's skepticism about the current natural-resource policy on coal is based on the age-old fear of eastern bureaucracy and big business. Some westerners perceive the federal energy crisis as a threat because at the same time it combines an increasing supply of energy with such conservation policies as the rationing device of the pricing system. Westerners can be characterized as doubting Thomases when viewing the nation's energy goals as outlined in the 1975 State of the Union Address. They do not see the nation achieving energy independence through a balance of goals. Instead they see a nation primarily dependent on western coal for its energy liberation.[58] The West contends that the federal government's national energy policy is poorly conceived and, at best, ineffective. Why should western coal supply the energy for the nation if the nation refuses to reduce its energy demands and conserve energy resources? Within these specious anagrams the westerner has a plethora of specific questions about the immediate and long-range effect of the nation's energy policy on his life and livelihood. Indeed, there is a rapidly developing confrontation in the West involving taxation, state and federal reclamation, energy programs, and corporate acquisitiveness.

One of the westerner's foremost worries springs from his mistrust of the legal mechanism—the leasing plans—for releasing the West's coal. The westerner's derision of the leasing system runs the gamut from castigating the royalty returns to lambasting the bureaucratic multireview procedures in Washington, which discourage all but the most persistent of developers.[59] In the last fifty-five years the national government has collected approximately $24 million in coal royalties, representing an average of $0.125 a ton. The westerner, to the constant frustration of government and business, wavers in his advocacy of what a just royalty should be. Most westerners, however, agree that the coal royalty should be double the current average.

Another western vexation with the leasing program centers on allowing the leaseholder to lease but not produce. Of the West's coal leases 90 percent are inactive at present. Under present legislatin a mineral lease may be held unproductive for nine years, after which a lessee can assign the lease to another would-be developer with overriding royalties. The assigned lease is not subject to competitive bidding.

The westerner views the coal entrepreneur who refuses to mine his lease the same way his grandfather regarded the eastern absentee owner who purchased large pieces of the domain and held it off the market until a price rise occurred. they are, so the westerner rants, members of the same family of exploitative species as speculators.

Not all westerners share one mentality on the subject of coal or anything else. As many an interviewer has discovered, there exists an enormous societal chasm between the rancher in Birney, Montana, and one in Gillette, Wyoming—a phenomenon that at first appears inexplicable. Neither Montanan nor Wyomingite will admit to the delirious "eastern" love of the land for the land's sake. One Montana rander irascibly commented:

It's mostly people in glittery suits that talk about loving the land. By God, you don't love the land when all it will give you is thistle hay for starving cows; and you don't love the land when all you're eating off it is porcupine and rattlesnakes and boiled weeds. But you get so it's a contest like. You say It's you or me and it ain't going to be me.[60]

When all is said and done, this grim game, accompanied by a fervent feeling of a generational patrimony to the land, goes far in explaining the Montana rancher's attachment to the home place. Most of the ranchers in the Colstrip-Birney area would like nothing better than to have the coal operator vanish forever. Although they may dislike admitting it to "foreigners," they are committed to ranching as their life-style. As a fraternity they are younger men who have inherited the mores of their fathers. Above all, they regard themselves as staunch traditionalists because of their preservation of the status quo and their past way of life. What are their alternatives? If they do not fight coal development, they are faced with the unpalatable decision of selling out or leasing. If they do lease, then they will be inviting the genuflection of mass industrialization and urbanization—a way of life totally antithetical to what they have known. Though they do not say it, the ranchers realize that the difference between selling and leasing is emblematic because in each case the land will be lost.

Some Wyoming ranchers, primarily the young, are as dedicated to their fathers' life-style as are their Montana friends fifty miles away. Most Wyoming ranchers who are selling out are in the over-thirty-five age bracket. In Montana many of the ranchers in coal districts are father-son operators. Montana ranchers tend to confront coal development head on, while ranchers in Wyoming evidence an acquiescence missing north of their border. Part of the difference in attitudes between the rural populations of the two adjoining states is that many Wyoming ranch families have either experienced or observed the economic compensation derived from mineral development. Gillette, for instance, has recently undergone an oil boom. Now, as in the past, Wyoming ranchers closely identify with big business, but not with big government. To some Wyoming ranchers the corporation is a natural and potent ally in fighting a common enemy—"encroaching" federal bureaucracy and regulation. The Wyoming attitude is essentially that ranching is a business, rather than a prototype for life. However, the variations in political, social, and economic outlook among Wyoming and Montana ranchers are wide and ever changing.

The urbanites in the coal country are as skeptical as the ranchers, but their distrust originates in a different premise. the townspeople are very contemporary in their outlook, with less concern for the past. In fact, they are more frightened of the future. Town meetings are filled with questions about the long-range effects of coal development.[61] One Billings resident capsulized his fears with the comment: ''In three years it [coal development activity] will be over for us. The coal companies will be located by then.''[62] In sum, the cocktail hour filled with fat bonuses and royalties soon will be gone, leaving a ''What will we do?'' presentist attitude. Many urban residents believe they are soon to be ''easternized.'' They foresee the future as bringing all the problems associated with eastern cities and industrialization—crime, overcrowding, and inadequate municipal services. A nightmarish scenario offers an impending loss of community with next-door neighbors unknown and feared. These western communities fully realize their insitutional vulnerability, but they are totally unprepared to deal with this precarious state.

Indeed, the growing recognition of their defenselessness only serves to increase their fears—rational and irrational. Typically secretive about their private lives, neighboring ranchers are even uncertain about each other's stand on the coal issue. The western social fabric, always delicate, is now being rent by rampant suspicion and a feeling of futility. The ancient dispute over whether the westerner lived by independence or interdependence is now being forcibly answered. One rancher cogently assessed his society:

We need each other in order to survive. Until this coal business entered our lives, we had been acting as though we were good neighbors but we had actually been drifting apart. Now we have to really be good neighbors again or we are going to be easy pickings for the coal people.

Tearing up one's roots to allow rootless people in is not a solitary act. It has a big impact on one's neighbors, on their water, on their ability to live as they wish, and so on. How can anyone justify selling out to industrialists as anything but an antisocial act?[63]

The westerner in coal country, unable to cope with the altered society and migration influx, is subject to frustration, depression, boredom, and divorce. The rancher, preferring independence, realizes, as his forebears did, that without collective action he is helpless. The magnitude of the problems demands composite judgment and action. The westerner, frightened by the pernicious effects of the social maladies forced upon him and unfamiliar with the rules of the coal-monopoly game, feels ill-prepared to cope with his situation. The divide-and-conquer tactics, the intimidation by rumor, but above all the enormous financial gains being offered are blandishments difficult for even the most resolute and land-attached westerner to resist.

The most hardened westerner concedes that the issue is not whether the West's coal resources will be exploited but rather who will govern the West's coal. The states, the federal government, the western people, and the corporations are all vying to provide the answer to that question.

Some states have passed more restrictive statutes on reclamation than those that presently exist in federal legislation. The federal government has hobbled the states economically by allocating financial resources to the impacted areas. At present states are restricted in their redeployment of royalites from federal and state school lands. The amount of population growth and the accompanying urbanization have confounded the prescience of all the problem solvers. Planning is a word with much surface obedience, but as yet the effect is hollow.[64]

The environmentalists are one group that cries out with a barrage of answers.[65] They consistently claim that more planning, more investigation, and more local and federal action are required before coal development should proceed. These ecosystem advocates argue that generalities do not apply to the reclamation of strip mining. Reclamation remains a one-site, on-site problem. What will work in one forty-acre plot will not necessarily work in an adjoining forty acres.

One of the most curious and intriguing facets of natural-resource dynamics is that the West focuses on environmentalists as radicals. Unfortunately, emotion-laden and politicized terminology engenders misconception. Environmentalists of today are unreconstructed traditionalists. These so-called radicals desire nothing more than maintaining the status quo, or even the status quo ante. Environmentalists heatedly maintain that they are conservers of the natural heritage for the future. As nearly as can be perceived through the fog of controversy, developers label the environmentalists as radicals because they are threatening to block the natural way of progress. Frequently, of course, that natural evolution coincides with the aspirations of the developers' *gemeinschaft*.

One of the extraordinary ironies of the controversy is contained in the environmentalists' selection of their allies. Accustomed to a lonely battle against economic progress under the banner of an eastern corporate image, the present-day environmentalists are startled to find antigrowth ranchers joining up with their crusade. Even town-hall meetings reveal the strangest faces in the same pew. Animosities are forgotten, if not forgiven, in a mutual search for the balance of power.

This is the western scene today. What of the twenty-first-century West? Until recently, the West assumed that, under the spell of growth, like the boisterous Americans appearing on the pages of Charles Dickens, all of its major difficulties would be solved by a larger regional economic product. Now the West, in common with the rest of the nation, must select from alternative futures. What annoys westerners, however, is that the nation at large insists on a major role in their choice for the future. And why not? The rest of the country has always participated in, if not dominated, the West's tomorrow. Westerners then constitute a rapidly shifting society in which commercial dislocations of distance and a colonial status are omnipresent—at least for the moment.

If we are to credit the recent polemic of Kirkpatrick Sale, the West's historic role as stepchild to the nation may soon be radically altered.[66] Sale argues that the Southern Rim—all the southern states from the Atlantic seaboard to the Pacific Ocean—could control the economic and political power of America. Sale characterizes Southern-Rim leaders as "cowboys" and as swaggering, sport-shirted *nouveau riche* fundamentalists. The past decade, according to Sale, has seen a contest for control of the nation's capital between the "cowboys" and the "Yankees"— the patrician New England-based Wasps of old family wealth.

Sale does not predict the outcome of the struggle between the Northeast and the Southern Rim. However, he leaves little doubt that the Southern Rim, with an economy of defense industries, tourism, natural resources, and agribusinesses, has the winning poker hand—to use the vernacular of the region's most recent spokesman, Richard M. Nixon.

Emotionally the West retains its image as the future of America. One of the major reasons for the West's increasing political influence is the booming population migration to the West. The West, specifically the subregion the Southwest, has the votes to influence national decision making. When they venture West, politicians and statesmen alike respond to what they feel is the excitement of the land of optimism and sun. In his February, 1976, visit to the University of Wyoming, Secretary of State Henry Kissinger began his speech by saying: ''It is good to be here in the West. The people of this land remind me once again that America is not the cynical, confused and tired nation so many in Washington would have us believe it is.''[67]

The West, with its new economic power, its population influx, its open spaces, and its brilliant atmosphere, has substantial advantages with which to move into the twenty-first century. In order for this future to be realized, however, westerners must balance their goals against those of the region's largest landowner, the federal government. In addition, westerners must contend with the presence of eastern financial and corporate influence and the recent and fervent concern of both easterners and westerners for the preservation of the West's environment and life-style.

Some western voices are strenuously campaigning for a regional planning approach in the West's struggle with the problems that will present themselves on the morrow. Events of the past demonstrate that one cannot be very optimistic about the West's chances for changing its outlook. The twin challenges of environment and natural resources may, however, push the West into forgetting its localism and joining in a potent and effective regional compact. Individualism has always been a hindrance to the West in its groping for regional leverage. Now, with the reexamination of western regionalism, old inorganic geographic concepts are of little value when man is confronting the organic planning of his relationship to his environment. Regions can and must clarify their needs in the context of national policy, instead of allowing the nation to provide answers to a nonexistent regional calculus.[68]

Historically, regional planning has been linked with conservation and rural harmony. The assumption was that planning by itself would bring vitality and happiness to the body politic. The West can no longer afford the luxury of debating the usefulness of regional mechanism. It must unite and promote the West's goals, or it will be swept away by the tide of national vested interests. Regional interstate agreements appear to be the effective option the West has in its search for the equalization of political power. The major failing of interstate compacts to date has been the insistence on adjudicating far too much in the present and far too long into the future. Born of compromise and nurtured in distrust, interstate compacts have been objects of derision and symbols of futility.

The West, particularly in its economic development, must transform its regional posture if it is to cope effectively with the federal system. Energy-resource development has made essential and inevitable the reordering of national priorities. In contrast with the circumstances of a decade ago, states are now being touted as the most powerful and fastest-growing level of government. Much of the shine on the states' posture is a reflection of their increasing concern with domestic obligations—a fiscal responsibility that has been heightened by revenue sharing.[69]

In short, the westerner, whose politics have been conditioned by a massive landscape, abundant natural resources, and a sparse population, is now placed in a position to counteract the centrifugal force of the national government. Federalism, as many have observed, is not a frozen body of stagnant principles.[70] The sharing of tax funds alone will not be sufficient to reverse federal magnetism. If the West dreams of a full and effective partnership with the nation in a political and economic decision-making role, then it must examine regionalism far more seriously than it has in the past. The nation's hunger for the West's wealth has handed it the power to be heard—at last.

Notes

1. Edward Abbey, *The Monkey Wrench Gang* (Philadelphia, 1975).
2. The bibliography of colonialism, in fiction and in fact, is long and wearing. Citations are made most often to Wendell Berge, *Economic Freedom for the West* (Lincoln, Nebr., 1946); Walter P. Webb, *Divided We Stand* (New York, 1937); Abraham G. Mezerik, *The Revolt of the South and West* (New York, 1946); Bernard De Voto, "The West: A Plundered Province," *Harper's* 169 (August, 1934): 355–64.
3. Geographically "the West," as defined in this chapter, denotes the region between the 100th meridian and the Sierras. The author subscribes to the view of Earl Pomeroy and others that the Pacific Coast historically is more "eastern" than "western."
4. The definition of regionalism depends on the discipline invoked. The geographer Preston E. James discovered regionalism thus: ". . . the face of the earth can be marked off into areas of distinctive character, and that the complex patterns and associations of phenomena in particular places possess a legible meaning as an ensemble which, added to meanings derived from the study of all parts and processes separately, provides additional perspective and additional depth of understanding." Preston E. James, *On Geography* (Syracuse, 1971), p. 78. The sociologist Howard W. Odum saw regionalism as possessing five attributes: ". . . first of all an area, a geographical unit with limits and bounds. Regionalism is, therefore, an areal or spatial generalization. Yet, in the second place, the region differs from the mere locality or pure geographic area in that it is characterized not so much by boundary lines and actual limits as it is by flexibility of limits, by extension from a center and by fringe or border margins, which separate one area from another. The third attribute of region is some degree of homogeneity in a number of selected characteristics. The definitive nature of the region and the aspects of its homogeneity will be determined by the fourth attribute of the region, namely, some structural or functional aspect or aspects through which the region is to be dominated. Yet there must be a limit to the multiplicity of regions, so that in general a fifth attribute must be found in relation to composite homogeneity of the largest number of actors for the largest number of purposes in view, to the end that a region may be a practical, workable unit susceptible of both definition and utilization." Howard W. Odum, "A Sociological Approach to the Study and Practice of American Regionalism, A Factorial Syllabus," *Social Forces* 20 (May, 1942): 431. The economist Henry W. Broude found his regionalism in ". . . some kind of a trade-off between geographic, sociological, cultural, or economic homogeneties,

which focus on him [the economist] the problem of setting up a priority list.'' Henry W. Broude, ''The Significance of Regional Studies for the Elaboration of National Economic History,'' *Journal of Economic History* 20 (March, 1960): 490. The historian Vernon Carstensen, with his usual felicity, blended all disciplinary definitions together in ''The Development and Application of Regional-Sectional Concepts, 1900-1950,'' in *Regionalism in America* (Madison, Wisc., 1951), pp. 99-118.

In this chapter I follow the Carstensen approach by incorporating an interdisciplinary definition of regionalism, borrowing from sociologists, geographers, economists, and historians. Others seeking some degree of regional accommodation and definition might peruse George B. Tindall, ''The States and the Future of Regionalism—A Symposium,'' *Journal of Southern History* 26 (February, 1960): 23-24; Lucien Brocard, ''Regional Economy and Economic Regionalism,'' *Annals of the American Academy of Political and Social Science* 162 (July, 1932): 81-92; J. O. Hertzler, ''Some Notes on the Social Psychology of Regionalism,'' *Social Forces* 18 (March, 1940): 331-37; ''The Conference on Research in Income and Wealth,'' *Regional Income,* Studies in Income and Wealth, vol. 21 (Princeton, N.J., 1957); Howard W. Odum, ''Regional Development and Governmental Policy,'' *Annals of the American Academy of Political and Social Science* 206 (November, 1939): 134-39; James G. Leyburn, ''A Critique of Odum's Regionalism,'' *Journal of Social Philosophy and Jurisdiction* 7 (July, 1942): 358-70; George L. Simpson, Jr., ''Howard W. Odum and American Regionalism,'' *Social Forces* 34 (December, 1955): 102-105; Alvin L. Bertrand, ''Comments by a Regional Sociologist,'' *Social Science Quarterly* 49 (June, 1968): 36-38; Edwin G. Flittie, ''The Delineation of a Region—An Alternative Technique,'' *Growth and Change: A Journal of Regional Development* 1 (January, 1970): 34-37; Donald G. Holgrieve, ''Frederick Jackson Turner as a Regionalist,'' *Professional Geographer* 26 (May, 1974): 161-63; and Charles R. Adrian, ''Regional Analysis in Political Science,'' *Social Science Quarterly* 49 (June, 1968): 27-31.

5. Mary Young, with her typical brilliance, develops this theme in *Western Historical Quarterly* 1 (April, 1970): 137-60.

6. Joseph Lynn Dubbert, ''The Puritan in Babylon: William Allen White'' (Ph.D. diss., University of Minnesota, 1967), pp. 9-11. The American ethic is dissected in Orin S. Kramer, ''The Death of the American Ethic,'' *Yale Review* 61 (Autumn, 1971): 69-75.

7. Reuel Denney, *The Astonished Muse* (Chicago, 1957).

8. Earl Pomeroy, ''The West and New Nations in Other Conti-

nents," in *Reflections of Western Historians* (Tucson, 1969), p. 243. Pomeroy time and again has demonstrated that he has more to say than most other commentators on the West. Other Pomeroy essays that have been helpful in this area are: "The Changing West," in *Reconstruction of American History* (New York, 1962); and "What Remains of the West?" *Utah State Hsitorical Quarterly* 35 (Winter, 1967): 39–55.

9. For various ways of turning concepts about the West upside down and right side up and examining the American character, the following are useful: John Greenway, *The Last Frontier* (Melbourne, Australia, 1972); Francis E. Rourke, *Bureaucracy, Politics, and Public Policy* (Boston, 1969); Russell B. Nye, *Midwestern Progressive Politics: A Historical Study of Its Origins and Development, 1870–1950* (East Lansing, Mich., 1951); Samuel C. Patterson, "The Political Cultures of the American States," *Journal of Politics* 30 (February, 1968): 187–207; Samuel P. Huntington, "Paradigms of American Politics: Beyond the One, the Two and the Many," *Political Science Quarterly* 89 (March, 1974): 1–26; Wallace Stegner, *The Uneasy Chair: A Biography of Bernard De Voto* (New York, 1974); Quentin Anderson, *The Imperial Self* (New York, 1971); John Greenway, *The Inevitable Americans* (New York, 1964); James Morris, "Out in Wyoming: Images of American Innocence," *Encounter* 38 (February, 1972): 30–37; Abigal McCarthy, "Out of Small-Town America; A Memoir of Teaching, Courtship, and Faith," *Atlantic* 229 (June, 1972): 75–93; and Eugene B. McGregor, Jr., "Politics and Career Mobility of Bureaucrats," *American Political Science Review* 58 (March, 1971): 18–26.

10. Vernon L. Fahle and Robert M. Rauner, "National Policy of Regional Economic Development," *Growth and Change* 2 (October, 1971): 9–15; Francis B. Francois, "The Dilemma of Regionalism for Local Elected Officials," *Public Management* 56 (January, 1974): 8–9; N. A., "From Community Studies to Regionalism," *Social Forces* 23 (March, 1945): 245–58; John B. Parr and Walter Isard, eds., *Regional Science Association Papers,* vol. 24 (Tokyo, 1970); Walter Isard and Thomas A. Reiner, "Regional Science: Retrospect and Prospect," *Regional Science Association Papers,* vol. 16 (Tokyo, 1966); and Edward F. R. Hearle, "Regional Commissions: Approach to Economic Development," *Public Administration Review* 28 (January–February, 1968): 15–18.

11. David W. Robinson, "Voluntary Regionalism in the Control of Water Resources," *Annals of the American Academy of Political and Social Science* 207 (January, 1940): 116–23.

12. Martin E. Ridgeway, *Interstate Compacts: A Question of Federalism* (Carbondale, Ill., 1971).

13. Ira Sharkansky, *Regionalism in American Politics* (New York, 1970).

14. William B. Munro, ''Regional Governments of Regional Problems,'' *Annals of the American Academy of Political and Social Science* 185 (May, 1936): 125–31; U.S., Congress, Joint Economic Committee, ''Regional Planning Issues,'' *Hearing Before the Subcommittee on Urban Affairs of the Joint Economic Committee,* 92d Cong., 1971.

15. Dewey W. Grantham, Jr., ''Regional Imagination: Social Scientists and the American South,'' *Journal of Southern History* 34 (February, 1968): 6–25.

16. Harry N. Scheiber, ''The Condition of American Federalism: An Historian's View,'' 89th Cong., 2d Sess., 1966, p. 7.

17. James T. Patterson, *The New Deal and the States, Federalism in Transition* (Princeton, N.J., 1969).

18. Frederick C. Mosher and Orville F. Poland, *The Cost of American Governments* (New York, 1969).

19. ''The New Deal in the West,'' *Pacific Historical Review* 38 (August, 1969): 249–345.

20. Martin Nolan, ''Walter Heller's Federalist Papers,'' *Reporter* 36 (June 1, 1967): 13–17.

21. Anyone who ''wanders'' into nineteenth-century economic history will soon encounter the amazingly fertile writings of James Willard Hurst. The pages of Hurst that will most frequently abe cited include James Willard Hurst, *The Growth of American Law: The Law Makers* (Boston, 1950); *Law and Economic Growth* (Cambridge, Mass., 1964); *Law and Social Process in United States History* (Ann Arbor, Mich., 1960); and *Law and the Conditions of Freedom* (Madison, Wisc., 1956). Scheiber is one of Hurst's more brilliant and perceptive critics; Harry N. Scheiber ''At the Borderlands of Law and Economic History: The Contribution of Willard Hurst,'' *American Historical Review* 75 (February, 1970): 744–56. See also Russell E. Brooks, ''The Jurisprudence of Willard Hurst,'' *Journal of Legal Education* 18 (June, 1966): 257–73; Earl F. Murphy, ''The Jurisprudence of Legal History: Willard Hurst as Legal Historian,'' *New York University Law Review* 39 (November, 1964): 900–43; and David H. Flaherty, ''An Approach to American History: Willard Hurst as Legal Historian,'' *American Journal of Legal History* 14 (August, 1970): 222–34.

22. Jack Kratchman, ''The Rise and Fall of Natural Resource Systems,'' *Land and Water Review* 8 (1973): 429–66.

23. First engraved in the legal code of the United States in Jennison v. Kirk, 98 U.S. 453, 461 (1878).

24. Act of July 26, 1866, 262 14 Stat. 251.

25. Act of February 25, 1920, 85 41 Stat. 437.

26. Richards' case is presented in a forthcoming book by Bartlett Richards' son (under the imprint of the Nebraska State Historical Society).

27. Wells A. Hutchins, *History of the Conflict Between Riparian and Appropriative Rights in the United States* (Austin, Texas 1954), 121–28.

28. Those who peruse literature about the public domain may soon be convinced that the investigators of this topic are trying to rival the enormity of their subject. Of most assistance were Wesley Calef, *Private Grazing and Public Lands: Local Management of the Taylor Grazing Act* (Chicago, 1960); Vernon Carstensen, ed., *The Public Lands: Studies in the History of the Public Domain* (Madison, Wisc., 1963); Marion Clawson, *Uncle Sam's Acres* (New York, 1951); Howard W. Ottson, ed., *Land Use Policy and Problems in the United States* (Lincoln, Nebr., 1963); James C. Malin, *Winter Wheat in the Golden Belt of Kansas: A Study in Adaption in Subhumid Geographical Environment* (Lawrence, Kans., 1944); Paul Gates, *A History of the Public Domain* (Washington, D.C., 1968); Leslie Hewes, *The Suitcase Farming Frontier* (Lincoln, Nebr., 1973); Henry J. Tomasek, "The Great Plains Agricultural Council" (Ph.D. diss., University of Chicago, 1959); William D. Rowley, *M. L. Wilson and the Campaign for Domestic Allotment* (Lincoln, Nebr., 1970); Great Plains Committee, *The Future of the Great Plains* (Washington, D.C., 1936); Walter J. Stein, *California and the dust Bowl Migration* (Westport, Conn., 1973); Charles R. Kutzleb, "Rain Follows the Plow: the History of an Idea" (Ph.D. diss., University of Colorado, 1968); Thomas F. Saarinen, *Perception of the Drought Hazard on the Great Plains* (Chicago, 1966); Paul W. Gates, "Public Land Issues in the United States," *Western Historical Quarterly* 2 (October, 1971): 363–76; C. L. Green, "The Administration of the Public Domain in South Dakota" (Ph.D. diss., State University of Iowa, 1939); and Ross D. Netherton, "Implementation of Land Use Policy: Police Power vs. Eminent Domain," *Land and Water Review* 3 (1968): 33–57.

29. A summary and final report of the commission is in *One Third of the Nation's Land* (Washington, D.C., 1970).

30. Ibid., pp. 41–63.

31. Ibid.

32. Milton A. Pearl, "The Public Land Law Review Commission: An Overview," *Land and Water Law Review* 6 (1970): 25.

33. Michael McCloskey, "The Environmental Implications of the Report on the Public Land Law Review Commission," ibid., p. 351.

34. Again, the literature on western agriculture is vast. Those items which have held some insight for me are Fred Shannon, *The Farmers Last Frontier, 1860–1897* (New York, 1948); Mary W. Hargreaves, *Dry Farming in the Northern Plains, 1900–1925* (Cambridge, Mass., 1957); James H. Shideler, ed., *Agriculture in the Development of the Far West* (Washington, D.C., 1975); Murray R. Benedict, *Farm Policies of the United States: A Study of their Origins and Development, 1790–1950* (New York, 1953); John T. Schlebecker, *Whereby We Thrive: a History of American Farming, 1607–1972* (Ames, Iowa, 1975; Gilbert C. Fite, *The Farming Frontier* (New York, 1966); John Bird, "The Great Plains Hit the Jack Pot," *Saturday Evening Post,* August 30, 1947, pp. 15, 17, 88, 90; John L. Shover, *Cornbelt Rebellion* (Urbana, Ill., 1965); Richard K. Olson, "Some Economic Aspects of Agricultural Development in Nebraska, 1854–1920" (Ph.D. diss., University of Nebraska, 1965); Yasuo Okada, *Public Lands and the Pioneer Farmer, 1850–1930* (Tokyo, 1971); Darwin B. Nielson and E. Boyd Wennegrew, "Public Policy and Grazing Fees on Federal Lands: Some Unresolved Issues," *Land and Water Law Review* 5 (1970): 293–320; Peter H. Lindert, "Land Scarcity and American Growth," *Journal of Economic History* 34 (December, 1974): 851–84; Blaine A. Brownell, "The Agrarian and Urban Ideals: Environmental Images in Modern America," *Journal of Popular Culture* 5 (Winter, 1971): 577–85.

35. *One Third of the Nation's Land.*

36. Stein, *California and the Dust Bowl Migration;* John Steinbeck, *In Dubious Battle* (New York, 1936).

37. Fred Floyd, "A History of the Dust Bowl" (Ph.D. diss., University of Oklahoma, 1950); James C. Malin, "Dust Storms, 1881–90," *Kansas Historical Society Quarterly* 14 (November, 1946): 391–43; Alfred B. Sears, "The Desert Threat in the Southern Great Plains," *Agricultural History* 15 (January, 1941): 1–11.

38. Willa S. Cather, *On Writing: Critical Studies on Writing as an Art* (New York, 1949).

39. Northern Great Plains Resources Program, *Effects of Coal Development in the Northern Great Plains: A Review of Major Issues and Consequences at Different Rates of Development* (Denver, 1975).

40. Saarinen, *Perception of the Drought Hazard on the Great Plains.*

41. Great Plains Committee, *The Future of the Great Plains,* p. 18.

42. Bernard Sternsher, *Rexford Tugwell and the New Deal* (New Brunswick, N.J., 1964), p. 14.

43. Hugh H. Bennett and W. R. Chapline, *Soil Erosion: A National Menace,* U.S. Department of Agriculture Circular no. 33 (Washington,

D.C., 1928); Marion Clawson, *Soil Conservation in Perspective* (Baltimore, 1965); Hugh H. Bennett and William C. Pryor, *This Land We Defend* (New York, 1942); I. R. Tannehill, *Drought: Its Causes and Effects* (Princeton, N.J., 1947); and Carl F. Kraenzel, *The Great Plains in Transition* (Norman, 1955).

44. Floyd, "A History of the Dust Bowl," p. 203.

45. Hewes, *The Suitcase Farming Frontier.*

46. John R. Borchet, "The Dust Bowl in the 1970s," *Annals of the Association of American Geographers* 61 (March, 1971): 1–21; H. E. Thomas, *The Meteorologic Phenomenon of Drought in the Southwest,* U.S. Geological Survey Professional Paper no. 342A (Washington, D.C., 1947); and R. L. Nace and E. J. Pluhowski, *Drought in the 1950's with Special Reference to the Mid-Continent,* U.S. Geological Survey, Water Supply Paper no. 1804 (Washington, D.C., 1965).

47. Donald E. Greely, *Land of Underground Rain* (Austin, Texas, 1973).

48. National Water Commission, *Water Policies for the Future* (Washington, D.C., 1973), p. 42.

49. William Lilley III and Lewis Gould, "The Western Irrigation Movement, 1879–1902: Reappraisal," in *The American West: A Reorientation* (Laramie, 1966); Roy E. Huffman, *Irrigation Development and Public Water Policy* (New York, 1953); Grant McConnell, *Private Power and American Democracy* (New York, 1966); Lawrence Lee, "William Ellsworth Smythe and the Irrigation Movement: A Reconsideration," *Pacific Historical Review* 41 (August, 1972): 289–311; and Vincent Ostrom and George O. G. Lof, *Technology in American Water Development* (Baltimore, 1959).

50. Norris Hundley, Jr., *Water and the West* (Berkeley, Calif., 1975).

51. Hutchins, *History of the Conflict Between Riparian and Appropriative Rights in Westen States;* Albert N. Williams, *The Water and the Power* (New York, 1951); Arthur Desko, "Political and Administrative Aspects of the Central Valley Project of California" (Ph.D. diss., University of California at Los Angeles, 1944); William E. Warne, *The Bureau of Reclamation* (New York, 1973); Gordon B. Dodds, *Hiram Martin Chittenden: His Public Career* (Lexington, Ky., 1973); Erwin Cooper, *Aqueduct Empire* (Glendale, Calif., 1968); Emmett K. Vandevers, "History of Irrigation in Washington" (Ph.D. diss., University of Washington, 1948).

52. William Lilley III, "The Early Career of Francis G. Newlands, 1848–1879" (Ph.D. diss., Yale University, 1965).

53. Ibid., p. 74.

54. National Water Commission, *Water Policies for the Future,* p. 38.

55. Ridgeway, *Interstate Compacts,* p. 45.

56. Northern Great Plains Resources Program, *Effects of Coal Development in the Northern Great Plains;* Institute for Social Science Research, *A Comparative Case Study of the Impact of Coal Development on the Way of Life of People in the Coal Areas of Eastern Montana and Northeastern Wyoming: A Final Report* (Missoula, Mont., 1974); Louis D. Hayes, ''Who Will Control Montana's Coal?'' *Montana Business Quarterly* 13 (Spring, 1975): 26–32.

57. K. Ross Toole, ''How Montanans View Independent Cusses vs. Glittery Suits,'' *Montana Business Quarterly* 13 (Spring, 1975): 33–38; Council on Economic Priorities, *Leased and Lost* vol. 5, no. 2, pp. 2–33; H. Hugh Hudson, ''Water for Wyoming's Coal,'' *Water Spectrum* 7 (Summer, 1975): 41–46; David D. Dominick, ''Oil Shale: The Need for a National Policy,'' *Land and Water Review* 2 (1967): 61–97; J. Leonard Bates, ''The Midwest Decision, 1915: A Landmark in Conservation History,'' *Pacific Northwest Quarterly* 51 (January, 1960): 26–33; Leonard J. Lewis and C. Keith Rooker, ''Domestic Uranium Procurement: History and Problems,'' *Land and Water Review* 1 (1966): 449–71; Fred P. Bosselman, ''The Control of Surface Mining: An Exercise in Creative Federalism,'' *Natural Resource Journal* 9 (April, 1969): 137–65; Don H. Sherwood and Gary L. Greer, ''Mining Law in a Nuclear Age: The Wyoming Example,'' *Land and Water Review* 9 (1974): 3–32; and Institute for Social Science Research, *A Comparative Case Study of the Impact of Coal Development.*

58. *New York Times,* January 13, 1975; John Walsh, ''Problems of Expanding Coal Production,'' *Science* 137 (April 19, 1974): 334–36.

59. Council on Economic Priorities, *Leased and Lost,* pp. 2–33.

60. Toole, ''How Montanans View Independent Cusses vs. Glittery Suits,'' p. 36.

61. Richard W. Poston, *Small Town Renaissance: A Story of the Montana Study* (New York, 1950); Thomas Griffith, ''Party of One: Show Me the Way to Go Home,'' *Atlantic Monthly* 234 (December, 1974): 29–31.

62. Institute for Social Science Research, *A Comparative Case Study of the Impact of Coal Development,* p. 47.

63. Ibid., p. 91.

64. Charles L. Leven, ''A Regionalist View of the Public Sector Planning in a Capitalist Society,'' *Regional Science Association Papers* 17 (November, 1965): 7–16; Johnny Booth Smallwood, Jr., ''George W. Norris and the Concept of a Planned Region'' (Ph.D. diss., Univer-

sity of North Carolina, 1963); U.S., Congress, Senate, *Hearings Before the Committee on Agriculture and Forestry,* 93d Cong., 2d Sess. (Washington, D.C., 1974), p. 296; ''Regional Planning Issues,'' U.S., Congress, Joint Economic Committee, *Hearings Before the Subcommittee on Urban Affairs of the Joint Economic Committee,* 92d Cong., 1st Sess. (Washington, D.C., 1971), pp. 303–536; and F. W. Johnston, ''The Evolution of the American Concept of National Planning Movement: A History of Cultural Change and Community Response, 1900–1940'' (Ph.D. diss., University of Pennsylvania, 1963).

65. Howard R. Lamar, ''Historical Relevance and the American West,'' *Ventures* 8 (Fall, 1968): 62–70; George Macinko, ''Man and the Environment: A Sampling of the Literature,'' *Geographical Review* 63 (July, 1973): 378–91; William R. Davlin, ''A Regional Contribution to State Administration of Natural Resources,'' *Public Administration Review* 9 (Summer, 1949): 211–18; Hugh Gardner, ''Goodbye Colorado,'' *Harper's* 248 (April, 1974): 14, 18–23; *Natural Resources Journal* 10 (April, 1970): 203–21; Donald C. Swain, *Wilderness Defender: Horace M. Albright and Conservation* (Chicago, 1970); and John Brinckerhoff, *American Space: the Centennial Years, 1865–1876* (New York, 1972).

66. Kirkpatrick Sale, *Power Shift* (New York, 1975).

67. Address by the Honorable Henry A. Kissinger, Secretary of State, University of Wyoming, February 4, 1976,'' Department of State press release, p. 1.

68. Neal R. Pierce, *The Mountain States* (New York, 1972); Rourke, *Bureaucracy, Politics, and Public Policy;* Raymond Gastil, *Cultural Regions of the United States* (Seattle, 1975); and Carl O. Sauer, *Land and Life* (Berkeley, Calif., 1963).

69. Ira Sharkansky, *The Maligned States: Policy Accomplishments, Problems, and Opportunities* (New York, 1972); Patterson, ''The Political Cultures of the American States,'' pp. 187–207; Daniel J. Elazar, ''The New Federalism: Can the States be Trusted?'' *Public Interest,* spring, 1974, pp. 89–102; Ernest A. Englebert, ''Federal-State Relationships: Their Influence on Western Regional Growth,'' *Western Political Quarterly* 16 (September, 1963): 686–707; and Ira Sharkansky, *The United States: A Study of a Developing Country* (New York, 1975).

70. Nolan, ''Walter Heller's Federalist Papers,'' pp. 13–17; Mosher and Poland, *The Cost of American Governments;* Patterson, *The New Deal and the States: Federalism in Transition;* Robert F. Adams, ''The Fiscal Response to Intergovernmental Transfers in Less Developed Areas of the United States,'' *Review of Economics and Statistics* 48

(August, 1966): 311–13; R. D. Dikshit, "Geography and Federalism," *Annals of the Association of American Geographers* 61 (March, 1971): 97–116; Harry N. Scheiber, "Federalism and the American Economic Order, 1789–1910," *Law and Society* 10 (Fall, 1975): 75–118; Arthur W. MacMahon, *Federalism, Mature and Emergent* (New York, 1962), pp. 97–155, 281–360; Norman Beckman, "For a New Perspective in Federal-State Relations," *State Government* 39 (Autumn, 1966): 261–69; Scheiber, "The Condition of American Federalism: An Historian's View"; Richard H. Leach, *American Federalism* (New York, 1970); Morton Grodzins, *The American System: A New View of Government in the United States* (Chicago, 1963); Robert E. Smylie, "Difficulties of a Small State in the Federal System and Suggestions for Dealing with Them," *State Government* 37 (Spring, 1964): 96–102; Walter H. Bennett, *American Theories of Federalism* (University, Ala., 1964); Maxine Johnson, "The Impact of the Federal Government Expenditure Programs on Montana's Economy," *Montana Business Quarterly* 2 (Summer, 1964): 12–27; and *Revenue Sharing and Its Fiscal Alternative: What Future for Fiscal Federalism?* prepared for the Subcommittee on Fiscal Policy of the Joint Economic Committee, vol. 3, *Federal, State and Local Fiscal Projections* (Washington, D.C., 1967), pp. 1229–1437.

CONTRIBUTORS

Roger G. Barker is Professor of Psychology at the Midwest Psychological Field Station in the University of Kansas, Lawrence. He is the author of many books; those most pertinent to frontier studies are *Ecological Psychology: Concepts and Methods for Studying the Environment of Human Behavior;* [with Herbert F. Wright], *Midwest and Its Children: The Psychological Ecology of an American Town* (Hamden, Conn., 1971); [with Phil Schoggen], *Qualities of Community Life: Measurement of Environment and Behavior in an American and an English Community.*

Ronald L. F. Davis is Associate Professor of History in the California State University, Northridge. With Harry D. Holmes he edited and contributed to the July 1974 issue of the Journal of the West, which was devoted to "Studies in Western Urbanization—Location, Transportation, Mining, Agriculture, Mobility."

Richard W. Etulain is chairman of the Department of History in Idaho state University, Pocatello. In Addition to several articles on western literature in the *Journal of Popular culture* and the *Western Historical Quarterly,* he is the author of *Owen Wister: The Western Writings* (Boise, Idaho, 1973); [with Daniel Alkofer, William Gibson and Cornelius A. Hoffman], *Interpretative Approaches to Western American Literature,* (Boise, Idaho, 1972), and [editor], *Western American Literature: A Bibliography of Interpretative Books and Articles* (Vermillion, S. Dak., 1973).

Gene M. Gressley is Director of the Western History Research Center and Research Professor in the School of American Studies in the University of Wyoming, Laramie. He is the author of *Bankers and Cattlemen* (New York, 1966); *West by East: The American West in the Gilded Age* (Provo, Utah, 1972); *The Twentieth-Century American West: A Potpourri* (Columbia, Mo., 1977); and [editor], *Bostonians and Bullion: The Journal of Robert Livermore,* Lincoln, Nebr., 1968).

Reginald Horsman is Distinguished Professor of History in the University of Wisconsin—Milwaukee. In addition to a number of articles on American Indian policy in the *William and Mary Quarterly,* the *University of Birmingham* (England) *Historical Journal* and the *Journal of the History of Ideas,* hi is author of *Expansion and the American Indian Policy, 1783 –1812* (East Lansing, Mich., 1967); *The Frontier in the Formative Years, 1783 –1815* (New York, 1970); and *The Causes of the War of 1812* (New York, 1962).

John C. Hudson is Associate Professor of Geography in Northwestern University, Evanston, Illinois, and current editor of the *Annals* of the Association of American Geographers. He has written a number of articles on frontier demography in the *Annals* of the Association of American Geographers and in H. Hollingsworth, ed., *Essays on the American West* (Austin, Texas, 1969); he is also the author of *Geographical Diffusion Theory* (Evanston, Ill., 1972).

John Opie is Professor of History in Duquesne University, Pittsburgh, Pennsylvania. he is one of the editors of the *Environmental Review.* he also edited *Americans and Environment: The Controversy over Ecology* Lexington, Mass., 1971); and is the author of *Jonathan Edwards and the Enlightenment* (Lexington, Mass., 1969).

Jerome O. Steffen is Assistant Professor of History in the University of Oklahoma, Norman. he is the author of *William Clark: Jeffersonian Man on the Frontier* (Norman, 1977); advisory editor of *Mid-American Frontier,* 47 vols. (New York, 1975); and coeditor of *The Frontier: Comparative Studies* (Norman, 1977).

INDEX

Abbey, Edward: 197
Atherton, Lewis: 107
Auraria, Ga.: 112–14
Axtell, James: 136
Becker, Carl: 11
Bennett, H. H.: 209
Bergson, Henri: 12
Berkhofer, Robert: 128–31, 134
British Georgia Gold Mining Company: 114
Brown, A. Theodore: 175
Brown, Dee: 126
Brown, George H.: 9–10
Cass, Lewis: 133
Cather, Willa: 208
Chandler, Alfred: 108–109
Change: model defined, 95; fundamental defined, 95
Clark, William: 101, 133
Collier, John: 140
Collingwood, Robin: 12
Colorado River Commission Compact of 1922: 213
Cook, Sherburne F.: 141
Cook, Warren L.: 144
Dahlonega, Ga.: 112–14
Dahlonega Mining Company: 114
Davis, W. W., Jr.: 3
Delaware Compact: 216
Deloria, Vine: 126–27
Denney, Reuel: 198
De Voto, Bernard: 152
Dobynes, Henry G.: 140–41

Doppler Effect: 166
Dykstra, Robert: 3–4, 175
Eblen, Jack: 43
Ecosystems: 20–25
Environment: ecological, defined, 68, psychological, defined, 68
Ewers, John, C.: 130–31
Faustian man: 13–16, 21, 24
Fisher, Vardis: 153–56, 169
Fogelson, Robert M.: 175
Frontier: undermanned, defined, 61–62, 75–77; new, defined, 62–63; unfinished, defined, 62, 66, 85–91; insular, defined, 96–99; cosmopolitan, defined, 99
Fuller, Margaret: 106
Fur trade: 100–101
Georgia gold rush: 110–15
Goetzmann, William: 115
Grasslands: 17–18, 22–25
Gressley, Gene M.: 3–4
Gross National Consumption, defined: 10–11
Guthrie, A. B., Jr.: 155, 157–60, 169
Heard, Gerald: 11
Hertzberg, Hazel W.: 140
Hickerson, Harold: 143
Hudson's Bay Company: 102
Hundley, Norris: 212
Hurst, James Willard: 207
Indeterminacy, defined: 19–20
Indian Reorganization Act: 140
Interstate Oil Compact Commission: 199

237